D0759963

A Good Life in the Inland Northwest:
A Collection of Columns from
The Spokesman-Review

To my wife Kate,
to my children Sarah and Cody
and to the people of Spokane.
All of you have enriched my life.

A Good Life
in the
Inland Northwest:

A Collection of Columns

from The Spokesman-Review

by

Chris Peck

NEW MEDIA VENTURES INC.

Spokane, Washington

A Spokesman-Review Book
from
New Media Ventures, Inc.

A Good Life in the Inland Northwest:
A Collection of Columns from The Spokesman-Review

1. Non-fiction   2. Social commentary   3. Newspapers
4. Newspaper columns   5. Spokane, Washington
6. Pacific Northwest United States

ISBN 0-923910-09-3

I. Chris Peck

New Media Ventures, Inc., Spokane, Washington

Series Editor: Shaun O'L. Higgins
Production Coordinator: Laura B. Lee
Typography and Design: The Oxalis Group

Printed by Lawton Printing Company, Inc., Spokane, Washington,
on Georgia-Pacific 70-lb. Valorem Natural Book paper.
Bound at the Lincoln and Allen Bindery, Portland, Oregon.

A Good Life in the Inland Northwest:
A Collection of Columns from
The Spokesman-Review

Contents

Spokane Traditions

Chapter One

Bloomsday

Carmen Hasse: One-legged runner who hasn't missed a race

Ten thousand Bloomsday runners will finish ahead of Carmen Hasse today.

She will be plodding up the Pettet Drive hill an hour after the winners hear the cheers of the crowd.

When she finally rounds that last corner onto Spokane Falls Boulevard the thrill of watching runners complete the final yards of the 7.5 mile course will have dissipated.

Still, I hope some of you stay to cheer Carmen Hasse after the thrill is gone.

Miss the first of the post-run parties and barbecues. It will bring the goose bumps to your arms when you see her.

I think no one exemplifies the Bloomsday spirit more than she.

When Carmen Hasse comes into sight a few dozen yards from the finish line she will be wearing only one jogging shoe.

She has only one leg.

From the time the starting gun sounds until she finishes the Bloomsday course, she will have planted her two Canadian crutches in front of her more than 13,000 times and swung her body ahead.

For two hot, tiring hours the 5-foot-3 mother of three will do the work of a weight lifter, lifting her 103-pound body off the ground with the crutches, planting her right leg ahead and moving another three yards toward the finish.

She will do it to make a point to those who laze about not just on Bloomsday Sunday but every Sunday.

With each swing of her arms Carmen Hasse hopes to jar the indolent from their angle of repose.

"My point in doing this is to encourage other people to get in shape," she said before the race.

"I want to share the benefits of physical exercise with others."

"If I get one person every year to begin an exercise program, or to get in shape for Bloomsday, I will go on. I love my purpose. I want to be healthy and encourage others to do it."

Carmen Hasse's children call her a health-natic. She is 44, born with only one functional leg, yet will not make excuses for flab.

Three years ago, in 1977, her husband, Dr. E. R. Hasse of Cheney, convinced her to start walking for health.

That began her training for Bloomsday.

"I started with half a mile and it seemed a terribly long distance," she said.

"I was self-conscious about my handicap.

"But I kept walking. My husband encouraged me.

"And, oh, my heavens, it's made a difference.

"I tell housewives, your whole attitude changes once you start getting into shape. I have a lot of energy. After I come home, I am ready to jump into my work.

"And in the springtime, with the smell of the wild roses, I can get high on exercise. It is a very different experience."

Carmen Hasse's life qualifies as a very different experience from the other mostly white, mostly non-handicapped runners in Bloomsday.

She was born in Mexico and has lived with one functional leg since infancy.

Since childhood she has not hidden her handicap nor let it slow her down much.

At three years old Carmen was given tow crutches but one afternoon she decided she wanted to pick up a cat and found she had no free hand to do so.

That day she threw down one crutch and picked up the cat.

Since then, she has mastered the art of walking with one leg and one helping staff.

She has raised her children, tended the house, taught a nutrition class in Cheney and still found time to train for Bloomsday.

And if that is not enough to make you stay to see her finish, then consider the friendly wager Carmen has going today.

"My husband is going to try to beat me going around twice this year," she said.

"He thinks he can run the course twice in the time I take to go around once. I think I'm going to beat him."

"I want to cover the course in less than two hours. I have walked almost every morning since November," she said. "In the winter I slipped on the ice and fell but I kept going.

"And I always try to take a friend with me. My neighbor has high blood pressure. She has begun walking with me every morning.

"We're making 17-minute miles together. Next week we will start on increasing our speed."

Today, four daughters and neighbors will travel the course with Carmen because she convinced them it would do them good.

That is the spirit of Bloomsday. It is the spirit of "yes I can" not "no I can't."

It is the thrill of knowing you have done something to make yourself feel better, the thrill of turning someone else on to the same idea.

"That's my goal," Carmen Hasse said. "I want people to say OK, if she can make it, I can make it.

"I am saying to them, you come with me next year. It would be so marvelous if they did. If everyone in the world would work on staying healthy, we would have a better world."

Be there at 2 p.m.

Carmen Hasse, the spirit of Bloomsday, is worth waiting to see and to cheer.

Bernie Babbitt: *MS victim whose friends pushed him through race*

There ought to be a monument to Bernie Babbitt and his friends.

A solid-gold running shoe or a crystal bead of sweat or maybe a wheelchair with Bernie's likeness in it and four friends huddled around.

There should be something. Because someday kids will wonder about Bloomsday, and puzzle at why thousands puffed and panted just to end up with a T-shirt.

When that day comes, the old runners could take the young to the shrine of Bernie Babbitt.

Old Bloomers would shuffle around the granite slab, and point at it and then it would all come back: the morning of May 31, 1981, Bloomsday V, and the sight of Bernie sitting in this wheelchair, wearing his gray Nike shoes and red Adidas warm-ups.

There would be no reason to tell the kids everything about Bernie.

The story might begin when Bernie Babbitt was a boy on the 1,200-acre wheat farm south of Colfax, Washington.

Bernie was introduced to running then. Early in the morning he would scamper after the dairy cattle and then race downhill to catch the country school bus.

The kids would like that.

But there would be no need to explain to them how Bernie, after he was graduated from Pullman High School in 1955, suffered through a bad marriage and did some drinking and took 15 years to finish college.

No, the story told at the Bernie Babbitt memorial would pick up in 1977 – the year Bernie turned 40.

He stood 5-6, 175 pounds then.

Someone dared him to run that new Bloomsday race in Spokane.

Bernie was a competitive son of a gun. So his wife hunted up an old pair of black tennies and Bernie borrowed some stinky gym shorts.

That first year he took 60 minutes to cover the 7.5 mile course and was rewarded with one hellacious set of blisters.

Yet the spirit of Bloomsday blossomed into nothing short of a change of seasons for Bernie Babbitt.

In the months after Bloomsday, Bernie kept running. He began to make new friends at events ranging from Harrington's Huff 'n' Puff to the Great Canal Caper in Ephrata.

His 40-year-old body sloughed 20 pounds and Bernie gave up junk foods.

After a few months, Bernie became so excited about running he dreamed up a run of his own.

"Run-to-the-Fair" he called it. Since 1978, kids from the wheat country have gathered at summer's end to run 3.5 miles as part of the Palouse Empire Fair in Colfax.

And in an odd sort of way, running made Bernie Babbitt a better father.

"I didn't mind his running," Kathy Babbitt said a few days before the fifth running of Bloomsday. "Running was a clean, healthy sport. We didn't meet a lot of people who were sitting around drinking and smoking. And the kids picked up on that. In fact, we chose runs where we could go as a family outing."

Always, Bernie returned to Bloomsday. His second year he hit 55 minutes. By the third he was at 52 minutes.

In 1980, the streak from the wheatlands tore from the pack and finished in 46 minutes and a few seconds.

At age 43 he placed 198th out of 14,000 runners, and in the top 10 finishes among men 40 to 44 years old.

That's why there ought to be a monument.

Bernie Babbitt's history typifies the history of a thousand other Bloomsday competitors.

Throw his old, old black tennies into a box, seal it with varnish and you would have the reliquary to the unknown runner.

And if that wasn't enough, the recognition that good health should be revered, the making of new friends and all the rest, well, there is something else that could go in the brochures at the Bernie Babbitt Memorial.

The most memorable chapter began to unfold October 12, 1980, the day Bernie drove to Yakima and ran all 26 miles, 385 yards of a marathon.

Afterwards, he felt sick. Bernie blamed his slightly queasy stomach on the race – and the hectic schedule he had undertaken the past few weeks.

It was harvest time on the farm. And Bernie was organizing the chicken and rabbit exhibits for the Palouse Empire Fair. Plus, he was driving school bus and working the graveyard shift at Safeway.

Five days after the Yakima Marathon, Bernie Babbitt was stumbling and having difficulty breathing.

By October 17, when he came to Spokane's Deaconess Hospital, he could no longer drive or walk without assistance.

Doctors tested him for neurological disorders and brain tumors. And they sent him home with a direct order to rest.

But Bernie couldn't rest. Nightmares kept him awake. He was often terrified that his pillow was attacking him.

By January, he developed a tremor. His coordination failed. He could neither feed himself nor walk.

Doctors finally concluded a scar had grown at the base of Bernie Babbitt's brain. It had nothing to do with running. It was just one more unexplained tragedy doled out by a largely unknown disease endemic to Eastern Washington.

In the spring of 1981, people on the rural running circuit of Eastern Washington began asking about Bernie.

One night Joe McManus, a Safeway manager in Ephrata and founder of the Great Canal Caper there, called to inquire about Bernie.

"We'd been running against Bernie since the first Bloomsday," Joe McManus told Kathy Babbitt. "Bernie was a friend and one gutsy competitor."

One night in late March, Joe McManus learned what had happened.

Bernie Babbitt had been hit with what his doctors called a "an unusually severe" case of multiple sclerosis and had quietly checked into the Pullman Convalescent Center.

Joe McManus spread the word. He called Jon Evavold, the organizer of the Harrington Huff 'n' Puff. He contacted Doug Miller, the force behind the Over-the-Dam run in Grand Coulee, Washington.

All runners were stunned. Bernie was just like them, someone who had taken to running to keep sane and healthy.

As the news sank in, Joe and the others begin to think that Bernie had to compete in Bloomsday, no matter what.

"Bloomsday was where it began for all of us," Joe told Bernie one night on the phone.

And he asked Bernie if he would let his old running buddies push him through the course in his wheelchair.

At first Bernie said no.

He didn't want to keep his friends from turning in good times.

"But I told Bernie it doesn't hurt to slow down once in a while and enjoy the scenery," Joe McManus recalled. "Because that's what Bloomsday is all about."

And so Bernie Babbitt finally agreed.

Even though he hit the wall, as they say in the running magazines, he kept going.

He displayed what his doctor described as a rare mental attitude toward his disease. He kept his spirits up and tried to go on living.

He worked out as best he could on a mat lying beside his bed. He arched his back and tossed a tennis ball from hand to hand to keep his joints loose and free.

"Because I loved running," he said one morning a few days before the race. The words stretched out like a voice on a tape recorder with the batteries going dead.

"It is very heavy, knowing that you may not ever part your hair again. But maybe if I can do this, it will inspire other people to keep at it," he said.

"I am very happy that my friends want to do this with me."

On that Sunday of Bloomsday V, Bernie Babbitt lined up at the front of the pack.

Two elastic bandages tied his legs to his wheelchair.

When the gun sounded, they were off – Joe McManus and Jon Evavold pushing; Doug Miller and Cline Sweet pulling the chair.

Down the asphalt, past the river, up the killer Heartbreak Hill they flew with Bernie Babbitt, a little four-wheeled, ten-legged band of Bloomsday spirit.

And that's why there ought to be a monument.

Kevin Proctor: Kid who pushed himself through Bloomsday, but whose name wasn't published

A few days ago *The Spokesman-Review* published the names and finish times of 51,000 Bloomsday celebrants.

One young man's vital statistics were missing. This is his story.

When Bloomsday first was staged in 1977, Kevin Proctor was eight years old. A rough and tumble kid from Spokane's lower South Hill, Kevin grew up around soccer and basketball and, most of all, his BMX bicycle.

In 1983 Kevin ran his first Bloomsday. The race was fun, and he finished in 1 hour and 10 minutes.

But he wasn't a devoted "Bloomie." Not then.

"Motorcycles were my major hobby," he recalled. "I loved the speed, the exhilaration of riding fast."

Through that summer, fall and into the spring of 1984, Kevin rode his motorcycle every possible moment. He took his machine off the pavement and roared along Latah Creek and the back trails near his home.

On March 7, 1984, he was riding south of Spokane on his way home. "There was no way to cross the creek except on the railroad bridge," he recalled. "So I went up on the tracks and over the bridge."

A train was parked on one set of tracks. Kevin veered his motorcycle away and jumped to the other set of tracks.

"When I went around the parked train, I saw the other train coming around the curve," he said.

When the train hit him, Kevin flew 90 feet and landed on the basalt near the banks of the creek.

When he awoke in the hospital, he was paralyzed below the waist.

There would be no Bloomsdays for a while. It took Kevin several years to rebuild his life.

He had to be fitted into a wheelchair. He had to return to Lewis and Clark High School to finish his classes. Toughest of all, he had to develop the inner strength not to wither under the stares of passers-by who acted as if they had never seen a teenager in a wheelchair before.

Then came learning to drive, living away from his loving family and, finally, getting a job.

Kevin found an apartment, bought an old car and landed a job with Telect, Inc., a company that manufactures telephone and telecommunications equipment in the Spokane Valley. Along the way, he has become a favorite around the company.

Last year, the Telect Boosters, an employee group devoted to community service, learned that Kevin wanted to race in Bloomsday.

"Kevin talked about how he would like to be in Bloomsday but that his wheelchair wasn't sufficient," Judy Williams, co-owner of Telect, recalled. "So, the Boosters got the idea of raising money to buy Kevin a racing wheelchair."

For months, Kevin's co-workers gathered scrap copper from the assembly lines, pooled their rebates from company vending machines and held car washes and other fund-raisers to raise money to buy Kevin a racing chair.

This spring, they ordered the $2,000 bright-pink wheelchair and presented it to Kevin at a special ceremony. Everyone was thrilled.

Last Sunday, Kevin pinned his number on his shirt and lined up with the other wheelchair racers.

From the moment the gun sounded, he felt the wondrous exhilaration of racing in his new chair. "It was like riding in a Porsche compared with a VW," he said.

Down the hills he zoomed to more than 30 mph. Uphill, he gritted his teeth and toughed it out.

"I gave it my all coming down Broadway," he said. "I pulled a muscle in my shoulder, pulled a muscle in my elbow and pulled a muscle in my forearm. But I was giving it everything I had for the people who were cheering me on."

At the finish, a race official tore off Kevin's finish tag just as it usually happens. Kevin gathered up his T-shirt and went home to wait for the race results to be published in the newspaper the next day.

But a glitch prevented that. When the Lilac Bloomsday Association began to tabulate the names of the more than 51,000 finishers, a handful of finish tags were misplaced.

"We think six or seven people in wheelchairs weren't included in the original list of finishers," Tom Cameron, the Bloomsday Association's wheelchair coordinator, said.

The people at Telect noticed that Kevin's name wasn't published; Kevin's mother noticed, too, and called the newspaper.

"As a mother, the hardest part about Kevin's accident is just seeing him struggle with the everyday," Barbara Proctor explained.

And, of course, Kevin noticed, too.

"Heck, this is just such a great community event. I wanted to be part of it and see my name in the paper just to sort of finalize everything," he said.

In a few days, the Bloomsday association will send Kevin a letter notifying him of his official time and offer an apology for missing him the first time.

Here at the newspaper, we want to set the record straight, too.

The following name and finish time should be stapled into the 1990 official Bloomsday results:

Proctor, Kevin – 49 minutes, 55 seconds.

Way to go.

Bloomsday's a big nuisance

She appeared about two miles into my Bloomsday training course.

After 13 years of spring training to prepare for the world's largest timed fun run, I felt confident in my technique for discouraging dogs with big teeth and a desire to taste sweat pants.

You stop. You say something unkind about the mongrel's lineage. You clap your hands or shout, and the cur slinks away.

But this hunk of bones wouldn't take the hint.

When I ran, she ran.

When I stopped, she stopped.

As I assailed her mixed breed background, her rear wagged like a metronome.

Not willing to allow a stray dog to interrupt a necessary day of working off a winter of too many cookies, I decided to simply carry on.

The dog would tire, grow bored, get lost.

So went the rationalizations of a confirmed cat lover.

Cat lovers don't understand dogs.

We can't comprehend their dumb obedience. Their unexamined loyalties. Their quick attachments, even to those who might loft small stones in their direction.

A mile later, I was panting like a pup myself only to look back and see a slobbering, loping ball of wet, muddy mutt on my tail.

Every long canine, bicuspid and incisor in her wolfish jaw gleamed white.

Her tongue hung like a limp slab of lox.

She was smiling!

We approached downtown Spokane, clogged with early rush-hour traffic.

I imagined a flattened, rug-like corpse as she foolishly burst into the busy lanes in pursuit of a robin, or a leaf or some other inane diversion.

I found myself calling out in a high voice that sounded like a bad imitation Vince Gill. "Here dog! Come here, pooch."

I bent over, wrapped my arms around this bundle of energy and walked like an old crone across the bridge as if I were wearing a huge dog charm around my neck.

My cat would have been ashamed.

Now we were far from where our paths had chanced to cross. Not wanting to be someone who abandoned a brain-challenged animal in the heart of the city, I now had sunk to encouraging this aggravation on four legs to keep up.

She gladly agreed.

On we went, down by the river, across the bridges, past the cemetery.

One of us was panting like a mutt. The other seemed serenely content to simply enjoy the scenery.

At Doomsday Hill, the big test for any Bloomsday runner, I imagined my opportunity to burst ahead and put some distance between me and my unwanted partner.

Instead, the dog sprinted to the top of the hill.

As I wheezed to the crest, she adopted an angle of repose.

She considered us friends. On the last stretch home she stayed close to my heel. Too close.

Our legs became entangled as I tripped and slid in the gravel, spewing venomous comments.

She scampered off in chase of a quail.

My biggest mistake was taking pity on her and filling a bucket of water at the end of the run.

Exhibiting timeless doggie etiquette, she slurped up a gallon of water and delivered a sticky lick to my face as I bent down to retrieve the bowl.

The cat didn't appreciate it one bit.

She climbed a telephone pole and spent all day there.

I climbed the pole about 11 p.m., thereby raising my life insurance premiums and adding to the scar tissue on my hands from the cat's claws.

My wife hid in the garage with the dog.

My wife's allergies erupted with an intensity that turned her eyes into overripe cherry tomatoes.

For a week now the dog has camped out on the back porch. The front of my little boy's clothes look like an advertisement for Save the Wildlife.

I try to sneak out each morning for a few laps around the neighborhood, but she is there in all her panting, wagging exuberance.

The dog has taught this lifelong cat person a lesson in tolerance.

Dogs live here, too.

They need love, and care, and attention.

In her annoying way, she has provided a lesson in family life, too. All of us need to find ways to make room for those unexpected things that show up as we travel this road.

We've decided to get a collar. And shots. And a license.

And somehow we're going to redefine our space and the picture of our family to include this mutt, assuming her other owners wherever they are, don't want her back.

My son named the dog Bloomsday.

As long as she is content eating cat food, we will get along just fine.

Why virtual Bloomsday can't exist

Virtual Bloomsday doesn't exist.

You can't go on-line to run this software.

This user group huffs and puffs in real time, real life.

The batteries can get low after an hour or two, but Bloomsday isn't a cyberspace community.

It's a real one, where the chat line extends back five blocks.

The differences between cyberspace and the Bloomsday race are important to consider right now.

Much smoke is being blown by Microsoftians about the value, the promise and the inevitability of a future world with little but Intel Inside.

In cyberspace, the vision of community begins with a bonding built around modems, our intellects stimulated by information sent via the Internet from all parts of the globe.

No need to leave home.

No need to run into people who don't think as we do.

This, the cyberspaceologists say, will be a huge part of community life of the 21st century.

Huh? This sounds as bad as wolfing down a big plate of sausage and eggs just before the race, an idea that could make all of us really sick.

The meaning of community happens on the streets of Spokane this morning.

The computer goes dark.

People leave their houses.

Friends of the Militia of Montana will rub running shorts with federal workers who have also come to run.

The community gathers not online and isolated, but in the streets for a common purpose.

Old and young, rich and poor, fat and skinny, Republican, Democrat, Independent, they show up to participate.

The community brings quite different people together in a public venue, where they agree to follow a few simple rules, then make their way at their own pace.

This combination of bringing diverse people together in a public place for a common purpose, where a few rules guide all on individual journeys, stands as an ancient and enduring model for community.

The alternative model is being much discussed and furiously promoted.

By the year 2010, three out of every four American households will be wired for interactive computer services, according to Strategic Futures, Inc.

At workshops and seminars in almost every industry and institution, this day 15 years hence is being presented as a liberated time when everyone can be their own mayor, own publisher and own at-home shopper.

Except that when everyone is a mayor, no one is.

And will this experience of going solo on all the communications, all the shared experiences of community, actually fulfill the heart, mind and soul?

Will it have the excitement of a Bloomsday morning, where real human beings press together, with real goose bumps at the sound of the gun going off?

In his book *Silicon Snake Oil*, which was reviewed recently in *Time* magazine, cyberspace veteran Clifford Stoll argues that the virtual community must never take the place of the real.

"Life in the real world is far more interesting, far more important, far richer, than anything you'll ever find on a computer screen," he writes.

At 9 this morning you will see the living, breathing proof on the streets of Spokane.

Real community events such as Bloomsday tap into something far more emotional, far more substantial, far more lasting than a world on a screen.

The computer, of course, offers a tremendous assist to a genuine community event.

Every finishing time will be sorted on a computer and then published in the newspaper tomorrow.

Reporters covering Bloomsday this year used the computer to crunch numbers and discover that more than 4,000 runners fibbed about their estimated finish times today by subtracting an hour or more from their actual finish times last year – in order to assure a better starting place this year.

Computers assisted the reporters in discovering that runners from Boulder, Colorado, and Big Timber, Montana, have the fastest average times for any townspeople in the race.

And tomorrow, the computer will calculate the fastest 100 Spokane residents to run Bloomsday.

The hardware and software of the electronic age provide powerful, imaginative tools to a community.

Family and friends can send e-mail about the race.

As early as next year, runners will be able to look up their times online as *The Spokesman-Review's* online service begins to be more active.

But to actually be part of this event in this place on the first Sunday of May requires you to be here in a genuine, living community.

Accept no substitute. There is none.

Allied Arts Festival

Playing in public, something all kids must learn

Shortly before noon last Thursday, Lindsey Nelson lost a key on the piano.

It happened to be the first note of the piece she had prepared for the 48th Greater Spokane Music and Allied Arts Festival.

All of us who witnessed her search for the missing key desperately wanted to help her find it.

Had it slipped underneath the pedals?

Was it hiding beneath the fragrant lilac bushes outside Gonzaga University's administration building where her performance was scheduled?

No one knew, least of all the frozen young pianist at the keyboard.

Thankfully, the adjudicator who held Lindsey's music gently described where the girl might find the first note of her piece.

It was a G above Middle C, I think.

With that small prompt, Lindsey Nelson suddenly found the missing key and plunged into her music with vigor.

Every kid and parent in the hall sighed with relief.

Lindsey had managed to recover from what we all most dread about public performance.

The lost page of the speech, the forgotten name during a toast, the slip on the dance floor when all eyes are watching – these are the true agonies of life.

Every year since 1946, hundreds of young people from all over the Inland Northwest have come sweaty-palmed and sleepless to Spokane to take part in the Greater Spokane Music and Allied Arts Festival.

As I feverishly sent telepathic suggestions to Lindsey Nelson on where she might find the first note of her music, I wondered, "Is this agony worth it for kids?"

Yes, said Barbara English Maris, the kindly woman who found the missing note and helped the terrified student get off to a good start.

Maris acknowledged public performances at Spokane's premier musical event could be either uplifting or a disaster. Either way, the day in front of the crowd can be a valuable experience.

All of us, she noted, need to understand what it takes for a good public performance. "Because we all are performing every day of our lives," she said.

"If we give a speech, if we have to introduce someone, if we are hosting a party at our homes, it is a kind of performance. We need to know how to do it well."

And every adult knows this task doesn't come easily. There is a knack to it, and before you learn you almost always take a spill.

At the same time, the value of knowing how to perform in public can be widely and readily observed.

The student body president of your high school had it.

So does Bill Clinton.

The guy at the piano on Christmas Eve always wins a smile because he can pound out a rousing rendition of "Rudolph the Red-Nosed Reindeer."

Mick Jagger and Thomas Hampson have made careers of the art of public performance.

Indeed, Hampson, the famous baritone of the Metropolitan Opera in New York who recently was named by *People* magazine as one of the world's 50 most beautiful people, got his start at the Greater Spokane Music and Allied Arts Festival.

In 1978 Hampson won best young artist in the voice division of the festival. He had talent and he didn't freeze on the stage.

Unfortunately, some parents and kids forget the importance of learning the full spectrum of skills needed for successful public performance and focus instead only on the judging of a particular talent.

That's a recipe for tears.

"I was working with a little girl who was so terrified about her score that she was just sobbing hysterically at the piano," said Victoria Wyatt, another adjudicator at the music festival. "I went up to her and told her that this day wasn't going to kill her. I said this was just one experience in her whole life and that sometimes we do really well on a day and sometimes we don't. I felt bad for her because no one had talked to this child about what it meant to perform."

Aimee Stormo, a young pianist from Moscow, Idaho, had her anxious moments, too.

Friday was her first day ever at the big music festival. But when her name was called, she calmly went to the piano and nailed a perfect minuet.

Later, her mother explained the secret. "First, she practiced a lot," said Mary Stormo. A key lesson: Practice in private what you eventually will perform in public.

"Then, on the night before we came up here she was anxious, but I told her to try to relax. I said the (judge) didn't eat children for lunch. She liked that." Another key lesson: Remember that today's public performance is only one day in the rest of your life.

Whether it's getting ready for your mother-in-law's visit or preparing for Carnegie Hall, performing in public requires a kind of balancing act between hard work, discipline and a desire to meet high standards on one hand, versus an easy-going, it's-just-another-day attitude on the other.

This balance isn't easy.

But it's the real test given the kids who for 48 years have come to Spokane for the music and arts festival.

It's not about who scored a superior and who had an excellent.

The festival is a place where young kids and their parents learn what it takes to get up in public and not make a fool of yourself.

The value of practice is apparent

Hayley Jensen, 15, was taking a break between performances.

She sat in the warm, afternoon sun on a bench outside Hughes Auditorium at Gonzaga University.

Sunning herself on a school day isn't what got Hayley Jensen here.

She won two gold medals this week in the fiercely competitive piano competition at the 52nd annual Greater Spokane Music and Allied Arts Festival.

Now, she waited for a playoff with other gold medal winners to see who would end up on stage at the festival's final concert.

"I practice the piano on the average of an hour and a half a day," Hayley said with her braces-perfect smile.

"Sometimes it's tough to fit in around soccer, tennis and basketball," said the Walla Walla High School freshman. "But that's what my teacher says it takes if I want to succeed. And I don't like to come all the way up here to perform and not do well."

Here rests the secret most successful artists, athletes and high achievers in every field know: The habit of good practice lays the foundation for great success.

The discipline of practice doesn't come naturally to most people.

Hundreds of children take piano lessons.

Only a handful won gold medals at the arts festival.

Certainly innate ability plays an important role in success at the piano or any area of human accomplishment.

If you don't have the voice, you really shouldn't expect to be on Broadway. If you stand 5 feet 4 inches, think computers not basketball.

But practice, practice and more practice separates those with potential from those with the gold medals.

And practice isn't something your mother makes you do.

Back at Gonzaga, only a few feet away from Hayley Jensen, mother Kandy Gore was pacing back and forth outside the glass doors of the auditorium.

Her son, Kyle Dresback, also won a gold medal for his piano playing.

"Kyle would never have gotten this far if I had to push him all the time to practice," she said.

"I could force him for a while, to kind of get him over the hump, but at this point he practices on his own. It takes a lot of discipline on his part."

For most kids and most adults the discipline needed to fit in regular practices amid the temptations of an entertainment-oriented, quick-fix society is a discipline as foreign as reading Latin.

Whether learning a language, or learning to rock climb, there are methods for practice.

Mary Toy, among the best-known and most demanding piano teachers in Spokane, even teaches classes in how to practice.

She had four students in the finals at Gonzaga. As her students began to take their places in the auditorium, she talked about some of what it took for them to be there.

"It's not just practice time," she said. "You have to have the proper procedures, the proper tools for practicing."

Baseball great Cal Ripken, Jr. put it this way: It isn't just practice that makes perfect, but perfect practices that make perfect.

Toy's guide to good practice includes these tips:
• Practice when your mind is alert.
• Focus on the hard parts.
• Play music slowly again and again until the brain has it memorized the right way.
• Don't keep running through the whole piece of music, but take segments and perfect them.

"Probably the most common mistake is that people practice without thinking or listening," she added.

"To practice well you have to actively use your mind to think about what the composer wanted. You have to be a detective. Study the music. Find out what is there," she explained. "Then, listen to what you are playing. Focus on what you hear."

Practice, in other words, isn't mindless.

It is a focused act, not to be confused with thinking about the boyfriend or whom you want to call when practice is over.

All of which explains why so few kids who start piano end up each May waiting to play at Hughes Auditorium.

Those who do end up there leave little doubt that practice can lead to a beautiful place.

All the gold-medal winners sat quietly at first, looking down at their hands on the piano keys.

Then, the hours of repetition, exercises, focused attention, right fingering and careful listening merged in their minds and bodies and they began to play.

Words cannot capture the mastery these young people displayed.

To listen was to be awed by their accomplishments and touched by their souls and intelligence.

At young ages they already could demonstrate a lifelong talent few ever achieve in anything.

Their hours of practice had resulted in artistic accomplishments that eclipsed any benefit that might have come from more time on the phone, or in front of the TV, or simply being like most of us who won't practice enough to make it matter.

Daily Life in Spokane

First Day of School: Daunting list of expectations for teachers

In eight weeks, my son will slick back his hair, put on his new sneakers and head off to first grade.

His classroom is all cleaned and ready but at the moment he doesn't have a teacher.

Early this spring, his school donated a prize elementary educator to bigger things in the district office.

That left a hole, a place for a new face.

The principal invited a group of parents to prepare questions for the prospective teachers and to sit in on the interviews.

For weeks, we parents met at night with poster paper and pens to discuss and write down the key attributes we wanted in a teacher.

Our list started like this: "Open, energetic, accepting, creative, organized, dedicated, likes Halloween, nurturing, healthy, positive, good thinker, honest, intelligent, and be a global citizen."

All we forgot was the often overlooked reason American education has been getting a bad rap.

We're asking a heck of a lot from teachers. In many ways, we're asking them to do much more than teach. They need to parent, provide discipline, set boundaries, establish values, counsel and hold troubled hands.

Teachers find themselves having to compensate for the shortcomings of a great many other people and institutions, including mom and dad, the church, siblings, politicians and extended families.

The list of ideal characteristics for my son's teacher went on: ". . . musician, adventuresome, bold, lifelong learner, sensitive, strong self-image . . ."

Would Bill Clinton, Ross Perot or George Bush be able to fill this job?

How about Hillary, Tipper or Marilyn Quayle?

Rather than a longer list of what teachers need to do, I think we need a shorter one.

Once interviews with my son's potential future mentors began, I sensed that three basics would do more to help him get started in school than the long list of "this would be nice."

No. 1 on the short list of teacher attributes: hire someone with a spark.

Our kids aren't dumber than all those kids in other countries with better scores. But they may be more bored.

After all, they watch a lot of sophisticated, entertaining TV and video. They know about entertainment before they learn multiplication tables. And they don't have long spans of attention.

Today's teachers probably could learn something from Ross Perot. They need to practice some sales and some preaching. Get the crowd fired up.

The best of the teachers who interviewed for my son's classroom spoke of this. They wanted to light fires beneath every kid, showing them the wonder of the world, not just read from the book.

Next on the short list: find someone who really believes all kids are special and don't learn in the same ways.

Of course I put my little boy in each prospective teacher's classroom. I imagined how his teacher would cope with his ants-in-the-pants style of learning that requires touching, feeling, experiencing.

Then I considered how my daughter learned. She observed, listened and watched.

Could they prosper under the same direction? I think so, as long as their differences were recognized and honored.

Yes. The best of the candidates for my son's class discussed such concepts as age-appropriate teaching, hands-on learning techniques and integrated curriculum that allows a kid a multitude of ways to catch on.

The third basic for today's teachers: find the ones who go out of their way to get parents involved.

This may be the key to it all. More than inviting parents to conferences or to join the PTA, parents need to buy into what happens in class. And, they need to be there or at least sit down before the year starts to plan projects and themes.

The principal in my son's school acknowledged that many teachers are still reluctant, if not outright fearful, of having parents in the classroom and having parents help design coursework.

The principal also said that many teachers have felt overwhelmed by the added responsibilities of the job.

So maybe it's time to get back to basics with our expectations for teachers.

They need to be charged up again. They need to understand the differences in each kid, and they need to work in partnership with parents.

That's what I want for my son.

Rachael Carver: One girl didn't make it to 4th grade

On Tuesday most young children of the Inland Northwest will be safely seated in school.

Rachel Carver will not be there.

The dark-haired girl who would have been entering fourth grade at Spokane's Ridgeview Elementary was assaulted and killed June 15, 1995 – the last day of school.

Her uncle, Jason Wickenhagen, is charged with her murder.

At a forum sponsored by *The Spokesman-Review* a few nights ago to discuss what can be done to reduce the risk of other child-abuse deaths, a chilling comment echoed through the auditorium at Shadle Park High School as the discussion began.

"There are many Rachel Carvers in Spokane," said Cheryl Steele, director of the city's community-oriented policing program. "We just don't know where they all are."

For too many kids, personal safety is a subject that must be learned at school because it isn't practiced at home.

The defining difference between a safe school and an unsafe home is that a school, regardless of its politics, educational philosophy or location, is a community.

Adults and children spend time together, watching one another, talking, walking and interacting every day.

And it is community that seems to make all the difference when it comes to the safety of a child.

In a recent *Time* magazine story, anthropologist Phillip Walker notes that in his study of bones from 5,000 children in pre-industrial cultures dating back 6,000 years, he has never found bruises that provide the skeletal hallmark of battered children.

In today's society, if tests were run on the bones of children in America's classrooms, one in 20 would show signs of child battering.

The reason?

Walker believes it goes back to community. Primitive children were raised under the watchful eyes of aunts, grandparents and friends in communities where little went unnoticed behind the mammoth-hide doors.

At the newspaper forum on preventing child abuse, Spokane Child Protective Services director Dee Wilson offered a similar perspective. Wilson noted that half the children who die from abuse and neglect in our region were children who were unsupervised much of the time. There was no aunt, no uncle, no caring, responsible adult from the community watching over them.

And when asked the best hope for preventing or reducing child abuse deaths, Wilson said this: "Home visiting is the best thing we know to do."

To visit a home requires someone to consider the neighborhood as belonging to them. But we know that few neighbors today bother to pay attention or even dare to intrude next door. Instead, the state has taken over that visitation – with limited success.

Given this assessment, could it be our politicians are baling too much political hay on the issue of needing tougher laws to fight and prevent crime?

Surely legal loopholes need to be closed that allowed Jason Wickenhagen to be free even though he had tried to rape a 16-year-old only weeks before Rachel Carver's death. To his credit, Representative Mark Sterk of Spokane has made closing this loophole a campaign issue.

But changing laws cannot create a community.

In fact, much of our anxiety over crime actually has led to more locked doors, high walls and threatening signs that all visitors should keep out.

In truth, we can't keep out of each other's lives.

The problems that lead to child abuse and neglect are community problems that affect us and cost us all. Our prisons already are overflowing with men and women who themselves were abused and neglected and who, in turn, abuse.

Our schools already are disrupted by children whose rage at abuse spills onto others in the classroom.

Our neighborhoods already are home to children at risk and parents who desperately need guidance.

We have to pay attention and be responsible for ourselves and our neighbors. No single best way exists for paying attention to neighbors and their children. Something as small as inviting yourself up to a troubled door with a plate of cookies might be a start.

Organizing a single mothers' support group at church could work.

Giving time and money to organized crisis centers in the region would be a step.

Reporting suspicious activities to the police is something we all should do.

What doesn't work is simply to pull the shades, turn on the TV.

All that will do is lead us once again to shake our heads in shame when the story of the next Rachel Carver flickers on the screen.

Last day of school: Valedictorians come in all forms

Jeff Burningham's brain has been bashed regularly with the music of Pearl Jam. Classmate Brandon Enevold's mind has been routinely invaded by Arnold Schwarzenegger's violent movies. Jeff and Brandon are 18.

They live in the Spokane Valley.

All through high school, they have been swimming in the American pop culture that pounds out endless entertainment images based on sex, drugs and violence.

This beat recently prompted presidential aspirant Bob Dole to describe today's music and movies as "nightmares of depravity," poisoning the souls and minds of American young people.

Are Jeff and Brandon poisoned souls?

"Gee, I hope not," Jeff said a few days after his graduation from University High School.

Although he could recite the words to "Jeremy," Pearl Jam's anthem to a nerd lost in school, Jeff Burningham doesn't fit a stereotype of a lost teenager.

Jeff graduated as a valedictorian from University High with a 4.0 average. His close relationship with the music of Nirvana didn't stop him from being elected student body president. He lettered in football and basketball all three years.

"And I still had time to go out with my friends to have some fun," he said.

A similar story can be charted for Brandon Enevold. His musical tastes run to Garth Brooks (who sings about a boy and a girl staying up all night in a pickup truck) and movies where big guns rule the world.

"Sure, some of it goes too far, but I guess the most important thing is for kids to know the difference between right and wrong before they go into the theater," Brandon said. "And while I don't really like the gangster movies, with all the bad language and stuff, I guess I can see that if that's the way life is in the big cities, then the movie is just trying to show it."

Brandon Enevold also pulled a 4.0 at University High School and shared the valedictorian stage. Besides perfect grades, he found time to win a power weightlifting competition and go bow hunting on weekends.

The stories of these 18-year-olds who managed to do well in school while listening to music and watching Hollywood movies suggest more thought needs to go into the relationship between popular culture and the disturbing attractions some young people have for drugs, sex and violence.

Surely the plague of teenage pregnancies, juvenile violence and below-average achievements presents troubling challenges to the nation's future. We know we need to do something about these trends.

But what?

After listening to Jeff Burningham and Brandon Enevold talk about their lives, it seems clear they have been influenced by forces more powerful than pop movies and music.

These young men found strength in their families.

They developed a youthful self-confidence based on their own sense of self. At a young age they focused on a point far beyond the next party or night out with their high school friends.

"I have a box in my closet I made in ninth grade," Jeff Burningham recalled. "Four years ago I wrote on the sides my goals for sports, school, church and family. And I have tried to keep to those goals."

The writing on the side of the box included such things as getting all A's, doing his very best in sports, avoiding drugs and alcohol.

"As I went to high school, I had to make a personal stand for these," he said. "Instead of going out to a game, I sometimes had to stay home and do some calculus. It was totally tough not to go out and party in my sophomore year. But once everyone knew that I wasn't into partying, it was fine."

Brandon Enevold described a similar, personal determination.

"I always got my homework done because I knew I wanted to get scholarships for college," he said. "I would tell kids coming into high school that it's not like you aren't cool if you don't party all weekend," he said. "It's your own choice and I chose not to."

Each of these valedictorians was molded early by a loving family that believed in them and set high standards. That molding and standard-setting happened before either Jeff or Brandon had watched many movies or owned their own collections of music. And, in their early adolescent years, when they moved into the world of pop culture and teenage peer pressure, each of these young men set personal goals and held to them.

Their road to success passed through the movie theater and by the record rack, but these amusements didn't lead them down a wrong path.

They already had a road map of where they wanted to go.

Shopping: Eagle Hardware has 146 kinds of hammers

I'm not sure women have a relationship with their hammers. Men do.

I would wager every man has a hammer.

He may not be able to put his hands on it at the moment, know whether it is safely tucked in his tool box or hanging from a nail in the basement, but somewhere every man has one.

In this life a man learns about many tools from computers to combs. Through all these lessons his hammer remains his oldest, most loyal friend.

This is because hammers are the first tools a boy learns to master. His first bottle is a hammer, also his first pencil, often his first younger sibling.

Long after he has gone to college, or put on a suit and tie, or retired from active hammering, the thrill of hammering remains.

This enduring fascination explains the crowd of men encountered on aisle 11 of the recently-opened Eagle Hardware and Garden store in Spokane.

We all were gathered at this sacred place for one reason: to judge whether the advertising was true.

Could it be that someone had assembled 146 different hammers to choose from? Was this truly the largest hammer selection under one roof? Many men went not believing hammers came in that many shapes and sizes.

Sure, framing, tacking, riveting, shingling and ball peen hammers would be there. But 146 different strokes?

We stood quietly just across from the 48 different varieties of work gloves. It was true. This was hammer heaven.

"I've looked everywhere for a hammer like this," said a quietly amazed collector of unusual and little-known mallets as he carried off a twin-headed, plastic-coated masher mall.

Every man seemed to be humming a different verse of that classic hit: "If I Had a Hammer."

There was the carpenter's version: "I don't pound so straight so I need a hammer that's good for pulling nails," said Charlie Staley, a commercial builder. "And I don't want to hit a nail 10 times. I want it to go in two."

Charlie went away with a 25-ounce Hart framing hammer.

The gentle soul's version: "This is just right for mounting tires," said Harry Reed. "Sometimes a guy doesn't want to leave bruises on the wood, or the tires, or whatever it is he's pounding." In his hands was a rubber mallet filled with buckshot.

The New Kids on the Block version: "My kid loves to collect rocks," said Tom Kynett of Deer Park. "This is great for chipping away at stuff." He left with a geologist's hammer with one flat end.

I'm not sure why men actually need the choice of 146 different kinds of hammers. The basics of hammering, after all, often come down to a simple formula: pick it up and wail on the sucker.

I suspect the awe felt when standing before this wall of at-rest destruction is linked to a deep-seated worry men have about being judged by their tools.

The wrong tool, handled inexpertly, all but guarantees low self-esteem.

The right tool, used with precision and grace, offers proof of one's mastery of a basic task of manhood. That is why I think Eagle Hardware will prove to be a colossal hit.

Sure, it is a hardware store, but it is also something else. This place brought out true passion and mystery for those on aisle 11, and elsewhere in the acres and acres of wrenches, fasteners, fixtures, blades, wires and rivets.

These things are practical, yes. They can be used to stop a leak or drive a nail. But there is something more. The sight of this opulence taps into a man's desire to build and create.

To understand the reverie just visit aisle 11 sometime, as I did.

Turn right at the 13-piece professional screwdriver set.

There they are – 146 different hammers and the men who love them.

How to pronounce Spokane: Everybody else calls it SpoCAIN

Luckily for his larynx, Francis Cook never flew from Spokane to the East.

Of course, he couldn't have flown even if he had wanted to.

Francis Cook published the first newspaper in Spokane. The year was 1879 and his city, which was called Spokane Falls at the time, had 75 people and no airport.

By the time airplanes were invented, Cook had lost his fortune and couldn't afford to fly.

Perhaps it was just as well he didn't touch down in Chicago or New York or Atlanta.

If he had, he likely would have been hauled off by the security police for screaming at all the ticket takers and bellhops.

You see, Francis Cook had one, consuming passion.

For 40 years, he fought against the mispronunciation of his hometown. "Spo-CAN! Spo-CAN!" he would shout in the faces of those who insisted on pronouncing his town Spo-CAIN.

At his frontier newspaper, he refused to accept the wholly-extraneous "e" in the spelling of his new town.

"There was never any sense to adding that final 'e'," he said in 1918, explaining why his newspaper always was called the *Spokan Falls Times*.

Often talking until he was hoarse, he made a simple, rational point.

No word in English which ends in "ane" is pronounced like Spok-CAN, he said.

The letters "ane" ring only one note in America, he said. It was the sound of a hurricane vibrating the membrane of even the most mundane ear.

Cook warned that persisting with the "e" at the end of its name would doom the little city on the plains to an eternal position of confusion and misunderstanding throughout the world.

With 100 years of hindsight, it is clear Francis Cook was absolutely correct.

"We get 40 or 50 people a day who mispronounce it," admitted a Pacific Northwest Bell operator.

"From all parts of the country they get it wrong. They all say Spo-CAIN.

"It's the 'e' that's throwing them."

Anyone who has traveled to the Midwest, the East or the South knows the drift to Spo-CAIN is growing more serious by the day.

Indeed, there is ample evidence that, unbeknownst to the people of Eastern Washington, the rest of the world has successfully changed the name of Washington's second largest city.

"Most people in the East don't say it the way we say it," said the Pacific Northwest Bell operator. "And I never correct people. The customer is always right."

The phone company isn't the only organization being humane, and allowing this place to be called Spo-CAIN.

In airports, ticket takers are letting hundreds of people board airplanes bound for Spok-CAIN.

On late night TV, the announcers who sell 14 songs by their original artists are constantly wrapping their records in cellophane and sending them to Spo-CAIN.

And honestly, if anybody here wanted to challenge this drift, not much ammunition can be found for the now-entrenched local spelling.

History is no help.

According to the late Reverend Jonathan Edwards, author of the authoritative *History of Spokane County, Washington*, of 1914, there was anything but a consensus on how the new town's name should be spelled.

Early fur trappers coined the name, "Spokane," to describe the Indians who lived here in the 1840s.

But the trappers were notoriously bad spellers. Some called the newly-discovered Indians the Spokeins, some the Spokanes.

The earliest reference to the place from anyone literate came from the famous Samuel Parker. And he bats for the other side.

"The name of this (place) is generally written Spokan . . ." the Reverend Parker wrote in his diary in 1836.

Nearly 150 years later, the English language has offered scant evidence to suggest local pronunciation is right and the world's is wrong.

The 1980 edition of the *Capricon Rhyming Dictionary* lists 46 English words that end in -ane.

All 46 are pronounced with a traditional "hard A" sound.

"Really, in English when you have an -ane, it should be pronounced with a long vowel," admitted Washington State

41

University linguist Geoff Gamble. "The rules (of phonetics) require that."

Since Francis Cook's demise, the people living along the banks of the Spokane River haven't shown much interest in what Samuel Parker said, or what the phone operators are doing, or what the rules of English require.

To them, Spokane is SpoCAN.

"And you always have to go with the local people," linguist Gamble was quick to point out, for fear of his life. "The people here take precedence. They will laugh off SpoCAIN for sure."

But is it really a laughing matter?

Think of it.

Most of the world doesn't know about this place anyway.

And the part that does thinks this city rhymes with insane, inane and profane.

That's wrong.

We know it's wrong. They should know, too.

I say revive the long-sighted views of Francis Cook.

Send that "e" to Wenatchee.

An extra one won't bother them.

Weather

Why we live here is largely due to beautiful summers

Consider the deep psychological importance of resin chairs.

What? You say there is no profundity resting in these four-legged icons of summer?

You have forgotten why you live here.

Maybe you have been chained in front of the TV watching O. J.'s preliminary hearing.

Perhaps you recently bought a home computer and now fiddle deep into the night making sure the Quicken software has accounted for your last five cents.

Could you be obsessing on your daughter's boyfriend or the neurosis of your boss?

Something is wrong if you haven't bought a resin chair and begun to sit in it yet.

This is summer in the Pacific Northwest.

Of course there are other seasons, of snow, and spring, and Hemingway, who best of all loved fall.

But this is when evening hangs still and cool as raspberry sorbet and the long twilight could serve as a backdrop to heaven itself.

To feel as if you have to sit and let summer nights wash over you like a freshened towel.

You must turn off the TV, walk away from the computer, leave the bickering and the trivia of life inside, and go out.

You must find a vista, a panorama, a view west where the high plains sky meets the vestige of Pacific rains.

This unusual mixture at the edge of one ecosystem, wet and green, bumping against another that is dry and high and clear, makes the summer here.

This is why resin chairs sell by the thousands.

Check the porches and decks of the rich and the not-so-rich and you will see them in white, or green, or possibly gray, all-plastic and identical, easy to nest this fall when their work is done.

They stand 30 high outside your garden or hardware store.

What a bargain. For $10 or less you may pack one home, despite the disturbing intuition that the chair, like last year's fishing rod, might spend all of July and August unused.

No matter.

It can stand the rain, the sun, even the inattention.

But seeing it there at dusk might remind you of a need to go out and sit.

This isn't about comfort for the backside.

Some resin chairs do just fine. Others offer a little dance when you settle in them. "Really, you've got to kind of sit down and wiggle around in it a little bit," advised Prisca Wilson, customer service manager for Ernst in the Spokane Valley.

Don't worry. Your comfortable chair waits in by the TV, a kind of coffin with a backrest where your senses dull.

A resin chair occupied on a Northwest summer night molds a different effect.

Just as staring at the Magic Eye suddenly brings a stunning new perspective into focus, an evening spent outside in the folding light of summer brings new insight about who we are and about this place where we live.

Cycles of warmth and coolness. Long days that begin with birds chirping at 5 a.m. and outlast us as we fade.

To comprehend summer nights requires each of us to extend, elongate and renew our schedules. From early June until late August, an extra portion of a day becomes affixed to the end of work and inserted before the beginning of sleep.

We must decide something to do just then.

Perhaps this is why no one buys just one resin chair.

The chairs almost always leave the store in twos and fours. The hours of summer nights compel us to share.

Notice your neighborhood and street. You will see people clumped together, family or friends renewing friendships, laughter and love.

No, this is more than molded plastic.

This is an idea, a notion, something easily lifted and set in place by ancient grandmothers or toddlers.

This is a promise of a sweet breath in a time choked by smoke, and haze, and the sweat of work by day.

On a summer night you just might forget all that.

Don't forget your resin chair.

Winters are long, and renewal is important here

The last weeks of winter aren't pretty in our part of the world. White snow turns brown. White people turn pasty.

Shoes carry a telltale ring of salty residue – a sure sign someone has stepped into slush for the 16th consecutive day.

Cars look as if nobody cares, because nobody does. Why bother?

Any attempt to wash off the thin film of late-winter grime only leads to immediate irritation once the tires turn out of the car wash.

Is this why 7,100 people turned out for the Spokane Chiefs hockey game on Wednesday night? A diversion in the big city, an alternative to cabin fever? It could be worse.

We could have spent the winter in Seattle. They molded beneath 32 inches of rain in the last 100 days – a record.

Or, we could have spent the winter in the Washington state Legislature where absolutely nothing happened. Not a record.

So, let's get on with this month, speed it up, roll it on through.

You feel this sentiment in classrooms. Children's eyes are beginning to look ahead on the calendar, counting the weeks until Spring Break.

You see it on the streets. A young woman waiting for a bus on Friday was wearing shorts – and her winter gloves.

Even the die-hard skiers are sick of the season. The snow may be great for another month, but the hills won't be crowded. It's just time to change from ski gloves to gardening gloves.

That is, unless you are a Republican running for president. Then you just take off the gloves in March and pound away. Yet another reason for the month to go out like a lion, a lamb or a lettuce, but go.

Having struggled with the recent loss of my mother, I am particularly looking forward to spring, to a time of renewal.

The idea of renewal, I think, is one of the most optimistic human notions. Renewal does not suggest everything is, or has been, perfect. Indeed, renewal first requires the act of being run down, drained or flattened.

To be personally renewed, or to renew a relationship or life's endeavor, suggests a period of decline, stagnation or failure that has just passed or will soon end. Like winter evenings, dark times are inevitable in this life. These same dark moments allow the seeds of possibility and renewal to germinate. Once renewal breaks through the dark earth, the energy, vigor and vision would be difficult to overestimate.

Think of Chicago after the fire, or Spokane after the rail yards left downtown, or Coeur d'Alene after silver dropped from $50 an ounce to $5.

Think of Bob Dole after the war injuries or Nelson Mandela after apartheid.

The comeback can, and often does, double the low mark from before.

Perhaps this is wishful thinking, but some signs suggest renewal is having a revival. In my office, the nasty letters to the editor have fallen off in recent weeks. In Spokane, the audience for the meanest of the talk radio shows has dropped way off.

In the nation, there are more voices than ever before suggesting we're overestimating our difficulties and must draw on personal renewal to get on with things.

Just as the alcoholic cannot be helped until he or she seeks it, renewal doesn't begin until a page turns in a life and a new beginning can be outlined.

I'm not sure cynics can be renewed. I don't think renewal can be triggered by deciding to make more money, get revenge or watch out more intently for Number One. Renewal, like Spring, comes a day at a time.

First a robin, then a daisy, then the warmth of a new day.

Ice Storm '96: These days were cold and difficult

Yes, other stuff happened last week.

The trade deficit went to $11 billion.

Boeing signed a contract to sell 103 new jets to American Airlines.

Some dogs and cats played football down in Pullman.

So what? A 100 hours spent freezing in the dark after the Inland Northwest's worst weather disaster in 50 years makes all that stuff seem about as significant as one more tree limb cracking beneath the weight of the ice.

When you are cold, in the dark and uncertain about tomorrow, the world narrows down. It's not the stock market you think about, but the stocking cap and whether it will stay on your head as you sleep.

On the first day in the office with stocking cap hair, everyone laughed and joked.

By day four, nobody was laughing at thousands of frozen workers who slept in their hats then straggled in to spend a few hours with heat, light and a shot at warm food.

Day one without electricity began as a lark. Everybody just went out to dinner.

Then came day two: cold sandwiches and cereal.

Day three: cookies and crackers.

Day four: vending machine food.

When it appeared likely my family would endure days five, six and seven without heat, lights or power, my focus on work abruptly changed. The tasks foremost in my mind didn't appear on the daily planner. I began to forget meetings, appointments, interviews.

One noon I suddenly jumped up from my desk and began driving from store to store looking for a generator or kerosene heater. I tried the Honda dealer where my lawnmower is serviced. Get a number, they said. Their two truckloads of gas-powered generators arriving Friday already were sold.

K-Mart, Target, Ted's Tools in Hillyard. Sorry. Sold out. Same story.

I missed all my afternoon appointments.

I canceled the meeting I chaired.

Instead of working late, I went home and huddled over a bowl of soup with my family and went to bed with my hat on.

The next day I visited Eagle Hardware & Garden early, hoping to beat the crowd to the heaters and kerosene. Dressed in a white shirt, stocking cap hair and new shoes purchased for the winter, I rushed home to assemble my new heater.

The box didn't contain a siphon. I could have returned it. But what if they were sold out?

I tried to pour in the kerosene. It spilled all over the new shoes. All afternoon I smelled like a lamp burning in an 1890s saloon.

I didn't care. My hands were going to be warm.

At night, I paced around the house giving orders to my kids, pretending to have control. There was no control – not for a guy with that kind of hair. This was finding a way to get by.

For just a moment I sniffed with self-pity and imagined I knew what it must be like for people in Rwanda and Zaire who don't have a safe place to live. Except mine was just a moment of discomfort, not a massacre or slaughter.

Still, the bare necessities of life, so often invisible in American middle-class life, were as clear as the frosty breath I could see in the kitchen.

Before you can ponder politics or polar bears or popular art, you need a warm place to live.

For thousands of shivering citizens, I expect this week shed a new light on the importance of nurturing a community that cares for its citizens. This notion of caring, of paying attention to those around you, matters. It matters most to those who find themselves on the short, hard end of the stick.

One day, any one of us could end up on that end, as 100,000 households found out across the Inland Northwest in the last week.

Being a good neighbor in the good days builds up some interest in the neighborhood account when things get tough.

Had I been a good neighbor or were my neighbors just saints in hats and gloves?

My neighbors and friends helped clear the downed trees. They called. They visited. They made it possible to get through a tough few days.

Soon, the lights will come back on. The news will speed up. We will get back to arguing and disagreeing and going our separate ways.

Let's just remember what it means to be a community that cares.

It will help us the next time things go dark.

Mount St. Helens' Eruption

We survived to tell story of volcanic eruption

In the beginning, God created darkness.

Most of us Northwesterners mistook it for a thundercloud building from the west.

Then the birds stopped singing.

On cue, we walked from our houses, illuminated by the eerie light.

Cool, black and silver light, the wattage of purgatory or Armageddon.

It was May 18, 1980.

Until the sky went completely black and street lights backlit the falling ash, disbelievers claimed it was but a summer storm.

It was a storm unlike any seen by man in North America.

Mount St. Helens, called the most beautiful volcanic mountain in the Cascade Range, had blown sky high.

The Indians called it Lawala Clough. The "smoking mountain."

For 32,000 years, no living thing had witnessed such a rampage from the mountain's depths.

Yet we have witnessed and lived to tell about it.

Survivors bear the duty of tending legends.

Legends for our children's children who will not likely see a blow from Lawala Clough.

Mostly, mountains stand alone.

In our lifetimes, one did not.

It fell before our eyes, crashing from 9,677 feet a week ago to only about 8,300 feet today, falling from the rank as fifth-highest peak in Washington state to a mediocre 30th.

But, oh, it dropped with a mighty bang heard 150 miles in each direction.

So, before the gripes of dusting for the 100th time obscure the picture of these last days, before we fall a-quarreling about who will pay for what and when, remember the history and the legend that has fallen in around us.

We have bested a gritty torrent that pelted us with 300 million cubic yards of ash, a blow bigger than Vesuvius when Pompeii disappeared.

Remember this. Remember the little things.

The tracks of the centipedes who circled, ran and doubled back leaving dainty footprints in their wake and then expired in their half-track patterns, choked in a half-inch sea of dust.

Cats and dogs fared faintly better. They hid and ran and took the form of walking mops and dust cloths.

Remember, too, the children.

They ran with wonder asking when the summer snow would melt.

50

And picture long the quixotic ones who rushed forth with brooms and dusted with a vengeance.

A continent lost the war for cleanliness with ash enough for every man to have one ton sprinkling down from the Western pines to the maples of Vermont.

In time, young and old straggled in for shelter, their hair touched prematurely gray by silica dioxide ash with a hardness surpassing glass.

From the first hours on, Northwestern cities clogged, sputtered and stopped.

Frontier times returned, with cowboy hats and scarves tied around many worried faces.

Isolation grew.

Phones were jammed when everyone tried to call everyone else. They were the busiest telephone days in Northwest history.

Radios still worked, linking households to the outside world, but the world didn't notice us at first.

Riots in Miami distracted many as the first cloud of ash slipped silently east across the Rocky Mountains.

Then the pictures were developed.

Pictures of a plume 50,000 feet above, pictures of the 100,000 acres buried in a mudslide, pictures of drifting ash three times the weight of the wettest snow on streets 600 miles from the mountain.

At first, we viewed it as a party.

The 10,000 stranded drivers packed beer into the churches.

Dizzy Gillespie took refuge in Spokane's nicest hotel and Senator Mark Hatfield finagled a $425 cab ride out of Spokane along backroads to Seattle.

But the dust began to settle along with the ashen facts of what St. Helens had wrought.

- More dust than a million vacuum bags could hold.
- More dust than every street sweeper could carry.
- More dust than could be washed away.

Water ran low in large towns and small. "We won't have enough water to take a leak," one mayor said.

And he was right.

After the water disappeared, only the big particles had washed away at all.

Half the bits set free when a cubic mile of rock blew east from Mount St. Helens were the diameter of a human hair or smaller.

Ashlets smaller than ragweed pollen, small enough to creep through every door ajar and into the deepest membranes of the lungs.

By the second day, all the surgical masks and respirators were gone.

Driving became impossible. Giant diesel engines and dozens of police cars went to scrap with dust imbedded in their cylinders.

Social gathering stopped. Small-town elections were postponed as were hundreds of DeMolay, Grange and Junior League dinners.

And what the gods created with an explosion equivalent to a 10-megaton nuclear bomb, man tried to explain by forming committees.

The enduring laws of "committology" prevailed.

On the question of whether St. Helens' ash was dangerous, Truman's Law took hold: "If you cannot convince them, confuse them."

Yes, the ash was dangerous, highly acidic and sulfurous.

Second reports said no. Ash was neutral and composed mainly of feldspar, glass and potash.

Third reports admitted no one knows what harm St. Helens set loose.

Mother Nature finally intervened.

Rains washed away the worst and settled down the rest, and when the president arrived, we knew the coast was clear.

He surveyed the scene in a three-piece suit and combat boots.

Stunned and quiet, he said it looked like the moon only 100 times worse.

Now, vacuum salesmen have 260,000 bags for dust.

Mayors have asked for half a million masks, and forces have joined hands to sweep and spray a path to normalcy.

Man at his best, as Kipling said:

"'Tain't the individual, nor the army as a whole

But the everlastin' teamwork of every blooming soul."

Yet the Northwest will not regain tranquillity soon.

For months, the iris will be ashen. Driveways will stay coated with a gray gossamer of the past.

And if 300 miles from Mount St. Helens we have managed to survive, it has not been without the memory of nearly a score of our neighbors who did not.

One of those was Harry Truman, the mountain man who lived half a century at the base of his volcano.

He spoke for all of us.

"We were content here," Harry said days before he died in the rumble of Lawala Clough.

All of us were content.

But now we have a legend to contend with, and other smoking mountains cast shadows from the west.

Forces towering above man's comprehension control this place.

We have seen too much to be altogether content again.

We worried about whether the masks helped save our lungs

Sending your lungs to Arizona would have been the best way to avoid breathing in bits of Mount St. Helens the last few days.

Unfortunately, most of us just wore masks.

Surgical masks, handkerchiefs tied around the nose and even old gas masks left over from World War II. It seemed logical they would filter out all the crud in the air.

Well, yes and no.

Last week's masks caught the big pieces of dust.

But the masks first worn all over Eastern Washington since the May 18 volcanic burst probably haven't nabbed the little particles of ash doctors now consider most hazardous to health.

No, it seems most of the surgical and common dust masks that sold like volcano cakes the last eight days put up about as much fight as a nose hair against the worst of the dust kicked up by Mount St. Helens.

Many masks purchased at hardware stores, surgical suppliers and the like were designed only for keeping noses free from the lint under the bed or keeping surgeons from sneezing all over patients.

Volcano dust?

Nobody in research thought there would be a retail market for masks designed to stop tiny, 3.5 micron or smaller particles of ash.

A micron, after all, is .000039th of an inch, one thousandth of a millimeter.

As luck would have it, Mount St. Helens did catch a few people off guard and as much as 50 percent of the nearly 300 million cubic yards of earth spewed forth by the volcano was 10 microns in diameter or smaller.

Equipment was too clogged with ash to measure the ash the day the mountain erupted, and the next day the particulate counts were as high as 35,613 – more than 500 times the normal count of 70 in Spokane.

Those bits were invisible to the human eye, bits small enough to fly through most masks, past nose hairs, down through bronchial tubes toward the inner sanctums of the lungs.

Even last Saturday, before rain knocked down the particulate level, there were more than 300,000 ash particles measuring one micron or less, in an average cubic foot of Eastern Washington air.

And a couple of days ago Dr. Paul Gross, an investigative pathologist who knows as much as anyone in the country about how scarred lung tissue develops, explained why these bits could cause trouble to people wearing the wrong masks.

"Anything from about 10 microns or greater would not get by the nose," the doctor said. "From 10 to 3.5 microns would be filtered out by the bronchial spaces (the upper region of the lungs).

"But particles less than 3.5 microns would be capable of reaching the air spaces."

In the alveoli, those tiny air spaces where blood is rejuvenated with oxygen, Dr. Gross said, volcanic particles could cause irritation that could lead to scarring, shortness of breath or worse.

The point germane to Eastern Washington is clear.

Masks that didn't filter out particles 3.5 microns or smaller last week didn't adequately protect anyone for the danger of Mount St. Helens.

Yet for some reason I didn't hear the radio deejays or the health officials make that point.

"Wear your masks," they cried, like Paul Revere.

They comforted us into believing we had cared for ourselves as 300 million cubic yards of glassy volcanic dust wafted our direction.

For days, no one in a high place pointed out the differences in masks.

The problem partly developed, of course, because the medical people in charge of public health had to become experts on masks right along with the rest of us.

"I'm not an expert," admitted Dr. Richard Stacey, president of the Spokane Medical Society, who, along with county public health officer Dr. Mohammed Marashi, charted the public pronouncements on masks.

Days rolled by and no one in higher places emerged as an expert, either. No one for the Washington Department of Emergency Services or even the National Institutes of Health.

Not until six days after the eruption did the emergency planners begin distribution of a mask that could protect three states from the fine volcanic ash.

It was 3M's Model 8710 (also sold as Model 6983), a mask used by uranium miners who worked around tiny particles as small as one micron in diameter.

A similar model is Deseret Industries' Model 530.

Saturday morning, after most people had spent may hours outside cleaning up the ash, 440,000 Model 8710s arrived in Spokane.

By Saturday evening, all 440,000 were gone, squirreled away by mask hogs who apparently had more than one mouth and one nose.

Another 180,000 of Deseret Industries' Model 530 arrived Sunday and are going out to the public.

And still mask madness continues.

The Red Cross received a shipment of 21,000 free masks from 3M only to discover 16,087 of them were Model 8500, a mask incapable of catching particles smaller than five microns.

A bewildered Red Cross official thanked 3M for their kind shipment of unacceptable masks but admitted she was "a little surprised" they were sent.

And don't forget the 91,000 surgical masks sent in Sunday by the Washington Department of Emergency Services.

They are "common, non-sterile surgical masks manufactured by 3M," according to Captain Colleen Nelsen of the Madigan Army originated.

These masks don't have a particle-size rating.

"Honestly, we don't know what they are," admitted civil defense deputy Lieutenant Earl Brown.

"They could be approved masks, but we don't know. It looks like they just sent us what was available."

Plus, the retail stores are still selling masks by the hundreds.

Some may catch the tiny particles, but as one 3M spokesman admitted from Seattle last week, "Ninety-nine percent of the masks sold for use in the operating room aren't concerned with this kind of matter (volcanic dust)."

It might just be another funny story, this trouble people have had getting information on the right masks, except that doctors don't know for sure what breathing lots of little volcanic dust particles will do to lungs.

The ash probably isn't dangerous, but there's still time to go to Arizona.

Some people make their living from dust

Every cloud, even a volcanic one, has a silver lining.

Four days after Mount St. Helens burped up 100 million cubic yards of volcanic ash, some businesses are crying all the way to the bank.

They are the people who make a living from dust.

Vacuum bag salesmen, parking lot sweepers and the sellers of auto and truck air filters have been blessed with an overwhelming gift from heaven.

"Our supply of air filters has sold out twice – they're going faster than our warehouse can supply," said a frantic Bob Demianew, manager of Spokane Checker Auto Parts on East Sprague.

"I've made three runs to the warehouse with my pickup and filled it up completely with filters. People are buying two or three at a time because they have to be changed every 100 or 200 miles.

"And by later in the week they'll all start coming out of their houses and driving!"

The gray dust casts an even more rosy shadow on Brian Lindaman, owner of Spokane Air Filter Cleaning Service.

The East Trent firm operates one of the few machines in Washington that can wash off the engine air filters used on big diesel trucks and buses.

"It's crazy, it's really crazy," Lindaman said Wednesday afternoon as the other phone rang with another desperate request for salvation from the dust. "I expect business will triple in the next three months."

Lindaman's machine washes used engine oil filters in soap and water and then dries them out, good as new.

"For five years the Spokane Transit System asked me to wash two filters a day. Now they want me to wash 60 a day," he said.

Lindaman made a $10,000 emergency order for more filters and cleaning gear Wednesday just to keep up with demand.

"The Spokane Transit System wanted 100 filters and said they would pay air freight from anywhere in the country if they could be here tomorrow," he said.

The dust in the Spokane city buses tells the whole story of Mount St. Helens' power.

Normally Spokane city buses change filters every six weeks. In that time buses accumulate about five or six pounds of grit and grime in a filter.

Wednesday, the bus engine air filters brought to Lindaman to clean were sucking in 25 pounds of grit every six hours.

"And we have loggers coming in, farmers coming in, everybody with a truck coming in. We slept down here last night," Lindaman said.

Across town at Mathis Super Sweep, Lindaman got no sympathy.

"At least he got to sleep," an exhausted Brian Mathis said.

Mathis Super Sweep's vacuum truck can suck up volcanic dust from parking lots.

For the last 48 hours the truck has worked non-stop.

"Holy cow! It's unbelievable," Mathis said of his business.

"I've got so many people calling me I can't call them back.

"I kind of wonder about the prayer I said in church Sunday, I really do. Things were kind of slow until this happened."

Some of the dust merchants have hiked their prices.

"We normally run at $30 an hour, but we're running at $40 now," Mathis said.

"It's not price gouging, it's just common sense. We're changing filters more often and running a risk to our motors."

The shafts in the gold mine of dust removal burrow into Eastern Washington households as well.

Hose and sprinkler sales have soared, and the vacuum cleaner dealers are licking their lips, dusty as they may be.

"We're looking forward to the next six months, we really are," said Eureka vacuum branch manager Bill Von Heeder.

"Anyone whose vacuum cleaner is teetering on the brink, this could push it over.

"And we've already ordered an extra (piggyback truckload) of bags.

"In one piggyback load we get 1,200 cases, and in each case we get 50 packages of bags, and in each package there are four bags. You figure out how many that is," he said.

It's 240,000 extra vacuum bags and it won't be nearly enough.

Scientists are saying there hasn't been as much ash dumped on a society since Mount Vesuvius buried Pompeii.

In southern Italy they let the dust sit. The people sweeping up under the cloud from Mount St. Helens won't.

So the dealers in dust could easily run out of goods.

They admit as much.

"By the end of this week there won't be an air filter found in this town," moaned the man for Checker Auto Parts.

"I've called Seattle and Portland, and they are all out of big truck and bus filters," said Lindaman from his cleaning service.

"It gets staggering," Eureka's Bill Von Heeder added.

If no filters can be found, commerce might stutter to a stop only days after it resumes.

Cars and trucks could stall after ingestion of too much dust.

Bus service could be disrupted; big diesels might not come to Spokane until the supply of filters is assured.

So there's even a cloud inside the silver lining in the aftermath of Mount St. Helens' roar.

Grass Burning

City folks setting agenda for once rural area

Environmentally driven urban politics of the 1990s have arrived in Spokane and Coeur d'Alene this past week.

City councils in those two cities voted to ban laundry detergents containing phosphates.

That's the city way to keep water clean.

The Spokane County Air Pollution Control Authority has served notice on Idaho and Washington farmers that their clouds of smoke from burning fields of Kentucky bluegrass won't be tolerated much longer.

That's a city way of keeping air clean.

Such acts help urbanites stay in touch with the environment. The cities can strike a blow for clean water and put the damper on eye-burning smoke which ruins the view from the patio.

But are city people genuinely interested in keeping water clean and air pure? Are they truly interested in supporting life-improving environmental change?

That remains to be determined.

"At the moment, emotionalism is driving the issues," said a miffed Michael Smith, public affairs spokesman for the FMC Corp., a Southern Idaho phosphate-mining company that lost two battles in one week to keep phosphate-based detergents available in North Idaho and Spokane. "Science and logic really have very little to do with what happened up there."

FMC had tried in vain to show that phosphate detergents aren't the primary reason why rocks in the Spokane River are growing green slime and algae has bloomed in Long Lake.

FMC officials are right.

Most of the phosphate-fed slime comes from the daily deposits city people make in sewers and septic tanks after flushing their toilets.

But it didn't matter.

Banning phosphate detergents allowed the local city councils to make an environmental statement, to act and to show concern about maintaining water quality, all without leaving the padded chair of the city.

And it's a start, a symbol – and very good politics for the 1990s.

These same forces also are fueling the drive to throttle grass burning by bluegrass-seed farmers who cultivate about 30,000 acres in the Spokane-Coeur d'Alene corridor.

Smoke from grass burning doesn't really add to smog. And while annoying, the smoke isn't particularly dangerous to people with respiratory problems, according to Dr. Michael Kraemer, a pediatric allergist who testified at the Friday hearing on the burning.

But smart politics all are on the side of banning the burning – and doing so soon.

"We're getting a lot of complaints," Spokane County Commissioner Pat Mummey said. "There is a citizen's initiative in Oregon to ban the burning. We feel the time has come in Spokane County to do something."

Farmers have solid agricultural reasons to burn their fields, but it is city people who increasingly are calling the shots on this issue.

And that won't change.

More people are moving from California onto Rathdrum Prairie every year. And as Spokane grows, new housing developments will bring hundreds of city people into new neighborhoods of the Spokane Valley.

These newcomers and transplants want a view of the hills. Their image of paradise is sitting with a vista and a sunset in the distance – not a guy in coveralls burning straw.

"We're seeing changing demographics in the region," acknowledged Dennis Carlson, secretary of the Intermountain Grass Growers Association.

"Twenty years ago, the people in government and making public decisions had some direct tie to agriculture. Their parents or grandparents had grown up on a farm.

"Now, we have decision-makers far removed from agriculture. They don't have any connection to it."

The grass growers find themselves pathetically under-prepared to engage in this battle for hearts and minds. Their fields lie directly in the path of the fast-developing commercial and residential corridor along Interstate 90. And oddly, very little effort is being made at either the University of Idaho or Washington State University to help find a mechanical or genetic way either to burn with less smoke or to grow new types of grass that don't need to be burned.

Only this winter did WSU receive a small grant to develop a mobile burner. In Moscow, the University of Idaho's only grass-seed specialist retired years ago.

That leaves the fields rather open for an assault by the urban population of Eastern Washington and North Idaho.

But the urban masses must be careful as they press their politics.

Preserving water quality, clear air and easy living will require a plan for the long term – not just posturing for short-term, symbolic victories.

Banning grass burning won't make up for the fact that more and more cars are bringing people from more distant suburbs into Spokane for work, giving the city some of the smoggiest skies in America.

Stopping the sale of phosphates detergents cannot take the place of building expensive waste-water-treatment facilities, installing sewer lines over the aquifer or simply keeping lawn fertilizers from running down into storm drains.

But industry and agriculture also must understand the changing political nature of this region.

Whether the issue is phosphates, grass burning or old-growth timber, the traditional coalitions and rural strategies won't carry the day anymore.

City people, fired up with their own brand of environmental activism, increasingly are calling the shots on wild waters and rural lands.

Rural businesses changing in urbanized world

What is a Cheney Weeder, anyway?

A college student from Eastern Washington University who pulls weeds for tuition?

A new kind of vegetarian sub sandwich?

A company in Eastern Washington you have heard about, but whose products are a mystery?

The last comes closest to the definition for most people.

For 87 years, Cheney Weeder built dryland farming equipment in Cheney and, since 1956, in Spokane.

Its most famous farm utensil, still known in farming circles as the Cheney reel, serves as a large rake on the front of combines at harvest time.

But big rakes on the front of combines are not the future of this long-standing company.

So a few days ago, Greg Paulus, the retired Air Force pilot and lifetime motorcycle rider who bought Cheney Weeder in 1993, took down the Cheney Weeder sign and put up the new company name, Metalite Industries.

"The new name represents the true capabilities of this country and the direction we want to take," Paulus said.

The name change at Cheney Weeder is one small detail in a very big regional shift under way across the Inland Northwest. It is a shift away from a resource-based, rural economy to something new.

"Today, our niche is snowmobile trailers in the country. We're expanding that market in the I-5 corridor and back east."

The company also is building the only handicapped-accessible pontoon boats in the country.

They are producing highly-stable, low cost floating docks for lake places.

True, their combine reels will continue to be manufactured and marketed through three new distributors across the U.S. and Canada.

But the company's future is pegged to recreation and customized metal fabrication and has moved a long way from being a business built around dryland tillage machinery popular back when everyone farmed.

Other signs of companies changing to meet a very different future abound.

Two weeks ago, the Jacklin Seed Company in Post Falls dropped a bombshell by announcing a pledge to phase out field burning on bluegrass seed fields near Spokane and Coeur d'Alene over the next 10 years.

Jacklin Seed is the biggest grass grower and seed processor in the region. It looked at its future and decided burning grass fields in an increasingly urbanized environment wouldn't work much longer.

As Glenn Jacklin explained, "Our company didn't get here without planning for the future and we're not going to get into the next century without planning for the future. Obviously, it will be difficult for us, but we must be determined to find a way to develop an alternative to what we had been doing."

Looking for alternatives, using ingenuity to fashion new business from current strengths, being willing to reshuffle the deck when the future isn't all that clear are characteristics of each of these companies.

Neither thinks the path ahead will be altogether smooth or familiar.

At Jacklin Seed, for example, future growth is pegged largely on China and other Asian countries.

The Chinese are building golf courses for foreigners and Jacklin Seed hopes to open an office in China this fall. "We think it's possible our China business can triple in the next few years," Jacklin said.

Others surely will try to sell grass seed to the Chinese, just as others will build pontoon boats and snowmobile trailers.

And, along the way, there always will be those who don't like the changes or, alternately, wish the changes were being made more quickly.

So, it didn't surprise Paulus when some of his employees decided they didn't want to work in his new company because he wasn't doing things the way they always had been done.

It has not surprised Jacklin that some farmers have complained bitterly that Jacklin Seed has given up the fight for field burning.

And when your friends, associates or family members start getting queasy about change, it doesn't make it any easier to press on.

"This decision (to support a phase-out of field burning) has been the most difficult decision I have made in 12 years at the company," Jacklin said.

At the old Cheney Weeder, Paulus believes some people aren't up for the challenge of coping with change.

"I was a test pilot," Paulus said. "I have been riding motorcycles since I was 13. I went out and bought a bankrupt business. After all that my wife said to me that I must like the risk, that risk is a part of who I am. She's probably right."

And, she likely has put her finger on the reason Jacklin Seed and Metalite Industries will be around in the 21st century.

Sarah Grows Up

Chapter Two

Birth of my first child

Excuse my gush, but my daughter – born July 20, 1982 – celebrates her one-month birthday this week.

I've planned a bang-up party: all the Similac she can drink; an extra hour of rocking at night; 36 Kodacolor snapshots of that red-faced bundle slumped in a variety of uncomfortable positions.

I realize a one-month-old's mind isn't keen on parties.

A babe that age has more pressing tasks to contemplate – such as keeping her head from flopping around like a sot on Saturday night.

No matter. Successful navigation of four weeks of life warrants a banner behind a biplane as far as I'm concerned.

You see, Sarah is my first child.

She also is the first grandchild on either side of the family.

And without going into all the teary details, suffice it to say she was eight years and half-a-dozen infertility doctors in the making.

My constant jibber-jabber about baby Sarah has baffled certain friends and acquaintances.

Uninitiated single people and married non-parents have grown very quiet at my house during recent heated debates over the ease versus cost of disposable diapers or the pluses and minuses of pacifiers.

It's a sign of our times, really.

Much of the Baby Boom generation lugs around prejudice against babies.

A University of Michigan study, for example, has found that in the last two decades the number of people who foster positive feelings about children has dropped from 50 percent of the population to 28 percent.

It isn't just talk. The 1980 census shows only four households in 10 even have kids in them today.

To the non-babied, the stock lines on neonates run something like this:

• Babies are a hassle. They slow you down when you might want to jet off to a Trident anti-nuclear protest.

• Babies are expensive. They eat up your disposable income just when you develop the need for a new stereo system.

• Babies require maturity. If you imagine cruising through life in an MG and not a four-door sedan, don't get anyone pregnant.

I know those lines. I used to spout them.

Today, I am astonished at how effortlessly Sarah has refocused my views and values.

Every day my daughter teaches me something. It's like going to college 24 hours a day, only this time I'm learning about life and about being a man rather than just faking it.

Sarah began teaching me the day she was born by tackling the avowed goal among many men today – that of overcoming their macho, tough-guy images.

The bookstores and TV talk shows are filled with advice on this subject.

All it really takes for a man to become reacquainted with his tear ducts is to hold his baby. When I stare down at that undifferentiated blob in the bassinet, it's like watching an endless rerun of the mushy scenes in *E. T.* Big, warm tears trickle all over a stubbly chin.

And that's only the beginning of what a baby teaches a man, or at least what my daughter has taught me.

A baby has a way of gently belittling selfish, me-first attitudes.

Without saying a word, Sarah has suggested I be an adult. "Grow up," she says, as I try to decide what the late-night fussing means. "I need your big hands to survive, your judgment to thrive."

Though my baby knows nothing of politics and war, she has brought into focus the surging emotional tide behind many of the social and political issues of our time.

Right away, a girl baby takes on the issues of abortion and equal rights for woman.

When we sit in our comfortable, middle-class bedroom together – she wrapped in material and spiritual wealth – I shudder at the travesty of denying Sarah birth.

Then I wonder: what if there were no comfortable bedroom? No grandmother with receiving blankets? What then?

I believe the answer is that my daughter came into the world at the right time and her luck likely will make all the difference for her – provided, of course, the male chauvinists give her a chance.

Most powerfully of all, my daughter has led me to a better understanding of the anti-nuclear sentiment sweeping this country.

At the celebration of her first month of life, my girl squirms in the shadow of having the equivalent of 10 tons of explosives aimed at the soft spot of her head.

In the year 2000, when she turns 18, military experts now predict there will be 20 tons of explosives reserved just for her.

Presidents are elected on issues such as these – issues intimately tied to the lives of babies.

Or at least such issues will affect my vote. The scales by which I weigh job, family and politics have been jiggled.

To veteran child-raisers, this is no revelation. It's just that if you haven't had one before, you don't understand how a baby gives you a new sense of time and place.

My daughter has made everyone in my family move a notch on the scale of human experience.

71

A dad becomes grandpa. An eldest son becomes dad.

And all who know Sarah now better understand the responsibility of humankind to take care of the babies.

Sarah turns one; Dad worries

The night before her first birthday, my daughter took seven wobbly, wonderful steps.

Arms stuck straight out in front, a six-tooth grin plastered from ear to ear, she swayed on her three-inch-long feet and then lunged across the living room.

That 10-second teeter made Neil Armstrong's small step for mankind seem infinitesimal.

Now, I can proudly boast, my girl is on her way toward exploring our strange, uncharted world.

Yet, if the truth were known, the months before Sarah's memorable first steps had me worried sick.

Like many young fathers, I have succumbed in the last 12 months to the habit of looking into other playpens.

Upon detection of other babies making progress in crawling, talking or walking, I felt it my duty to instruct my girl on how she should make her way.

In February, Sarah and I began our crawling practice.

Each night after work, I faithfully scuffed up the knees of my pants and dragged my tie across the floor demonstrating basic crawling to my puzzled slow learner.

She responded by dropping her head in despair and wailing at her belly button.

Then, around the first day of summer, she suddenly was scooting everywhere on her palms and kneecaps. Soon, she was even pulling herself up.

I was relieved. So was my dry-cleaning shop.

Since June, a horrible knot has taken hold of my stomach.

Now I watch my young Evel Knievel dive headlong into couch legs or practice her backward spine flops onto the concrete.

And on the eve of her first birthday, I felt a powerful urge to whisk her to a foam-padded, hermetically sealed tree house (no, underground bunker) where she might grow up without the benefit of sharp edges, stairs or MTV.

A friend, who has two older daughters, tried to reassure me that this urge is nothing new.

In 1806, my friend noted, James Mill felt the terror at seeing his precocious son growing up in a difficult world and decided to personally undertake the education of his boy.

The younger Mill was removed from the mainstream of British life while his father taught him Greek at age 3 and tutored him endlessly in the philosophy of Plato.

What resulted from this ultra-protectionist, highly channeled childhood?

John Stuart suffered a nervous breakdown in his 20s and fell into deep depression.

Case closed, my friend said.

Unfortunately, the case wasn't closed.

John Stuart Mill recovered from his breakdown to become the most influential political thinker of the 19th century. His IQ was estimated to be 200, and his political writings are standard reading in a hundred universities now.

Yet in some ways, John Stuart Mill's childhood represents the very dilemma faced by modern parents.

Many fathers and mothers of the '80s are single-mindedly targeting and training their children for success.

The shaping begins early with Lamaze, then La Leche, and finally, Lacoste pajamas.

Youngsters from infancy on take kiddie swimming classes, eat low-fat kiddie diets, exercise their brains in exclusive kiddie nurseries.

Childhood currently is viewed as the minor leagues of life. It is the place where you teach babies to be smarter, thinner, more athletic.

The Library of Congress this year lists 42,000 separate titles on improving and raising a child.

The careful planning to create perfect babies will lead to some remarkable achievements.

One day, a kid who learned to read *Megatrends* at age four or who listened to Mozart since birth will write the new constitution for Zimbabwe or invent a microchip that stores all of John Stuart Mill's works on the head of a pin.

But in creating 21st century geniuses, some kids likely will suffer a modern version of Mill's breakdown.

And that's the problem, according to some child-development experts.

"Because we don't make our kids smart," explained Dr. Brian Gipstein, a Spokane adolescent psychiatrist.

"They come into this world with a certain biologic potential, and every child is different, with different learning skills, different cognitive styles."

Gipstein and others don't suggest that children be allowed to sit like blobs to develop on their own.

Early exposure to books can help children read more quickly. Lively interaction with parents and teachers will advance social skills and define boundaries.

"But the process can become distorted if parents expect too much and the children don't respond as hoped for," he said.

And under certain conditions, the push to make infants and young children learn fast ultimately might retard development.

"In terms of conditioning and negative reinforcement, if you ask children to do something they can't, something they don't understand, they can develop an aversion to it.

"(Trying to learn) becomes a negative experience.

"Then, when a child finally develops to a point where it can learn, it doesn't."

Gipstein had a tactful way of saying that I shouldn't have forced all that crawling practice onto my daughter.

My girl wasn't programmed to crawl at six months – or even 10 months.

Instead, she concentrated on the verbal side of babydom, blurting out words like "book" and "dog" and "cock-a-doodle-doo" long before Dr. Spock said she should.

Still, I know the push to build an even better baby will continue to run deep among modern families.

I mean, good grief, Charles Brown, if mom and dad have only a few chances to sculpt a life, why not go for a brainy Diane Sawyer instead of a neurotic Phyllis Diller?

But on Sarah's first birthday, I am reminded again how often a child becomes the teacher and a father the student.

In her fierce little way, my girl taught me that it isn't parents who decide when a baby crawls or walks or reads *Utilitarianism* by John Stuart Mill.

Instead, every person has her own timetable, even at two-feet-six.

Sarah turns 2; Dad up at 4:30 a.m.

On the morning before her second birthday, the crack of dawn jolted my daughter into 100 percent consciousness.

The battery-powered bedside clock read 4:30 a.m.

Suffice it to say that the crashing arrival of another day didn't register with me.

But my Sarah's biological timepiece works toddler hours. From earliest light, she hears the clarion call to live and breathe, touch and taste all that surrounds her.

Robins are abuzz in the dewy dawn.

A freight train ("choo-choo" in toddler talk) rumbles by.

Sunlight washes across the faces of teddy bears and dollies waiting, just out of reach, to be jostled, tickled and fed imaginary breakfasts.

"Daddy, Sawah awake," bellowed a tiny insistent voice from the crib.

Then she started jumping.

What floors me about raising my girl is that just when I think I have it wired to be the straight-A daddy, something changes and I'm scrambling to learn a whole new curriculum.

Sure, when she feels hot, I've learned to take her temperature. If she smears the raspberry jelly on her chin, I know to wipe it off.

But the morning when she decided she wouldn't eat yogurt anymore, I was stumped.

And the mystery continues over why she wants to wear only her pink tennies and screams when fitted with black patent leather.

And what, in heaven's name, should be done for a girl at 4:30 a.m. who is awake, jumping and calling out, "Daddy, Sawah get down?"

If my girl were a lion cub or baby elephant, she would be out of the home this month.

If she were a squirrel, she would be old enough to be a mother.

Only human kids need so many years to grow up. And unlike bamboo, the growing doesn't happen all in one night.

Sarah's growth sputters along, from diaper to diaper, interspersed with meteoric leaps to be a "big girl" on the potty followed by a terrified plummet back to the crib, daddy's arms and the blankey.

Yet, at 4:30 a.m., none of this calm reasoning about growing up filled my head.

Only gritted teeth and an old Danish proverb did.

The proverb goes: "Give into a pig when it groans and to a child when it cries out and soon you will have a fine pig and a bad child."

The far-too-early morning hours are, I expect, among the times when child abusers come unglued.

All parents, I'd wager, have felt angry at their darling monsters who simply do not understand when daddy or mommy need sleep or private time or an evening of something besides watching baby dance to Michael Jackson.

"But then, you don't go into parenting with everything all planned out," said Eunice Snyder, a Spokane social worker and author of a professional child-protection guidebook, *Deciding to Place or Not to Place*.

"In fact, the people who are on the far end of abusing their children are the ones who have that notion out of alignment with reality. Abusive parents think their needs are absolutely first. They never see the needs of the children. They are just not tuned in."

In the thin and quiet hours of the morning before Sarah's second birthday, the whole neighborhood could have tuned in to her.

"Daddy, Sawah needs bottle of juice," she hollered. "Bottle of juice, Daddy. Juice."

For the sake of the marriage and because I'm a wimpy soft touch, I stumbled to the refrigerator and brought her the juice.

"Bottle of milk," she said upon spying the juice.

Child psychologists have spent careers writing about the maddening struggle for independence waged by 2-year-olds.

A basic truth always emerges from their research: a kid's relationship to her parents at around age 2 goes a long way in deciding how the girl will turn out later.

"We know that people who have trouble with their teen-age kids, who say they can't talk to them or deal with them, usually didn't talk with them or deal with them when they were young, either," wise and published Eunice Snyder said.

"By age 2, a parent simply must realize a child is a separate person who needs time, attention and pleasure. And that means if she likes to be read to, the parent must suggest that they read a book. If she likes to go out to the pool, the parent must suggest that they go swimming.

"And if that doesn't happen, then that child very rarely learns how to enjoy other people, how to relate."

I'm dog-tired writing this. That's the toll of being up and relating to my little girl.

The last few days, we've talked about the sunrise, the paperboy, the birds.

Yet, she has been the real teacher. She has instructed me in the discipline of a mule trainer, the patience of a steelhead fisherman, the understanding of a preacher.

My Sarah is the best and brightest twinkle in the sky.

Even the red sky at morning.

Sarah turns 3, is fearful of world; Dad still worried

"Daddy," my daughter called out a few nights before her third birthday, "where are the garden bunnies?"

The fearsome bunnies had made a brief guest appearance in a bedtime story I've all but forgotten.

They were the bad bunnies who didn't mind their parents, who hit their friends, who tended to spill carrot juice on the just-cleaned burrow floor.

They seemed a metaphor useful to real little girls who sometimes ask for cookies before finishing dinner and who occasionally forget to put away their blocks.

Except in a mind unfamiliar with metaphor and still trusting in what the big people say, the garden bunnies became too real.

My girl imagined, I expect, 10-foot-high, pink-eyed lopers pounding down the irises, crushing the wading pool and lurching thump-thump, thump-thump, toward the lighted window of her dim and door-closed bedroom.

I have yet to see a garden bunny.

On occasion, I venture out into the hot summer night looking for them, only to return to Sarah's room with a "no-sightings" report.

Yet, she worries.

To think of adding to my girl's worry, of plugging her into stress and fear at 3 years old, has been a most difficult part of fathering these last 12 months.

How daddies would like to shield their little ones from The Bomb, the brutality of mankind, the garden bunnies.

But we cannot. The truth of being a dad requires you to raise your daughter's ire once in a while, risk searing her soft soul occasionally with some guidance on how to grow up.

Besides giving Sarah a phobia of rampaging rabbits, I have added to her anxiety in a variety of other ways this past year.

My girl endured a swat on her rear for spitting at her mother.

She has been sent to her room in tears for repeatedly interrupting adult conversation.

On vacation, she was carried to the car, kicking and screaming, after throwing a fit in Yellowstone National Park's Old Faithful Inn.

My expectations have been high. She is to be a good girl, a big girl – and all the definitions are mine.

Yet, she is only turning 3.

And on the eve of her birthday, I wonder if parents might be capable of molding tiny personalities into angry persons who suffer the ills of too many expectations and the sores of having been given too little room for imperfection.

Can, in fact, a hard-driving, Type-A parent produce a hostile, possibly heart-diseased child?

The answer, according to a Stanford University education specialist who studies stress in children, appears to be a troubling and powerful "yes."

In the last five years, Dr. Carl Thoresen has observed hundreds of children with the behavioral characteristics of a high-stress, Type-A personality. Those include traits such as rapid speech, extreme competitiveness, a quickness to anger.

"And in high-stress children," Thoresen said from his office on the Stanford campus a few days ago, "we have observed many, many parents who are high-stress, Type-A people themselves."

Highly stressed kids live a childhood far less than perfect.

Thoresen has discovered highly stressed kids suffer more colds and viruses than low-stress kids do.

Their hearts beat faster, their intestines churn more.

They can't sleep and are fatigued during the day.

Powerful hormones known as catecholamines and corticosteroids, which are produced during chronic periods of stress, have been found in kids and linked to increased cholesterol in the blood, reduced resistance to disease and irregular heartbeat.

Thoresen says stories about garden bunnies don't really impose much stress on children. But parents' failure to recognize and accept the frailties and immaturity of their kids can inflict significant strain.

"What seems to distinguish parents of high-stress children is the way the parents respond when the child does not do as well as the parent thinks he or she should," Thoresen said.

"Parents of high-stress kids seem to be more disapproving of failures. And by failures, I mean relative things, like getting a 'B-plus' instead of an 'A' or maybe even getting an 'A' but not being the best kid in class."

What parent doesn't want his child to achieve?

It's just that the research now being done on children suggests that building a love relationship based on a child's success creates high-stress kids, not necessarily high-achievers.

"In our studies, we could find absolutely no differences in the performance of highly stressed and low-stress kids," Thoresen said.

"High-stress kids were no better in their grades, in athletics, in the social activities."

Thoresen didn't offer an answer for fending off the garden bunnies.

But he did have a suggestion for keeping the stress level in young ones under control.

The key is for parents themselves to lighten up.

"Parents would do well to remember that there are enough pressures and demands imposed on young people from the media, peers and school that it's not usually necessary for them to create pressure on their kids," he said. "It's far more important for a child to feel loved and accepted for who he or she is."

Love without contingency – that's what my daughter has tried to teach me as she frets about the garden bunnies.

They may not be there, but I must allow her room to think they are.

On my darling girl's third birthday, I plan to be on bunny patrol.

Sarah turns 4, watches TV, learns evil things

A few nights before her fourth birthday, my daughter was introduced to cocaine.

Our family was enjoying family home night.

A quick game of Candyland was being played against the backdrop of a Robin Williams 99-cent video.

Williams was doing one of his funniest routines. He was bouncing around the stage, parroting the inane conversation of a coked-out baseball player. Lots of four-letter jive talk about sex, drugs and the life of an abuser.

Good stuff. Funny stuff in this weird world of ours in which people mistake drugs for happiness.

"Daddy," my daughter said amid the laughter, "what's that man doing on TV?"

Her small, innocent voice popped the bubble of tranquillity.

With a mind hungry to embrace the meaning and significance of every new word, my daughter had just lofted me a simple question that, for me, defied condensation to the level of a preschooler.

Daddy made a snap decision. He changed the subject.

Up to bed my daughter went for her goodnight stories about princesses who live happily ever after, witches who never are wicked and our favorite make-believe character, Cynthia, the un-scary ghost.

But the diversion was an uneasy one.

Today, as my Sarah turns the corner from baby to little girl, I face with trepidation the wicked witches of reality, the scary ghosts of hardships still to come.

Preparing your kid for the best challenges of her life is easy. When children learn to ride a bike, play the piano or count to 10 in Spanish, all parents, I'm sure, feel as if they have succeeded.

But getting a kid ready for the worst of life? I'm beginning to see how that can throw you.

The little things come up all the time.

Kids at the YWCA use "ain't" instead of "isn't."

Kids at the park now use all seven of the words you can't say on the radio.

Big kids hog the swings, and mom and dad don't want Sarah playing doctor with the door closed.

"Why?" she asks.

But then come the unexplainables – the bad men who might touch her in the wrong places, why people shoot each other with guns, where grandpa goes after he is buried.

It seems to me that today's kids have fewer places to find shelter in the world we big people have created.

It's not just that nearly half of America's kids under age 6 are in day care.

No, the toughest place to find safe haven in many families is right there at home.

Divorce. Drugs. Poverty. Junk food versus Brussels sprouts. Most of this now walks right in the front door and into the bedroom with parents.

For a while, when the kid was a blob in the bassinet, maybe she didn't pick up on what was happening.

But a 4-year-old listens. A 4-year-old watches. A 4-year-old knows what is going on. And if she doesn't, she'll ask.

Then, too often, we're left speechless – or running for help.

In the publishing industry today, children's books lead every other category of best sellers.

Many parents, having introduced their children to the real world, apparently find themselves groping for the language and symbols to explain it to young, fragile, innocent minds.

On the shelves of Spokane's outstanding Children's Corner Bookshop are titles such as *How It Feels When Parents Divorce* and *No More Secrets for Me*, a book on sexual abuse.

They have colored pictures and big type. They are kids' books about the adult world.

"Sexuality, disease, death, all kinds of tragedies – now we have books about it for kids," said Susan Durrie, a partner in the Children's Corner.

"This is all rather new. In the past many adult subjects were kept from children; children were not brought into the problems of the adult world. Anymore, children are living them."

Those of you who have raised six kids may consider my concern over my girl's introduction to the real world overblown. After all, generations of parents and grandparents have managed.

83

The first comic book in the United States was published in 1911. For the next 30 years, parents and child-development authorities claimed that comic books would rot the minds and disturb the psyches of children.

They must have been wrong. At least, my parents and grandparents generally turned out OK.

But they weren't confronted with television. And that's a difference.

Today, in every household and in every classroom of the public schools, a TV set can be found.

Knight Rider offers some peculiar driving habits.

Saturday-morning cartoons suggest that sugar stands for the most important ingredient in children's food.

And when Friday night comes and mom and dad rent a video, a kid at age 4 can hear all about cocaine. Ask me – I know how innocently it can happen.

And there is something even more insidious.

More and more researchers now believe that children who watch hours of television at ages 4, 5 and 6 may suffer lifelong difficulties in their reading and thinking habits.

"What seems more and more apparent is that kids who watch a lot of TV before they go to school do less well in certain areas of development," Dr. Francis Palumbo, an associate professor of pediatrics at the Georgetown University School of Medicine, said when I called to ask him about television and my girl.

"Some people have proposed that because TV is such a very simple sort of process that children who watch a lot start to learn that way. When it comes time for them to learn more complex processes (such as reading and writing), they may not be able to do it."

Turning 4 is a big deal for my girl.

On this birthday, she is looking ahead, looking around, looking at me for answers.

84

If she doesn't get the answers from mom or dad, she will get the word from other kids or television.

On this, her fourth birthday, she taught me the importance of being a dedicated, thoughtful, tuned-in guide to the rest of the world.

Sarah turns 5, gets bicycle; Dad is tough

When my daughter discovered her first bicycle on the morning of her fifth birthday, I knew she was headed to a place far, far from home.

She doesn't know it yet. Only the night before her birthday, she had hugged me and said, "Daddy, I'm going to live here with you forever!"

It won't be like that.

She will get on her bike, ride down the driveway, around the corner, and one day I will call her with birthday greetings only to hear the answering machine say Sarah can't come to the phone because she is out riding bikes with her boyfriend, her husband or her kids.

Dads know, deep inside, this is best. Still, I turned my head on her birthday to shield my girl from the trickle on my cheek as she set off on her pink beauty with training wheels.

This business of growing up and away threw my daughter and me for a tumble last year. Her being 4 turned out to be the "terrible 2s," only doubled. Our family struggled for a balance between doing things Sarah's way, our way or the right way.

No, she couldn't cross the street without an adult looking on.

Yes, she must ask to be excused.

OK, we'll discuss under what circumstances she can make her own peanut-butter-and-jelly sandwiches and determine how much jelly on the counter constitutes too much.

Once, I imagined that raising children would proceed in an orderly, unfolding pattern of greater responsibilities, activities and independence.

Ha! Bringing up the kids reminds me of bucking a Jeep up a logging road. You bump along, spin out, shoot forward, alternately hitting your head on the roof liner and then being thrown back by a rush of acceleration.

The process requires a parent's full attention or a child runs the risk of a damaging crash.

Luckily, over the last year, my girl has educated me about our struggles. She has taught me my role: give clear direction on what is expected and then make sure she has places to practice her good behavior.

Seeing my girl jump on her bike that first day left me feeling stunningly satisfied. A balance had been struck. She had practiced on her smaller trike, been rewarded for not going into the street, told of the need to move on to the wheels of a big girl. Neither intimidated nor oblivious to the danger, she took to the pedals with thrilled anticipation.

If only the preparation for eating your broccoli went as easily.

But with both bikes and broccoli, the requirements for a parent are the same. Keep your messages convincing and clear, offer encouragement and allow room for a kid to grow.

I've come to think that fudging your role as an authoritative, consistent parent represents about the worst sin a parent can commit.

Alternately, when I have slipped on the iron glove of a dictator or shown the spine of a marshmallow, my daughter has fallen into fits of anger and confusion. "What the heck is going on?" she seems to be asking as her feet flail and her cheeks turn red.

Research at Stanford University suggests the importance of sticking to a steady plan. A study of 8,000 California highschool students found that children whose parents set rules firmly and stick to them, yet encourage discussions, ended up earning far better grades than children of parents who were rigid dictators or permissive marshmallows.

Children are crashing and burning all around us as a result of parents who either are dictatorial or mushy. One in four kids drops out of high school partially as a result of this kind of parenting. Teenage suicide, often brought on by poorly formed self-images in young people, is the second-leading cause of death for people under 20 today.

Fathers, in particular, still appear to be fumbling away their responsibilities to send clear, warm messages to their offspring. Analysis of young people with serious drug problems reveals that most addicts come from homes in which the father is hostile, emotionally distant or simply gone.

In my view those fathers are missing out. There is nothing in life more spiritual or more rewarding than being a father and watching your young ones sprout wings.

My daughter imagined that being 5 would bring with it suddenly larger shoes and the need for an extra-long bed.

"Dad," she declared, "when I turn 5, I will grow big all at once."

I imagined the opposite. She would forever be a little girl, clinging and in need of an all-protective shield.

Sarah is closer to being right.

The morning my girl struggled to swing her gangling, long-boned leg over the seat of a Schwinn, I understood how much there is to learn about being a parent – and how little time there is to learn it.

Sarah breaks elbow, has surgery at 6

A few days before her sixth birthday, my daughter fell and broke my heart.

I didn't see it happen.

Sarah was horsing around in a rented condominium with a baby sitter while her mother and I went out to dinner.

What the baby sitter was doing when the accident occurred, I don't know. My girl was playing kids' games with her little brother; turning somersaults on the floor, rolling on the couch, jumping off a table.

On her last jump, Sarah's feet slipped. Off balance and airborne, she began a free fall of about 36 inches.

Feet up, arms back and with the full force of her 48 pounds, she smashed elbow-first into a hard slate floor.

Her screams lasted four hours as police in Sun Valley, Idaho, searched in vain to find mom and dad and tell them they were needed.

Walking up the sidewalk toward the condominium at midnight, I sensed something was wrong.

All the lights were blazing. An unfamiliar woman, the baby sitter's boss, was sitting in the hallway.

As I turned the key and opened the door, a high, painful whine drifted through the summer air.

The sound of a child desperately in pain never leaves a father's ears. It is an animal sound, related in some way to the yelps of dogs that have been kicked and to the frantic shrieks of newborn birds that sit in downy terror as a snake crawls up the tree.

Shortly after dawn, the doctor in the emergency room at Moritz Community Hospital brought the news. My daughter had dislocated her elbow, broken her elbow, fractured her arm and suffered nerve and muscle damage from the fall and subsequent swelling.

"It's an extremely significant injury," he said. "She could lose use of her arm."

The words hit like a .45-caliber cartridge.

Lose the use of her arm?

My girl, who only has begun to learn to write and play the piano, could lose the use of her arm?

I walked into a small, windowless room where my daughter would not see me cry. No pain can match the all-consuming, growling sorrow that ate up my thoughts.

"Daddy," Sarah called from the emergency room.

I went back to her.

"Look what they did," she said with quivering lip.

I looked at her mangled right arm. It reminded me of a salesman's display for Ace bandages.

"No, not that arm," she said. "This arm."

At the bend of her left arm, a nurse had taken blood. A tiny red pinprick remained.

"Look at that dot!" Sarah said. "I need a Band-Aid."

Six weeks and three surgeries later, her cast has come off.

Sarah's arm looks like a piece of beef jerky.

A seven-inch scar runs from her wrist to her elbow, while a second curved scar wraps around the elbow.

Sarah cannot extend her arm, cannot straighten two of her fingers, cannot lift or carry much beyond a Popsicle.

At night, she lies with her arm cautiously curled beneath her as if to protect it from goblins in her sleep.

Seeing her struggle with her fork or fumble with the buttons on her blouse, I often quietly must leave the room to gather my composure. At night, my wife and I lie long into the hot summer darkness and turn over the events again and again. Why didn't we stay home? Why didn't we go to the hospital sooner? Should we seek medical advice elsewhere?

Dr. Mark Olson, her Spokane orthopedic surgeon, and Dr. Charles Miller, her plastic surgeon, speak optimistically of the next 12 months.

With therapy, they say, Sarah's arm and elbow likely can recover into a useable limb. The nerves slowly regenerate. The stiffness ought to recede.

In the meantime, my girl is playing "Puff, the Magic Dragon" with her left hand at the piano. At swim-therapy class, she politely declines to share her swim mask with other girls because she says swimming practice is important for her arm and she doesn't want to go back to the hospital.

In five weeks she will be entering first grade.

She is worried about her desk. But her arm?

Don't worry, she tells me when we talk.

Once again, she teaches me what it means to be strong.

Sarah turns 7, Dad remembers 10

Ten years, a thousand columns, a million memories in Spokane.

Ten years? Couldn't be.

I have a daughter who turns seven in a few days, and a son who is nearly three.

Ten years in Spokane? A daughter and a son?

I will remember always the scorching day in 1979, when the U-Haul truck growled down Sunset Hill and I sweated with every downshift.

Partly that was the result of the family cat being wrapped around my neck like a panting fur coat.

Mostly it was the tingly fear that comes with facing something very new.

Spokane isn't so new anymore.

Five cats, two children and a car wreck later, I no longer sweat down Sunset Hill. It's just a pretty drive home.

But where did the time go?

Wasn't it only yesterday that I sat with a road map and asked a gas-station attendant the pronunciation of "Sprague Avenue"?

A day in a life passes slowly. But 10 years scamper by like a frisky tabby on a slick floor, barely touching down and then disappearing around a corner in a fleeting blur.

Ten years.

I didn't hear a clap of thunder or see a flash of light to mark their arrival and departure. There was only a stream of moments strung together.

A job brought me here. The assignment: write newspaper columns, have opinions, stir the pot of ideas.

Ten years later, I think the spoon is still wet, the ideas still flowing. But when the well goes dry, I pray someone gently will tell me to turn off the computer and pick up a good book.

The first column I wrote for this newspaper talked about heroes. Back in August 1979, near the end of Jimmy Carter's gloomy presidency, *Newsweek* magazine said this country had run out of heroes.

Spewing the false confidence of somebody who had been in town all of three weeks, I opined that the magazine was wrong.

Ten years ago, my heroine was Cris Embleton, a founder of Heal the Children. In 1979, that organization flew its first six children from Guatemala to Spokane for medical care.

Ten years later, Heal the Children has brought medical assistance to a thousand Third World children.

Time passes. The work of heroes becomes the daily business of life.

I have written about a thousand columns. What has come of them?

My vain hope is that the words have activated the minds of others, lifted faint arms to action, helped stop bullheadedness in its overblown tracks.

Selfishly, I know that 10 years of such work have allowed me to earn a Ph.D. in the study of human events.

I have learned about love and hate, fear and courage, human triumph and human tragedy.

I remember the lesson of Walter Kinsey who, at age 98, decided to be married in a Spokane rest home. He taught me of the enduring power of love.

I remember the eyes of Kevin Coe, convicted as Spokane's "South Hill rapist." His gaze brought me the chilling comprehension that some men simply cannot feel.

Ed Lindaman, deceased president of Whitworth College, taught me the necessity of trying to imagine the future.

Robin Lee Graham, youngest person ever to sail alone around the world and someone who now lives quietly on a mountainside in Montana, reminded me never to hold too long to past triumphs.

Some half-formed ideas have floated through this space. Some people unintentionally have been hurt or confused. I sincerely regret those occasions when I have failed to uphold the privilege of having access to the power and beauty of the printed word. It is appreciation of that privilege that I hope to instill in all reporters and editors who work with me.

Lately, my children have appeared regularly in this column. My apologies if you are tired of hearing about them. If I have learned anything in 10 years of living and working, it is that your children continue to be the best story you ever can write about.

Their lives require attention at the moment. Kids need attention now, when they fall, or grow fearful, or need a dad.

Ten years have had the result of refocusing my life away from external events and in the direction of internal ones.

Ten years ago, there were no children in my home. Writing newspaper columns was the most important part of life.

It isn't most important now.

What matters now is understanding that rosebuds bloom and need to be enjoyed. Balance is the key.

Ten years of doing a job and living in a place call for the attributes of the middle-distance runner, not the sprinter. Life is loping along at a brisk pace, still aiming for a personal best, but with a realization that the race is half over and the moments left mustn't be rushed.

A few nights before my daughter's seventh birthday, she told me how much she likes her home.

Home? In my mind, I saw my childhood in Wyoming, college in California, jobs in Connecticut and Idaho and then places on the map where I have not yet lived.

But for her, this place is home. Purely, unequivocally home. Ten years.

At night, I lie in bed and wonder.

Sarah turns 8, reads first column

I have waited eight years and a thousand bedtime stories to write this.

On this birthday, my daughter will read most of the birthday column that I write for her.

When and how she learned to make sense of the alphabet remain as mysterious as watching the night sky for a meteorite.

For a long time she simply looked at the hieroglyphics of *Pat the Bunny* and *Charlotte's Web* and listened as the stories were told through other voices.

This pre-loading of her brain led first to memorization of famous lines from children's classics. She would shout them out at exactly the right moment: "He huffed and he puffed and he blew the house down."

"And the glass slipper fit perfectly!"

Her yearning to read arrived about the time of her front teeth.   Finally, one night this spring, her confidence was sufficient that she volunteered to read *me* a bedtime story.

The joys of a child reading are revealed many ways.

This summer we traveled by car through Idaho and Wyoming.

The long, dry days were made quick and exciting by books – *A Little Princess* by Frances Hodgson Burnett, *Ramona the Pest* by Beverly Cleary, *Secrets of a Summer Spy* by Janice Jones.

Now, at restaurants, my daughter picks her own lunch from the menu.

This summer she can go to the phone and find the number of a friend to call without asking for help.

How odd to think her struggles to sound out place names and sandwich specials already put her ahead of 25 percent of America's school children who, at age 9, still haven't mastered basic reading skills.

More frightening is to consider that by age 13, forty percent of American kids have slipped so far behind in their reading abilities that they likely cannot make sense of a newspaper column like this.

And at high-school graduation, nearly 60 percent of American 18-year-olds are estimated to have difficulty understanding the wording of job applications, basic contracts such as are used for buying a car, and other documents basic to modern life.

I don't want my kids to be part of these numbers. Much of what I read suggests that kids who don't get hooked on reading stand a significantly higher chance of being hooked on other stuff.

Eighty percent of the teenagers who end up going to Juvenile Court can't read.

Most of the people who end up in prison can't read.

When social workers document the lives of families living on public assistance, they find most of these people have a hard time reading.

Reading extends a line to a better life. People who read well land better jobs, earn more money, give themselves more opportunities to succeed.

Beyond its economic and social benefits, reading is a basic and necessary skill for simply getting through the day.

Sometimes parents say, well, the world is becoming more visual so we might as well let our kids watch television or a rented video. Problem is: visual images, while stimulating and exciting, don't often help answer the big questions such as

"What do I want to be when I grow up?" or "How shall I live a good life?"

The major-league abstract issues of life require thought. Thought always demands careful consideration and study. Learning about the meaning of life comes from living and reading, pure and simple.

Reading requires work. A dictionary becomes a heavy, yet essential, accessory.

Reading demands undivided attention. You can't read and ride a bicycle or read and play soccer.

But in the end, fifteen minutes a day spent reading to your child, or having your child read on her own, knock down barriers as if they had been hit by an Army tank.

The awesome power of the written word, copied and circulated for other eyes, changes history every day.

That my daughter now reads reminds me again of what it takes to be a parent.

Her success was built on many hours spent, night after night, with books.

I know *Sleeping Beauty* by heart. And *Danny and the Dinosaur*. And *Arabian Nights*.

Sometimes I didn't want to read those books; I wanted to read my own books, or watch television, or simply go outside and be done with children.

But being a parent means thinking not just of yourself, but also of your child and what you hope she will become.

I hoped she would become a reader. And she has.

Sarah turns 9; Dad learns about child abuse cases in Spokane

The week of my daughter's 9th birthday, a Spokane doctor spent an hour venting frustration at trying to cope with a shocking case of child abuse.

The juxtaposition of these two girls' lives shocked me.

One morning I was shopping for my not-so-little girl whose dreams still are filled with idealized images of Ken or Prince Charming.

She has her torments, but life is unfolding at a pace that allows for innocence, dreams and the promise of future happiness.

In that way she is like thousands of other children these days who, despite the stresses and strains of family life, are allowed the essential privilege of being concerned primarily with the tasks of growing up.

Then, I visited the office of Dr. Jim States, a specialist in adolescent and young adult medicine.

He read me the short life history of a girl who, at age 9, had been sexually attacked by her father and her uncle.

The girl has no more images of Ken or Prince Charming.

The authority figures in her life attacked her at home, in her bed.

They photographed her, threatened her, committed acts of violence and degradation.

At 9, she already had tried to contact police in an Eastern Washington town to ask for protection. But she was a kid. They discounted her story.

At 9, she went to her mother and tried to explain what had happened. Frightened and poor, mom told her it was her own fault and to do what her father asked.

Eventually, the girl ran away.

She lived on the street after a judge in Idaho found insufficient evidence for her to be taken from the home and to have her father prosecuted.

By 18, the girl herself was charged with assaulting children.

Jim States met her in a hospital room where she lay unable to digest food, unable to eat and close to death.

Her life was on the verge of ruin.

Yet, even after so much bad had happened, this young woman had one more chance.

The doctor tried to intervene.

He called the deputy director of a state agency asking for assistance.

He contacted law enforcement.

He wrote and called a judge.

Somehow the evidence, the history, the life story didn't quite fit anybody's job description.

Because she was 18, Child Protective Services said the young woman wasn't covered by state child protection law.

Now that she was hospitalized and safe, law enforcement and the courts said they couldn't help.

But as a high-risk, low-payout adolescent without a medical plan, she wasn't welcome as a long-term medical patient.

Instead, she was shipped to a correctional facility.

Jim States was left wondering what is happening in our society.

"Kids these days have a hard time asking for help – or finding it," he said. "I tried to help. But I was worn out."

And that's what got to me.

Kids assume their parents – at least one of them – will be there to help them if they are in trouble.

The point isn't that parents have to be perfect, or rich, or never wrong.

What parents must do is just be there, without abuse and neglect, to provide support.

When they aren't, the shortcomings of our nation's jerry-built system of external support and childhood maintenance appear all too obvious.

The system is built to deal with symptoms, such as adolescents breaking the law or acting out their attempts to medicate the pain in their lives through drugs.

Most troubling of all, our society still hasn't found good ways to adequately deal with severe problems of early childhood.

Instead, we end up locking away the grown-up results of impaired childhoods.

A few days ago, the final report of the National Commission on Children explained the support system for children coming out of severely damaged families this way:

"If the nation had deliberately designed a system that would frustrate the professionals who staff it, anger the public who finances it and abandon the children who depend on it, it could not have done a better job than the present child welfare system."

What kids need is a loving, safe and nurturing family in a stable, secure home.

We know that is the answer.

What we don't know is how to make it happen for more than seven million kids in this country.

A good place to start is one kid at a time – your own.

Sarah talks politics at 10

Riding in a pickup truck on the night Bill Clinton became the Democratic nominee for president, my daughter asked her first question about politics.

"Does Bill Clinton care about kids?" she wondered out loud as the radio speakers reverberated with the words of the Arkansas governor's acceptance speech.

I launched into a far-too-complicated explanation of what I knew about Clinton's educational reforms.

"Was Geena Davis the star of any other movies besides *A League of Their Own*?" my daughter asked.

End of politics, on to the movies.

That was my 10-year-old's thought process.

That images, pretty faces and the cult of fame matter more to her than Bill Clinton's plan for better-trained teachers is easily understood.

At 10, it works.

Children occupy a world of magic, spells and powerful God-like figures.

But we don't.

In our world the magic ends about the time the checkbook balance slips into the red.

God-like figures most often emerge after years of understudy, hard work and tough decisions.

Yet for weeks, the voting adults of this country fell under the spell of a magician who waved wands on TV.

Ross Perot made for a great movie script.

With squeaky voice and quirky face, he became a kind of Pee Wee Herman in politics, instantly a hit among people who grew up on Donald Duck and Mickey Mouse but now wanted a new cartoon character.

And that was the problem with Perot.

Maybe he didn't become the caricatures of Democrats and Republicans that have emerged, but he nonetheless was a caricature protest candidate.

This man didn't have the stomach for politics. As he said this week when he pulled out of the race, "I have no drive to be president of the United States."

And when the people who understand modern politics came to his side and told him what he needed to do, Perot didn't want it.

He had no positions on the economy, no clear ideas on foreign policy, no agenda for the underprivileged.

Instead, he reminded us of Sly Stallone's *Rocky*, who rose up out of nowhere to challenge the big boys at a game they thought they owned.

This is a fine script.

But it isn't really politics.

When he pulled out of the race this week, Perot himself alluded to the difference between the Hollywood aspects of his campaign and the reality.

He looked at the numbers. He brought to bear an engineer's analytical mind and concluded that he couldn't win.

And if he couldn't win, he would simply hang it up.

That's the most important lesson of Perot's remarkable run.

In the end he dealt with the hard facts and their consequences.

He couldn't win. His continued campaign could throw the nation into an electoral crisis by denying any candidate a clear majority and putting the selection of the president into the House of Representatives. That would be a disservice to his country, and he wouldn't do it.

Ross Perot's decision was based on sober realities, not the magic of it all.

Sure, we all need to believe in a savior. The nation needs a vision; it needs hope.

Ross Perot tapped some of that.

But the stark realities of facing up to what needs to be done to balance the budget, make the tax system more equitable, improve education and get a grip on health-care costs will require hard choices from all of us.

To fix what is wrong will be difficult, painful and take a lot of time.

And that's not much of a movie script.

My daughter didn't want to hear about all that stuff.

But she is only turning 10.

She can live in a world of make-believe where the movies matter more than a president's plan.

The rest of us, though, need to flick on the lights, quit eating candy bars and try a cold dose of reality out on the street.

Make Bush and Clinton accountable. Don't buy platitudes or vague promises.

Taxes will need to go up and spending will need to come down.

Docs will make less, and those who are covered by health insurance will have to pay more.

Congress needs to quit filling pork barrels and go back to the infrastructure.

I think these are hard truths that somebody needs to speak about and be accepted for saying.

In the end, Ross Perot dealt with reality, the hard truths, the tough choices. He knew the difference between the steak and the sizzle.

Let's hope Bush and Clinton can make the same good judgments as they stand before the grill of presidential politics.

Sarah wants to be a grown up at 11

Six flowers unfolding and a pesky little brother buzzing them like a bee.

This was my daughter's 11th early birthday, a day of touching contradictions.

The night before, she slept with her bunny.

Then she privately told her mom the other girls all had bras.

She is on the edge of that place where her eyes, her mind and her attention turn away from childhood and toward grown-up things.

To me it seems all too early.

She is an early 5-foot-2, an early 100 pounds, an early size-8 shoe.

And her 11th birthday came early, as it often must for kids whose grandparents, cousins and aunts live far away.

We will be a family on a distant vacation on the day of her actual birthday this week. Already she is asked to understand the trade-offs of living in a place where daddy followed a career that led far from what once was called a hometown.

On this birthday I was troubled by all that seems so early for kids.

101

Little human beings require the longest period of care and nurturing of any creature on the planet.

The reasons are not only physical, but mental and emotional.

My daughter will look grown-up at the end of her 11th year. But she isn't.

She will have only begun to understand the big world around her. She will have been exposed to a great deal, but not have lived long enough to have experienced much.

So many kids soldier into too-early appointments with real-world predicaments like sex and AIDS, divorce and broken families, the choice between working hard and hardly working.

The problems are as big as the 20th century, but the skills my daughter has developed to deal with the world all have been honed one decision at a time by someone who was born in 1982.

For many kids, the symmetry is off. Too many big projects coming at them, too few tools to handle them.

Sometimes my wife and I roll our eyes and wish for respite from pre-teen logic, but we understand the necessity of letting our daughter exercise her willfulness on us, only to then run for the shelter of our arms and her room.

As a father, I feel uneasy as the next curtain is about to rise in the passion play of child-rearing.

Just as the actor wishes for one more read through the script before the curtain goes up, a father longs for one more day to impart wisdom.

The world of little girls doesn't always allow for much more of that.

Already my daughter announces that she thinks the old man isn't so wise.

He's getting some back talk.

And in a larger context, I fear that the combination of male-bashing in many feminine circles and the very real lack of male role models in the lives of many families has resulted in fathers being marginalized as a memory or a parody.

Too bad, for dads can often tell little girls some things about the world that moms can't. We know about competition, and rules, and the value of rising up from defeat – things that men face.

Mothers and daughters don't have it all that easy during this time of a child's life, either.

In our house I watch bemused as my wife's I.Q. seemingly drops precipitously by the day as our daughter discovers her own voice and opinions.

And I see my girl's classmates and peers taking more of the front-row seats in her life.

They enthusiastically rush to that place, ready to burst out of childhood and into being teenagers.

The girls who came to my daughter's early birthday slumber party brought with them some very adult thoughts.

They wondered if their mom's new boyfriend would like them.

They debated whether they were fat and if it was really important to eat food with no calories.

They didn't want their pictures taken without combing their hair and made sure the doors were closed when they changed into their nightgowns.

They all screamed at the spiders and were little flirts.

"Here he comes to save the day," they sang as I, the lone father in the group, approached with the tools necessary to assemble a birthday gift.

This was the Mighty Mouse theme song.

Sometimes I feel dads need super strength and a bulletproof veneer.

But then, we moms and dads are the grown-ups.

This isn't the time for self-pity.

The little girls and boys of today may need our protection and guidance more than ever.

Girls at 11 need to be told they shouldn't be worried about diets.

Girls at 11 should be thinking about the boys in their own class, not the boyfriends of their mothers, aunts and grand-mothers.

Even if they are straining to take a run at being more grown up, they still need someone on the reins.

I think they know that. I think they tell us that every day.

On my daughter's 11th birthday, she taught me that I mustn't turn her loose too early, even if she asks me to do it.

Sarah turns 12 at Disney movie

A sublime idea can give children the power to dream.

On July 20, 1969, the world sublimely watched and children dreamed as men landed on the moon.

On July 20, 1994, the day my daughter turned 12, we went to *The Lion King*.

In air-conditioned darkness she searched for her power to dream, a reminder of how exercises for the imagination can change.

Movies occupied an important place in imaginations and culture 25 years ago. *Butch Cassidy and the Sundance Kid* was big in 1969. But not as big as the men on the moon.

On that July evening children looked outside and up and imagined that was where they wanted to be.

Of course you can be an astronaut, parents said. Fly, fly to a distant, risky, chunk of rock. There you will conjure up adventure, inspiration and achievement.

On her birthday, my daughter and I talked only briefly about the landing on the moon.

Her imagination went somewhere else.

She took flight in thoughts of a movie that would be most instructive on this totally awesome day of life.

Would it be *Forrest Gump*, *Ace Ventura: Pet Detective*, *The Lion King*?

I think the movies, including music videos and old TV shows from the '50s and '60s, now provide the most accessible reservoir to fuel a child's imagination and drive her search for meaning.

The search at 12 is no different from what it was 25 years ago, but the view of the outside world has changed.

Today, my girl is just peeking over the edge of what life might become just as children always have done at 12 or 13.

She is alternately frightened and exhilarated and knows there is no going back to Barbie.

But I don't think it just my imagination to suggest she and many of her friends are mapping their approach to the future in a different way than children did 25 years ago.

They aren't looking at the moon or the outside world for much guidance or inspiration.

In 1969 the world wasn't all that peachy. Remember Vietnam, and Woodstock and Richard Nixon.

Though the times were divisive, the people were somehow more engaged. Whether you approved or disapproved of what was going on around you, it was a part of life. Woodstock was a public/private issue. The Vietnam War was a public/private debate. Richard Nixon, in his first year as president, evoked strong feelings both in public and at home.

Now, the connections between the outside world and the inside are purposefully severed.

In 1994, we watch music videos at home.

The events in Rwanda, though highly accessible, are pointedly left on the screen. Only Bill Clinton seems to arouse the passions of past politics.

I sense my daughter's search to find herself and her place in the world has become a much more personalized, internal journey than I remember.

And she wants it to be fun.

Entertainment, pleasure and meaning have melted together, and this puts a special burden on the media.

Vapid music videos can burn like a laser beam into the soul of a young girl, but to what end?

Luckily, the Disney people have gotten onto this. Their highly moralistic movies have matured and now bring very modern themes to young minds through incredible animation and song.

In *The Lion King* the songs tell it all. First comes "Hakuna Matata," sung by a warthog in warthog heaven:

"Hakuna Matata,

What a wonderful phrase;

It means no worries for the rest of your days."

Eat dessert first, channel surf, watch out just for me and my paradise comes through as the message here, and kids recognize it as a seductive part of the world around them.

But every other song in *The Lion King* cuts against this notion. The other singing lions talk of being prepared, of being a king in one's own world, of feeling what Elton John calls the rhyme and reason of life in his chart-topping "Can You Feel the Love Tonight."

The night we left the theater, a full moon shone above.

I looked up and realized my daughter's imagination was being shaped in an opposite direction from imagining the moon.

But it can work for her.

Inside the world of music and film she can find hope and courage and purpose.

Perhaps her generation is right to sense that the real world has become so troubled and disconcerting that Hollywood is the last refuge and only substitution available to fill the void left from a time when dreams were built by "One small step for man, one giant leap for mankind."

Sarah becomes a teenager

"I'm a teenager, Dad," my daughter said with a lilting voice and melt-a-heart smile on the morning of her 13th birthday.

I was grateful for the merry words and show of teeth.

Becoming a teenager compels many perfectly normal girls and boys to experiment with a variety of other verbal tones and facial expressions.

Grunts, screams, scowls and disdainful glances come to mind, along with animated crying, personalized yelling, loud stamping and slamming and, my favorite, the hysterical laugh.

Though still trying to be an optimist, I'm worried.

This symphony of teenage attention-getting devices could begin to wear on a person and turn a loving father into a psychotic with an ice pick.

Was this the reason summer camp and vacations without the kids were invented? I was relieved when my daughter suggested Wolffy's as a place for her party.

This '50s-style joint with a loud jukebox, clattering plates and menu that invites you to "walk a cow across the grill and run it through the garden" (or otherwise order a hamburger deluxe) offered the perfect venue to experience the full range of 13-year-old exuberance.

My daughter's exuberant 13-year-old friends were invited to share the experience.

For an hour or more we all squealed, whispered and stuffed ourselves with burgers, fries and milkshakes before heading for a movie.

The activity worked up quite an appetite in the girls.

Just after Wolffy's, and just before entering the movie theater, they stopped to order enormous tubs of popcorn, big rolls of candy and more Coke to make sure no one expired of hunger.

In some ways, the whole birthday was something of a throwback to the '50s.

For one day, Elvis still reigned supreme.

The girls didn't worry about being thin but about whose sundae would arrive first.

They all sat together without boyfriends to watch a love story.

The next day my daughter floated a stretch of the Spokane River as a rite of passage. She navigated a few rapids, looked at the sky and the birds, taking a moment to consider her place in the natural order of things.

Along the way, some punk kids threw rocks at the innertubes. When we arrived back at the truck, someone had stolen our new beach towels.

This was a lesson, too. There is always a next day after a perfect birthday.

And in the next days since 1982 when my daughter was born, the number of arrests in Washington state for crimes committed by teenagers has more than doubled.

By the time she turns 18, my daughter will, God willing, have lived through the largest increase in teenage homicides seen during any period in our nation's history.

She will have watched a record number of girls have babies without husbands.

She will have seen more lethal drugs, more AIDS, more violence among her peers than any generation before her.

In her book, *Reviving Ophelia*, psychologist Mary Pipher describes the struggle American girls must undertake to maintain a sense of themselves as adolescents today.

"Adolescence is harder now," Pipher says, "because of cultural changes in the last decade. The protected space and time we once called childhood has grown shorter.

"There is an African saying: 'It takes a village to raise a child,'" she said. "Sadly, most girls today no longer have a village."

She will need your assistance for that.

She will need mentors and coaches and teachers in her school, her church, her neighborhood.

She will need the police, the doctor, the student driving instructor.

She will need music that speaks of women's power and heart and intellect.

She will need poems from writers who have thought hard and deeply about life.

She will need long walks on safe streets, full nights of sleep without boys, a friend or two who will be there no matter what.

She is the reason to vote, to clean up the neighborhood, to fight poverty and ignorance and fear.

And for now, she still needs her mom and dad, dumb, stupid and mean as we are, to help her navigate in a village where she, and all of us, must find a way to work together, prosper and thrive.

Sarah goes to New York on 14th birthday

The night she turned 14, my daughter went to the top of the Empire State Building. At 14, a young woman imagines the big, bright world out there.

A dad's job must be to help a teenager begin to see it.

Seeing the world requires more than an elevator ride up 86 floors on a summer vacation.

The disciplines needed to truly picture the world, grasp it, occasionally understand it, take a lifetime to master.

Fourteen-year-olds curse the cataracts of childhood. My daughter demands that she be allowed to look at a world larger than her bedroom and her bunny.

Assisting her in this task might be compared to performing laser eye surgery on a self-conscious kitten who is watching everything in a mirror. Go too fast and you get scratched. Too slow, and the kitten yowls in impatient agony.

My daughter, along with most of her 14-year-old girl-friends, spends a considerable part of each evening trying to see the world by looking in the mirror.

Her smiles, hairstyles and each tiny blemish are examined, questioned and discussed. Who am I? Where am I headed? How will I get there?

Some answers can be found staring, self-absorbed in that mirror, mirror on the wall.

Picasso painted his first masterpiece at 14. Bill Gates was messing with electronics at that age.

As my daughter searches the mirror for her inner soul and talents, I hope she sees a mouth that is filled with the voice of a rich mezzo-soprano. I hope she sees ears that capture the nuance of foreign language. I hope she knows that she combs her hair over a brain that can keenly solve algebra problems the way her father never could.

These are the gifts I see in her.

My role, most assuredly, is not to see for her.

This distinction between being the eye surgeon, not the Seeing Eye Dog, is difficult for a father.

My 14-year-old often asserts she has 20/20 vision – particularly on such teenage matters as sex, drugs and music.

To assume she is right would be as foolish as sending the visually-impaired into a crosswalk with no understanding of traffic sounds.

Still, she must see the colors of life with her own eyes, even as she bumps into familiar objects like dad, mom and family.

Hillary Rodham Clinton wrote a book in which she spoke of the African idea that it takes a village to accomplish the task. In his acceptance speech as the Republican presidential candidate, Bob Dole disagreed. It takes a family to raise a child, he proclaimed.

I think they are both right.

A family can give a girl a safe place to dream. A village can give her a safe place to venture out and make her dreams come true.

Atop the Empire State Building a few nights ago my daughter asked me, "Dad, do you think I will ever sing on Broadway?"

Some girl just like her will.

At 14 you begin to think rollicking, audacious thoughts. That is if you manage to see beyond a pair of fashion jeans and getting kissed.

This is a dad talking, remember?

Very soon now, my daughter's eyes will turn away from mine. She will seek out others in the village.

Because she isn't a fly or fish or crocodile, her eyes can look in only one direction at a time.

She is turning now. She is teaching me how to watch her go. High school is but fifteen days away.

For her I pray one day she will look back and say, "I've found a path for me, the one you helped me see."

Sarah discovers boys at 15

Today my daughter turns 15.

One thing stands out. There is no going back to the day when she was daddy's little girl.

Not when your little girl is 5-foot-8 and has a mind of her own.

She is looking forward.

She is looking out.

She is looking at boys.

Oh, God.

Boys.

Boys call day and night.

Boys ride their bikes over. Neither snow nor sleet nor the fury of Ice Storm '96 could keep them away.

This summer, through a bureaucratic snafu, some of these boys got driver's licenses.

I think a nice mom in the family van has stopped by for a visit. Then I learn, in a panic, that a nice mom has lent the family van to a 16-year-old boy who has spent a considerable amount of his private time thinking about my daughter.

Thinking about my daughter in the family van.

Thinking . . .

Who knows, exactly, what 15-year-olds think?

For clues, I have asked my daughter.

"What are you thinking?" I say in my most non-threatening fatherly voice.

"Nothing," she replies as if I were applying thumbscrews under a white-hot light bulb.

I know at 15 she is thinking and dreaming about a great deal. Some hint of her thoughts can be found inside the covers of *Seventeen* magazine, copies of which are strewn across the floor of her bedroom.

The other morning I ventured into that bedroom. Next to a well-worn pair of Doc Martens I found the February issue of *Seventeen*.

February was "the love issue."

Topics in the special love issue include: "Does he like you? Seven ways to tell." And "Quiz: Is he crushworthy?" And "How we fell in love; real couples talk."

The region of the heart occupies a good portion of the mind at 15. Young women need good hearts. The 21st century will be achingly long for strong women who can provide care, comfort and concern.

There was one other story pitched on the cover I hope my daughter, and other girls her age, managed to find.

The headline read: "Playing it smart: Girls who refuse to act dumb." It isn't just a strong heart young women will need as they move toward 30 and 45 and 60.

Brains will matter more than ever.

In the next century the great divide between opportunity and diminished hopes will hinge on knowledge. Sadly, I think too many 15-year-olds aren't getting that message.

Here's a clue from an old guy.

Being cool in the 21st century won't have much to do with smoking cigarettes and piercing your navel.

Being cool will be knowing how to make your computer do tricks and how to speak to your business partners and neighbors in Spanish or Chinese. Young women with both good hearts and keen brains will rule.

But work must begin now, in high school, with the development of a self that honors not just good hair and a good heart, but what is percolating in between.

Thankfully, my daughter shows a glimmer of understanding about this balance. A few nights ago my daughter went to see *Annie Get Your Gun* at the Coeur d'Alene Summer Theatre. The songs inspired her. She dreams of hitting Broadway one day. I hope she does. She has a voice.

When Annie Oakley intentionally missed a target so the man in her life could win a sharpshooting contest, my daughter was outraged. Why would a girl do that? Why would she intentionally not do her best so a man could win?

Why, indeed.

Doing your best as a young woman sometimes means putting up with people who put down accomplishment. Accomplished 15-year-olds, I am learning, must perfect a variety of poses, costumes and phases.

113

One day a 15-year-old can strive to be an A student in math and score points with the parents. The next day a 15-year-old practices the art of keeping a guy's attention with nothing more than a laugh into the receiver.

The problem is that a winning telephone personality is more easily accomplished and seems far more rewarding than struggling through calculus.

As a result, more than one girl in high school has opted to drop tough classes so she can work harder and spend more time on the phone. I think that is the wrong message and the wrong choice for girls.

I worry about girls who feel they must be average and aim low to be popular.

I share these worries with my daughter, even though she no longer is my little girl. She doesn't listen much and sees me more as a set of car keys and a checkbook.

So, my job now is to clear a path for her.

Out of her room and out of sight from her friends, I am left to hack away at the vines and false images that could pull her down.

The potential of her generation is awesome.

But girls, always remember two things that your fathers tried to teach you: Hard work can be lonely. Big dreams take guts to achieve.

Hot Topics Across the Inland Northwest

Chapter Three

Seattle vs. Spokane:
One's hot; one is still warming up

Spokane – Seattle.

Dry side. Wet side.

East vs. west.

For 100 years, Seattle and Spokane have been Washington's two largest cities.

As far back as 1900, when Seattle's population stood at 80,671 and Spokane's residents numbered 36,848, the two cities have been compared and contrasted to define Washington state.

In the last decade, however, the dynamics playing off the two cities have changed dramatically.

For most of this century, Spokane could conceive of itself as having a big brother/little brother relationship to Seattle.

They had minor league baseball; we had minor league baseball.

They had a world's fair; we had a world's fair.

Some years they had the political and economic upper hand; some years we did.

But we were, in essence, part of the same family.

In 1997 the relationship is on the brink of becoming more like that of a first cousin who has migrated to a new land, grown rich and famous and now rarely sends a postcard to his distant shirttail relative back in the old country.

That's the bottom line of a stunning, fascinating report done by *The Spokesman-Review* over the last five months.

In the last decade, the divide between Washington's two largest cities has grown vast in terms of economics, political clout and vision.

In a special section entitled "The Great Divide," *The Spokesman-Review* examined the forces at work in Spokane and Seattle.

As in all honest analyses, there are some painful moments in the telling of this story.

Some hard facts emerge about Spokane and some candid feedback is offered about Spokane's economic, political and cultural realities.

The underlying theme of many of these comments is that a culture of poverty has begun to shape Spokane.

An astonishing 45 percent of the jobs in Spokane today pay $14,000 a year or less. In Seattle, the average wage is now $48,727.

Spokane political tone now often reflects this culture of poverty. We're prone to a we-don't-want-it, we-can't-afford-it attitude.

Spokane voted no on a science center. Spokane voted no on computers in schools. Spokane voted no on street repairs. Some in Spokane are fighting downtown redevelopment, yawning at efforts to expand the local museums, ignoring pleas for rebuilding core infrastructure.

Meanwhile, in the last decade Seattle has built three new art museums, won approval for both a new football and baseball stadium, and warmly endorsed the revitalization of downtown around a Nordstrom.

The civic and political attitudes of the two communities have always been different. But the differences seem more pronounced than before.

Spokane seems less ambitious, even as Seattle seems more.

Spokane seems less sure of its ability to be a place of note, even as Seattle grows more confident.

Seattle vs. Spokane:
One's hot; one is still warming up

Seattle, of course, has benefited immeasurably from the thousands of people who, a decade ago, went to work at Microsoft and now are millionaires because they bought as few as 200 shares of stock in 1986 and held them.

Seattle has been boosted a second time by the huge run-up in Boeing company employment and business. Today, Boeing employs a staggering 91,000 people in King County.

Spokane, by contrast, has enjoyed a modest echo of this resounding blast of success. Boeing employs about 550 people at its Spokane fabrication plant.

This is better than Microsoft's Spokane presence, which is only an 800 number in the phone book.

Spokane cannot rewrite history.

Neither Boeing nor Microsoft is likely to move its headquarters here anytime soon.

A vision finally needs to be crafted from what is possible here.

Right now, it is unclear what is possible.

Will Spokane gather its strength and become a vibrant second city, a kind of smaller San Francisco to Los Angeles? A Colorado Springs to a Denver?

Or will the city fall, like a tired track star, behind not only Seattle, but a host of other second-tier cities from Boise to Bellingham?

This is not to suggest that Spokane can become, or should aspire to become, a Seattle.

As *The Spokesman-Review's* series documents, there are some things about Seattle we would like to avoid.

We sent Paul Turner, author of "The Slice" column, and cartoonist Milt Priggee to the West Side, and they came back with some amusing anecdotes.

Spokane still has a big heart.

Spokane is resourceful, livable and a great place to raise a family.

119

Historically, Spokane has taken pride in being a strong number 2.

To stay there in the 21st century will require a rekindling of Spokane's soul as a place solidly rooted on hope and active optimism, not reactive negativism and despair.

This is the hope the newspaper wants to rekindle as it presents "The Great Divide."

Sam Donaldson is stinking up news business at WSU

Sam Donaldson, the in-your-face co-anchor of *PrimeTime Live* is articulate and funny.

He is also wrong when he says today's TV journalism is really no different from the broadcast journalism of 50 years ago.

A few nights ago Donaldson visited Pullman to deliver the keynote speech for the Edward R. Murrow Symposium.

The symposium is named for the Washington State University graduate too often forgotten by TV viewers.

Murrow rose to fame on radio in the 1940s for his broadcasts from London during World War II and then on his own interview show on CBS television in the 1950s.

Upon his death in 1965, then-President Lyndon Johnson led the nation in mourning when he said of Murrow, "We knew him as a gallant fighter, a man who dedicated his life both as a newsman and as a public official to an unrelenting search for the truth. He subscribed to the proposition that free men and free inquiry are inseparable."

Will some future president be saying that about Donaldson?

In Pullman Donaldson made an entertaining case that journalists have never been loved, that their work always has been controversial, and therefore there isn't much difference between Ed Murrow's day and today's TV news.

Donaldson only drew one distinction between then and now – today's broadcast journalists must make the news more interesting because people are distracted and the media are far more competitive than before.

To make news interesting, Donaldson explained, sometimes requires a journalist to spruce up the story a bit – maybe use a hidden camera, maybe even lie.

These practices certainly have made Donaldson a topic of conversation.

People wonder if his hair is real. Women in Pullman shamelessly posed with him at the reception following his speech. After all, he is a celebrity.

But the fame of Donaldson really doesn't matter much in terms of what is or isn't news.

It's the story, stupid, not Sam's hair, or his pointed questions, or even the shock value of what he and his cohorts find out.

News involves facts, implications, complicated pros and cons. These don't always bring high ratings. And that's the problem with Donaldson's argument.

To make the news interesting and to build ratings often results in a type of news gathering and news presentation that does a disservice to both journalism and the public interest.

Donaldson said he thought Ed Murrow would probably be using hidden cameras and dramatization to fill his broadcasts if Murrow were alive today.

If the hidden camera would have ended the bombing of London, perhaps so. But would Ed Murrow have used a hidden camera and deceptive reporting practices to catch a grocery store re-wrapping a few fish?

That's what Donaldson's cohorts at *PrimeTime Live* did in the now infamous Food Lion case.

When Food Lion sued, a jury awarded them $5.5 million in punitive damages. The damages were awarded not because the story was false. The facts broadcast were never in dispute. The verdict came because the jury didn't agree with Donaldson's logic that it's OK to lie, deceive and use hidden cameras to find a few re-wrapped fish.

Good journalists don't lie to get a story. They don't secretly film them or cast them in a false light.

The best journalists make judgments on the importance of stories and try to give a complete picture.

In this month's *American Journalism Review*, reporter Marc Gunther notes that the *Richmond Times-Dispatch* newspaper dug out the records to show Food Lion had the third-best cleanliness ratings among eight national chains. The TV broadcast didn't report this.

The *AJR* story also noted ABC's own crews had recorded, but not broadcast, conversations with unsuspecting Food Lion workers who said their boss urged them to be on the lookout for spoiled food and throw it out.

PrimeTime Live found some problems. They raised valid questions. But the story wasn't whole. It wasn't complete, and it was built on a foundation of deception.

Murrow developed the genre known as eyewitness accounts. Murrow perfected what we now call the in-depth interview.

Murrow wasn't afraid to stand up to demagogues. Fifty years ago when Senator Joseph McCarthy tried to put a communist label on everyone in Hollywood, Murrow simply asked for the proof.

The substance of what Murrow did then and what the best journalists try to do today isn't much changed.

But the style and tone of Ed Murrow then and Sam Donaldson now couldn't be more different.

Violence is not a constitutional issue anymore

I don't want to register anyone's gun.

When my son turns 12, we're going to the rifle range and learn to shoot responsibly and with good aim.

But recent events in Moses Lake and downtown Spokane suggest why people who support the right to keep and bear arms need to begin waging the war against violence and quit focusing so intently on the right to have a gun.

One more impassioned speech about what the Constitution allows doesn't move our society one inch closer to finding a way to both allow gun ownership and reduce the havoc guns can let loose.

The real struggle, the heroic struggle, is to find a way to keep a 14-year-old boy from walking into his junior high school and killing his teacher and his tormentor.

This wasn't a drug death in a big-city ghetto.

This kid got good grades.

He didn't use a Saturday Night Special. He used a .30-.30.

The question isn't whether he has a right to a gun.

The question is why a kid had a message in his brain that the way to get even with a rival in school is to shoot him.

Spokane hosted a regional conference on youth violence recently.

A theme spoken time and again was that our society is shaped by too many images that say shooting people for little slights is OK.

"They watch that stuff. They act it out. It's reality to them," junior high school counselor Mary Cady explained as she sat and listened to the presentations at the Ridpath Hotel.

Remember the Ridpath? That's where a 78-year-old gunman walked in one Tuesday and shot a waitress and the restaurant's manager.

Why? A witness said the shooting might have been the result of the gunman feeling insulted when others in the restaurant complained that he smelled.

A boy is tormented in junior high and kills his classmate.

An old man can't keep himself clean and kills his waitress.

Do these stories have anything to do with the U.S. Constitution? No.

The issues here have to do with anger, isolation, revenge and hate.

So enough, already, about rights, freedoms and the Constitution. We get it. Most people don't rob or steal or commit murder with guns.

But the law-abiding people who passionately believe in a free society's right to have a gun need to focus every ounce of that passion on ways to reduce the violence that guns enable every day on our streets, in our businesses and in our homes.

Fighting government restrictions on firearms is a bonding experience.

It makes people feel good as they do right by the Constitution.

Fighting the causes of despair isn't fun.

It's gut-wrenching and messy. But that's where the true battle needs to be waged.

In 1990, guns were used during 80 felony assaults and 84 robberies in Spokane County.

By 1994, guns were involved in 300 felony assaults and 184 robberies in Spokane.

In Switzerland every adult male remains in the military reserves until age 50. Most of these men own guns. Most Swiss households have guns.

In Switzerland last year, fewer than 100 people died from handguns.

In the U.S. more than 35,000 died from guns.

This is the issue.

Remember the bumper stickers that read, "Guns don't kill people; people kill people"? Well, legislators and the public buy into this.

It is politically difficult and practically impossible to take away guns. Time spent arguing about it is time wasted as we chillingly go about murdering our society.

The Swiss have guns and you don't hear about someone there walking into a school or a restaurant and opening fire.

Gun owners and gun supporters need to work harder to find out why.

In the meantime, wouldn't it be something if every time a troubled youth used a gun to kill, a gun-rights group came forward and donated money for counseling or anger control at the school?

Wouldn't it be heartening when an old man seeks attention through firearms, to have gun supporters speak up for services to assist those who are lonely, mentally ill or who otherwise cannot care for themselves?

Gun owners, this society needs your passion, your involvement, your hard work to help us address the real problems associated with guns.

Don't let fanatics steal Halloween tradition from schools

Freddy Krueger could cause a nightmare on Elm Street.

The devil might exist, and evil most surely does.

None of this adds up to a reason to rain on Halloween.

Yet a number of schools in Eastern Washington and North Idaho spent the last days of October trying to dampen down a truly fun day into something soggy, like Harvest Fest or Parade of The Fuzzy Bunnies.

Don't let it happen in your neighborhood school.

Resist the worried voices who say kids' minds are being bent by seeing a bloody rubber mask or somebody dressed up like a witch.

Kids need tradition.

They love costumes.

Ancient symbols of ghosts, goblins and deathly skeletons are rooted in a child's attempt to cope with issues of life, death and the hereafter.

Of course, schools will be tempted by the allure of trying to wring all controversy out of the halls.

When a misguided parent complains about the evils of scary masks and ancient rituals, the temptation would be to just cancel Halloween parades, ban scary faces, and nobody will be upset.

Wrong. People will be upset.

"My family is extremely disappointed to hear that Halloween costumes and parties will be phased out," wrote second-grade parent Susan Bresnahan to the principal of Spokane's Roosevelt school.

"Halloween costumes, poetry, stories and songs are especially effective in developing imagination in children and provide a safe experience to explore fears," this mother wrote.

"I do not believe a majority of parents fear for the souls of their children because they have an opportunity to enjoy a Halloween party at school. I become angry when my children are denied experiences because a small percentage of parents can make life miserable for administrators and school boards."

These sentiments weren't brewed up in the basement of someone with a broom and a coven. Susan Bresnahan works as a school psychologist. "And Halloween is just a highlight of the school year for my daughter," she said.

In the coming weeks parent-teacher groups at Roosevelt Elementary and dozens of other schools will take up the issue of future Halloween parties and festivities.

Meetings will be called. Compromise will be advocated. During these discussions, a few core principles need to be recalled.

To begin with, the tradition of Halloween matters simply because most families don't have many traditions left.

Halloween beats watching *The Simpsons*. This is a day when moms, dads and kids share something. They have a bit of family life, some joy, a sense of neighborhood and community.

"I think honestly that some schools perhaps took this too lightly when they started talking about changing Halloween," said Joan Kingrey, a Spokane School District Area Director. "Something as silly as Halloween has symbolic value to us, and to many parents it matters a great deal."

That's right. And parents who like Halloween but are otherwise concerned about too much violence in our society mustn't be tempted to think that keeping scary masks off kids makes much of a dent in the amount of maiming and killing children must endure in movies, pictures and real life.

Honestly, a second-grader seeing an older student in a bloody mask has very little to do with TV having too many murders and government overusing the military.

And what a mistake to plant the idea in children that Halloween is somehow linked to worship of the devil.

This is truly a scary thing for a parent to do, and it's a far too narrow view.

Some cultures used this time of the year to honor the dead. Others used it to mark the passing of the seasons.

And clearly in America, Halloween has been a 100-year tradition of candy overload.

Talking through the value and meaning of Halloween is fine. Suggesting that Freddy Krueger masks aren't the best way to help second-graders enjoy hot lunch is OK, too.

And as Spokane Hutton School principal Deborah Johnson explained, "I think our primary focus should be on how we can celebrate learning at the time of this holiday."

That's a fine idea. Link up school celebrations of Halloween to a study of the Middle Ages, or of human skeletal structure, or the economics of candy manufacturing.

But let kids feel the power of imagination.

Let them pretend.

Let them ponder the possibility of goblins and things they don't understand.

Halloween, after all, is for kids and not a place where the neuroses of adults should intervene.

Don't let Easterners steal Montana's dinosaur eggs

CHOTEAU, Montana – After 125 million years, nest robbers have poached Montana's dinosaur eggs.

The pirates from Princeton University have purloined the paleontological prizes.

And in this little town on the Atlantic side of the Rockies, people are positively fried over the loss of the eggs.

"If dinosaurs had wanted to live in New Jersey, God would have put them there," wrote one Choteau youngster after learning the eggs were gone.

I think the kid is right. The dinosaur eggs lasted 125 million years in Montana. How long will they survive in New Jersey?

The scrambled case of the pilfered eggs literally began ages ago.

It was the late Cretaceous era when some early Montanans were raising families on the shore of a great inland sea near Choteau.

Those reptilian pioneers stood 40 feet tall and ate, not beef, but only green plants with their duck bills.

One afternoon the Choteau marshlands began to flood.

Adult triceratops and duckbilled dinosaurs lumbered to higher ground, but the babies and the unborn were inundated under mud and limestone.

For the next 125 million years the baby bones and the unhatched eggs hard-boiled under the weight of geologic time.

The Rockies sprang up, the sea drained off and today the 1,600 residents of Choteau look out on a desert.

"We're on the road to Glacier Park," town librarian Thelma Nauck said of Choteau.

But last summer the pirates from Princeton put Choteau on the map for another reason. The New Jersey fossil diggers uncovered the first intact baby dinosaur bones ever found. It was one of the little ones caught in the flood a few epochs back.

Around the world people began to talk about the baby reptile and the town where it was found. Choteau was on the map at last!

The eminence was short-lived. Paleontologists abducted the bones to New Jersey and locked them in a display case at the Princeton Museum of Natural History.

Finders, keepers, they told Montana.

That brought a cloud over Big Sky Country.

In 1910 the New York Museum of Natural History filched Montana's *tyrannosaurus Rex*, the first ever found in the world. Now the first baby dinosaur bones had been lost to New Jersey.

The legislature decided enough was enough. It rewrote the Montana Antiquities Act to make it difficult for any more of Montana's dinosaurs to be carried off to some dusty museum in the East.

"Our collection of dinosaurs has been scattered to the far winds for 100 years," Montana Historic Preservation spokesman Edrie Vinson said, "and this new law will stop that."

The revised Montana Antiquities Act declared fossils in Montana property of the state. Removed bones were only on loan to museums, not the property of those who dug them up. Or so the law said.

So, this summer the people of Choteau felt better when the outlaws from New Jersey again pulled into town with their picks, screens and geologic maps.

This time, the Montana Antiquities Act would protect the Choteau pioneer dinosaurs from the gravediggers.

Still, the pirates dug. And one day in late July they hit a treasure of unbelievable good fortune.

Near the top of a small hill outside Choteau, a digger stumbled across the fossil of a century: a six-inch, goose bump-textured, duckbill dinosaur egg without a crack in it.

One hundred twenty-five million years after the flood, the nest robbers discovered the first intact dinosaur egg in North America.

Again, the news spread about Choteau. The *Washington Post* wrote about the egg, along with *The New York Times*.

Around town, people buzzed about the new find being a boost for tourism and to Choteau's image.

The egg and fragments of other imperfect eggs went on display in the Choteau Public Library. Hundreds of people came to see them.

"We had tourists from Texas and from all around Montana," librarian Nauck said.

Recalling the disappearance of the baby dinosaur only last summer, many Montanans added a note beside their names in the library guest book. "Keep the eggs in Montana," they scribbled.

"Everybody said the same thing," Mrs. Nauck remembered. "If scientists wanted to examine the egg, that was fine with us. But people knew if the egg stayed here people would get to see it. There was a great deal of pride the egg was found here and people thought it should stay. This is where it belongs."

As you can guess by now, the pirates from Princeton thought differently.

No Ivy League university spends $10,000 on a fossil-hunting expedition to spiff up some provincial Montana library.

No, this is science. This is discovery based on the British model of tomb-robbing. You dig, you find, you carry back as bounty anything unearthed.

"It's like an oil company drilling well," explained Jack Horner, the Princeton paleontologist who led the egg-hunting trip to Choteau. "If you hit oil, do you leave the town the well?"

Answering his own question, Horner loaded up the dinosaur egg and fragments from the Choteau library and left for New Jersey.

The Antiquities Act? Well, it contains a loophole. The law only prevents commandeering of relics from public lands.

By chance, the only dinosaur eggs yet found in North America ended up, for this brief century at least, on the private cattle ranch of Jim Peebles outside Choteau.

Yes, the Peebles family feebly tried to demand that the pirates from Princeton leave something behind this time. They got a token.

A fake plaster cast of the dinosaur egg will be sent to the Choteau library.

Librarian Nauck, and much of the rest of Montana, is unimpressed with the offer.

"It's a shame we can't have the Real McCoy," she said. "I mean, who really is going to see those eggs back there? We could put them on display right here in Choteau and everyone could see them. We're open every day."

Unpacking the eggs in a Princeton laboratory, Jack Horner explained why Princeton thinks Thelma Nauck is wrong.

Montana isn't equipped to examine dinosaur remains, he said. The state doesn't have the facilities to care for the eggs.

"Dinosaur remains take up a lot of room," he said, "and in Montana they ran out of room for storing dinosaurs."

Ran out of room?

A state with 147,138 square miles, five universities, two natural history museums and a nice public library in Choteau doesn't have room for a six-inch egg?

Montana's dinosaur eggs have been rustled, pure and simple.

Will Tom Foley come through with the goodies?

In Texas, tears shaped like dollar signs fell from the eyes of friends and beneficiaries of the late, great Jim Wright.

"He had an enormous economic impact on this area," said Tom Vandergriff, former mayor of Arlington, a suburban city of 250,000 between Dallas and Fort Worth. Reflecting on Wright's resignation as speaker of the U.S. House of Representatives, Vandergriff added, "Jim Wright was a major reason for the tremendous economic growth in this part of Texas."

As a pushy Texas congressman, pushy majority leader and then pushy House speaker, Wright brought home not just the bacon but also many whole pigs for his constituents.

Wright helped funnel hundreds of millions of defense dollars in the direction of Fort Worth-based General Dynamics, builder of the F-111, a plane often grounded and labeled a death trap but still funded.

For years, Wright kept alive the V-22 helicopter, called by its critics the wrong aircraft at the wrong time. No matter. Its prime manufacturer was Bell Helicopter, located in Wright's congressional district.

And remember the superconducting super-collider? Washington state tried to win the $4-billion federal contract for that experimental physics laboratory for a site in Eastern Washington near Davenport.

Washington state lost. Instead, the project was sited just down the road from Jim Wright's offices in Texas.

But that is history.

In a couple of days, Jim Wright will step down as speaker of the House, forced out by activities a congressional ethics committee considered unbecoming of the top officeholder in Congress.

His replacement will be the lawmaker from Eastern Washington's 5th Congressional District, Representative Tom Foley of Spokane.

So, the question will be asked: "Will Tom Foley deliver a federally-funded economic renaissance to the Inland Northwest?"

The answer depends on whom you ask.

"I would say Spokane and the state of Washington are about to enter a golden era," predicted former Arlington Mayor Vandergriff. "We lost our chief spokesperson, the man who could open any door in Washington, D.C. And you are gaining that position. I think the best is yet ahead for you."

But Vandergriff, who also served a term in Congress with both Wright and Foley, acknowledges that Foley doesn't operate as Jim Wright did. Foley has not been interested in pork-barrel political projects nor has he shown much inclination to use over political pressure to get his way.

George Reitemeier, president of the Spokane Area Chamber of Commerce, isn't counting on any big federal boondoggles to be located in Spokane. "I think if economic development comes to Spokane and the region as a result of Tom Foley, it will be because the best way for a business to get close to a congressman is to have some sort of operation in that congressman's district," Reitemeier said.

The sudden presence of the Boeing Company in Spokane likely is an example of such an indirect economic benefit. Boeing acknowledges that other Washington cities wanted the company. But it was Spokane that had the majority leader of the U.S. House of Representatives, and it was here that Boeing, a major defense contractor, decided to expand.

The power of the speakership won't be lost on companies doing business with the federal government. Indeed, both the Spokane Area Chamber of Commerce and Foley's office in Spokane say they already sense the subtle, increased pressure from businesses hoping to gain access to the 5th District congressman.

"It's happened a number of times already," Reitemeier said. "Businesses that aren't headquartered here but have operations here now are interested in trying to use their Spokane contacts to get to Foley."

This presents a dilemma for Tom Foley – and for Spokane.

Foley's ascent has put Spokane closer to the levers of political power and influence than it ever has been before.

However, the success of Tom Foley will depend, to a significant degree, upon his ability to set a new example as speaker of the House.

Indeed, new rules and attitudes in Congress will assert that political leadership not be as arbitrary, as self-serving or as greedy as in the past.

Tom Foley isn't as arbitrary, self-serving or greedy as some who have filled the speaker's chair before him. Those are reasons why he may become a highly successful, perhaps legendary, speaker of the House.

Yet, the irony of his rule is that because Tom Foley is the right man for the job, Spokane may not feel his power the way Texas felt the speaker's power in the now-marred era of Jim Wright.

Gonzaga Law School grads advised to become janitors

Good morning, distinguished members of the Gonzaga Law School Class of 1983.

Thank you for not inviting me to speak at your commencement last night.

I would not have wanted to have ruined the glorious graduation ceremonies for 176 idealistic yet still-hoping-to-afford-a-BMW law students.

My message could wait until today. For it is only today, after 19 years of schooling, that most of you are entering the real world.

What an odd place, the real world.

People out here live on things other than pizza.

Many residents perform constructive tasks rather than spending all day reading thick explanations of how to finagle, cajole and wheedle human beings.

And a lot of your new neighbors despise law school graduates.

I'm not one of them.

For my mind, law school represents one of mankind's finest achievements.

Law schools provide hundreds of mixed-up young people with a safe place to grow up. For those egos troubled by the transition from adolescence to adulthood, law school provides a kind of finishing school for the confused.

In addition, law schools offer a foolproof way to keep moms and dads happy. To the folks back home, law always has been a good alternative to sending a son to the Army or having a daughter run away with a punk rock band.

There is only one problem with law schools.

They inevitably produce a new batch of lawyers that this country doesn't need.

That's what I want to talk to the Class of 1983 about today.

Reality therapy has to begin somewhere. And I think it should begin with the most basic question of all: Should all 176 graduates in the Class of 1983 actually try to become lawyers?

I think not.

Lawyers share a status similar to goldfish in our culture.

Both are pretty in pairs and have their place in a home.

But when allowed to propagate without regard to the water in which they swim, each is a deadly nuisance.

Evidence of *de facto* overpopulation of lawyers is clear to anyone who will look into the American cultural pond for it.

Washington state, for example, has 12,000 attorneys.

The number has doubled in 10 years while the population of the state has grown by less than 25 percent.

This state now has one attorney for every 350 residents – a ratio nearly double that of California, which generally is considered to be the most over-lawyered state in the nation.

More than half the attorneys practicing law in Washington today have passed the bar since 1973. The state not only is overcrowded with lawyers, but it also is overcrowded with *young* lawyers.

That means the job market is exceedingly tight.

Despite yeoman efforts of the Gonzaga placement office, records suggest 20 percent of the Class of 1982 couldn't find a law-related job last year.

And now comes the Class of 1983.

But that, I fear, is too practical a reason for this year's graduates to shred their degrees and open vegetarian restaurants or learn to mount radial tires.

So I will suggest a more compelling argument for the 1983 law graduates to take up bean sprouts or white sidewalls: many of them would enjoy those pursuits more.

In 1981, the American Bar Association surveyed recent law school graduates in America, asking new, young lawyers if they are happy in their work.

Forty percent said no.

The real world of law, it seems, contains all kinds of surprises law schools rarely talk about.

First among these surprises is the discovery that law often is confined to what the ABA-surveyed graduates described as "trivial matters." There is only one Supreme Court, but half of America gets divorced.

A second surprise identified by the recent graduates is the realization that a significant number of older lawyers now working are, in the words of the ABA survey, "incompetent."

Perhaps incompetence and triviality would be acceptable to the Class of 1983 if the money were right.

Money can't buy happiness, but it can at least buy the kind of misery a person prefers.

Yet here again, the facts of the real world suggest that the misery of being a law graduate in 1983 isn't worth that much.

The average salary of the 1982 Gonzaga graduate was $20,500. Not a BMW salary, but enough for a nice Honda.

For the 50 percent of recent Gonzaga graduates who enter small private practice, however, the salary figures are significantly lower. The graduate who hung out his own shingle without a partner earned only a pitiable $8,000 last year.

For those selfish reasons, I would ask the Class of 1983 to reconsider the career path ahead.

Law can be boring and unsatisfying, and you can starve at it.

And if that is not enough to make some of the class reconsider, then there is one last argument against going on.

Simply, this nation could use some bright minds in areas other than law.

For a decade now, law schools have siphoned the best young minds in the country away from other noble and needed pursuits.

Nineteen-eighty-three is no exception. While 176 students received law degrees at Gonzaga this year, only one student received a master's degree in English that could lead to a professorship at a university or to the writing of a great novel.

In time these lawyers will be forced to try to make a living in their crowded career field, even though our society can't rationally absorb them.

It's already happening.

The federal court caseload has risen 137 percent in 20 years while the national population has gone up 13 percent.

In Washington state, the number of superior court cases has doubled in a decade.

And despite all the noble talk from law deans, it is not primarily the needs of the poor, the disenfranchised or the underrepresented which are being addressed by these suits.

Those groups have no money to pay the latest batch of attorneys. Even the government is becoming less likely to finance legal help for them.

No, the need to eat continues to force many attorneys to poke wads of legalese into the carburetor of working society, gumming up the political, social and business worlds with torts and claims that shouldn't be pursued.

The cycle will continue until that special day after graduation when law school students make a different choice of careers.

That day of decision has arrived for the Class of 1983.

So what will it be, graduates? Law or lentil soup?

The country could use one more good lunch counter.

It can't afford any more attorneys.

Thank you, and good luck.

Downtown Spokane decaying while city dithers

Doug Sutherland has been to a place where the economic sun doesn't shine.

We know it as Tacoma.

Sutherland was mayor there.

In Spokane the other day, the former mayor recalled that 20 years ago his city could fit into every stand-up comedian's routine.

Tacoma: I didn't see it, but I smelled it.

Tacoma: Where they put the Velveeta in the gourmet food section.

Portrait of a loser: Harold Stassen driving an Edsel down the streets of Tacoma.

Tacoma is a loser no more.

Once downtown closed up, once the close-in neighborhoods became infamous for their crime, once the tax base had eroded to a point where the city couldn't pave the streets, people in Tacoma said, "We gotta fix this."

And they did.

The fix-up formula involved three key elements:

• A wealthy family (the Weyerhaeusers) pledged millions of their own money for a major redevelopment;

• Elected officials applied for millions of dollars in federal and state grants to help finance the project;

• A new public-private partnership was forged to help spread the risk and the benefits of among other things, a downtown hotel and parking garage.

In Tacoma, it worked. Doug Sutherland was there to see it.

So, he was invited to Spokane to hold some hands here and let people know that a big project designed to save a city can be pulled off. Sutherland, a Rogers High School graduate, had this message for Spokane: don't wait until things get as bad as they did in Tacoma.

"In Tacoma, it has taken 20 years and hundreds of millions of local, state and federal dollars, but the city has been saved," Sutherland said. "It takes a very long time to repair damage once it has been done."

Now county executive for Pierce County, Sutherland noted that Spokane has a chance to miss the worst of what happened in Tacoma.

"You have an opportunity here that we didn't have," Sutherland said. It is the opportunity to save the retail core before it craters.

CHRIS PECK

"You have a family (the Cowles) that has stepped forward and is willing to make a major commitment to your city," he said.

"You have people who wholeheartedly believe in your downtown," he explained.

"And you seem to have a City Council that understands the benefits that will come to all if they make a courageous political decision to move ahead."

Sure there will be people who will try to knock Spokane's redevelopment plan down. Why help out a rich family? Why help out a rich company like Nordstrom?

Doug Sutherland faced these things, too. For him, the answers were clear in Tacoma and are obvious in Spokane as well.

The Cowles family, which also owns *The Spokesman-Review*, is putting at least $45 million of their own resources into the project. Sutherland asked, what other family or bank would do that?

Sure, Nordstrom is getting a good deal. But the former mayor noted, "If you don't have the retail core, including the plum of Nordstrom, the result will be a steep decline in property tax collections and sales tax collections. Everybody loses."

Conversely, if the project goes, the city of Spokane gains what appears to be an additional $2.5 million in property tax revenues, plus other gains in sales tax from a revitalized shopping district.

"And in Tacoma," Sutherland said, in a reference to Northtown owner Dave Sabey's opposition to Spokane's downtown plan, "the Tacoma Mall continued to improve on its investments as the downtown continued to improve. Everybody won."

Sutherland outlines a vision for Spokane that appears obvious to someone on the outside.

To him, Spokane is poised to become a city with one of the most vibrant, successful urban centers in the country.

It can do it without having to go through the terrible cycle of hitting rock bottom.

Private developers are putting up the majority of the money and paying off the federal loans.

"As I see it," Sutherland said, "this is the best thing Spokane has on its horizon. It will send a signal that Spokane is ready to take a step into the next century. This is one of the lightning rods for the city. It's just critically important."

If Sutherland had one regret about what has happened in Tacoma, it is that the redevelopment there started too late to allow much retailing to return downtown.

"Retailing is absolutely critical to the success of other kinds of projects in the urban core," he said.

Keeping shopping downtown, in fact, will drive much of what else can happen in Spokane, including redevelopment of the Davenport Hotel, adding more downtown housing, and keeping the close-in residential neighborhoods from decay.

The ex-mayor laid it out clearly for all to see.

Either a city seizes the opportunities before it, or a city slides back.

Spokane hangs right there, right now, and the comedians don't have Tacoma to kick around anymore.

Kids can buy their own condoms, not get them at school

Over the lunch hour I went shopping for condoms.

I had nothing planned that required them.

This was simply research to see whether purchasing the suddenly much-promoted devices was easier today wearing a suit and tie than it was years ago as a teenager in tennis shoes.

It isn't easier.

Boys were embarrassed about condoms 25 years ago. They are still embarrassed today.

"A lot of young guys come in to look at the condoms, but just can't go through the checkout counter," said Janice Jennings, a helpful customer service representative at a downtown Payless Drug store in Spokane.

"They come in, stand there in front of the displays for a long time, then try to steal them," she said.

"But they have a hard time buying. They always put them face down on the checkout and make sure nobody gets behind them in the line."

Perhaps this explains why the Washington governor's advisory council on HIV/AIDS has suggested condoms being distributed in schools. Easy access, no fuss, no muss.

Wrong choice, in my view.

Young people don't have a problem getting condoms.

Visit any drug store, grocery store or variety store and you will see 15 varieties of extra large, ultra slim, mint-flavored and multi-colored packages.

Besides, access to condoms doesn't address the essential, difficult issues about when to have sex and with whom.

That's the job of adults. Grown-ups who advocate passing out condoms to teenagers are sending the wrong message.

Adults who want to give out condoms to teenagers seem to be suggesting that adults can protect kids from the consequences of risky sexual behavior. We can't.

Distribution of condoms to teenagers also assumes the recipient is ready to use them. We don't know that.

Making it easier for young people to get little foil packages of prophylactics is like passing out aspirin and barf bags before the beer party.

It assumes the decision to have sex is inevitable, already has been made and that somebody else will take care of the safe-sex details.

Young people must challenge these assumptions.

Grown-ups can't protect kids from bad sexual experiences, nor can they decide when a young person will become, or should become, sexually active.

Adults should stick to what we know. We know now that sex changes your life, leads to complicated relationships, can produce children, and for all of its wonder, often is heartbreaking and disease-ridden.

The message young people need from the sexually experienced is that the decision to have sex is a grown-up decision that should be based on facts and heavy thinking.

Schools can, and should, help with these.

Elementary and junior high classes should discuss the medical effects of AIDS and sexually transmitted diseases.

Social studies and history teachers should detail the economic and social costs of teenage pregnancy.

English classes could discuss the centuries-old struggle to find a balance between responsibility and pleasure.

The moral issues raised by sexual activity probably are best discussed by church leaders, coaches, scoutmasters and families.

Some will preach abstinence and that's fine.

Some will advocate waiting, another good option.

A few will say, be prepared.

Then, adolescents will still decide when and where to have sex. An estimated one in three boys now become sexually active by age 15. For girls, it is one in four.

When the time comes, an essential element of this highly personal decision should include an appreciation that a sexually active person carries the responsibility for reducing the risk of unwanted pregnancy or disease.

Let young people buy their own condoms. It's a part of one's sex education. Adults shouldn't do it for them.

And while teenage boys apparently are still having a difficult time with this responsibility, many teenage girls aren't.

"The girls are buying most of the condoms," said drug store service representative Jennings. "They come in and buy eye shadow, blush and a condom. It's all on the list for a big date."

Maybe this is progress in a mixed-up world.

Fred Coe, South Hill Rapist

Chapter Four

Women are frightened on the South Hill

Women on the South Hill are frightened.

A rapist is preying on their classic, middle-class neighborhood.

He has been portrayed time and again as a white, slightly husky male in his early 20s, with dark hair.

Since September, at least six women have been attacked by someone who roughly fits that description.

Police have a number of suspects. They think there may even be two men of similar build terrorizing one of the nicest residential districts in Spokane.

Three detectives are working the cases, and they concede the South Hill rapist is not yet in custody.

So, women on the hill have stopped going out alone at night. Others have quit walking home. At Rosauer's and on the Cannon Hill bus, they talk uncomfortably about the attacks.

When women read the story of Susan Jones, they will be more frightened still of what lurks in their neighborhood.

Susan Jones lives on the South Hill.

And she thinks she knows who the rapist is.

If she is right, it means the fulsome, frightening man is on the loose again, because Susan Jones saw him just a few days ago. She saw the man who attacked her on the South Hill on December 5, 1979 – and he is free.

Her real name isn't Susan Jones. When we met in the parking lot of a South Side cafe, she said again she was too frightened to have her real name used.

And, she explained, for the sake of her family, her husband and her mental stability, she has not yet signed a formal complaint against the man she has identified for police as her attacker.

Susan Jones is a new mother. She has a good job downtown. She has considered the ordeal of a rape trial too much for her to bear. She has tried hard to forget that night.

The memory might have disappeared with the winter skies if she had not seen that face again.

The day she saw him, she called me at home.

She said she wanted to let a judge know he had made a mistake and would tell me a story to prove it.

"I was jogging in the Hamblen Park area," she began. "I recently had a baby and I jogged for health. I was running in the evening between 6 and 7. I was running in the middle of the street in an ugly outfit, not form-fitting."

It was a winter evening on a well-lit street in a nice neighborhood. At the time, almost no publicity had been released on the string of South Hill rapes. There were no pictures in the papers, only a few short stories.

Coming down the street toward her was a man in jogging clothes and a down jacket. The two runners passed a few feet from each other. Then he turned and grabbed for her.

"He came up behind me and got his arm around my neck," she said. "I was yelling for help. I yelled four or five times, but nobody heard.

"He said, get over in the yard and shut up. I grabbed and started pulling his hair. He hit me a couple of times in the face."

She was bleeding from the nose, and her eye was swelling and black as he dragged her 10 feet away into a yard by a fence.

"He tried to rape me," she said, describing the disgusting fantasies and imaginations of her attacker, who climbed on top of her but couldn't complete his foul deed.

He asked her ugly, personal questions about her husband and her private life. "He wanted me to urinate on him and have a bowel movement," she said.

"I was crying at this point. I thought how much I wanted to see my husband and my child again. It just seemed to go on and on and on."

After 15 or 20 minutes of his feculent violence, the South Hill sicko ran.

Her attacker had made only one mistake. He put his face directly over Susan Jones during his violence, and his features were burned into her brain forever.

In the following days, Susan Jones told no one but her husband and her doctor about the attack.

The doctor wanted to alert the police, but she held back. "I could hardly talk about it," she said.

A week later, she decided to contact a rape crisis center. The center suggested she call the police. She agreed, but refused to give the detectives her real name.

At the end of December, police convinced her to look at a few photographs of some suspects in the South Hill attacks and of some men who weren't suspects.

She instantly identified a picture of her assailant.

The detective pleaded for her to come forward, but she couldn't.

Her courage sank in a flood of tears.

"People think you have nothing to lose if you make it a matter of public record," she explained. "But you do have something to lose. I have something to lose. I have a career. I have friends. To me it was excruciating to have other people know."

She didn't file charges.

Then a couple of Tuesdays ago she saw him again. She learned the man she had identified as her attacker was out on bond, even though she knows he has been convicted of one rape and has been charged with another.

"I was so angry, so very, very angry," Susan Jones said. "And I was frightened. You think you are safe and that things are going along OK and then you see him again.

"The reason I called you is that I am worried there is another gal who is out there jogging. It could happen again," she said.

For now, all Susan Jones can bring herself to do is tell her story this way.

She is a quiet woman, married nearly 10 years; a woman who has never so much as been in a police station before. And she has grown cynical about justice.

"He could get bargained away," she said. "That makes me wonder very much about justice. The thing that is so incredible is that there's nothing like this that can happen to men."

Today, Susan Jones is home, with her husband and her first child, thinking.

She didn't ask to be a heroine. She still cannot speak of that night without choking on her tears.

If she doesn't come forward, most women will understand.

Yet the only way she can even the score with the man who attacked her is to make him face a jury.

For the good of Spokane and the women on the South Hill, I pray this helps her find the gumption to face the face that is on the loose again.

Gretchen's harrowing story of being raped

Clear and cool at 7 a.m., it began as a beautiful morning.

Gretchen looked out the window of her High Drive home.

She scribbled a note to her kids: "Mom is running . . ."

For fun, she sketched a stick figure in tennis shoes on the notepad.

Half an hour later, she would think of that little runner.

"I thought what a schmucky way to die, with the kids home reading that cute, little note and me being killed by some horrible creep," she said.

A horrible specter is back on the South Hill.

In jogging clothes, threatening with a knife, it has begun again to strike at women in one of Spokane's classiest neighborhoods.

"Yeah, it's back again," sighed Spokane Police Lieutenant Gene McGougan a few days ago.

That morning he had pulled the file on South Hill rapes.

In the last two weeks he has added three new assaults, bringing the total assaults and rapes to as many as a dozen in the last year.

For a time, the South Hill seemed safe.

All last winter a jogging rapist hid among the wealthy houses and apartments, preying on high school students, housewives and working women who live on the South Hill.

But in March, the heat was on.

Police toured the neighborhoods. Women organized support groups. A highly publicized rape trial raised consciousness among female joggers that they shouldn't run alone.

The attacks died down.

Five months passed and the South Hill rapist, or rapists, were too frightened to slither from the shadows.

Time lulled a neighborhood into lethargy – until the clear, cool morning of August 26, 1980.

That Tuesday was to have been a busy day for Gretchen and her children.

After her jog, she and the kids planned a tour of the Walk-on-the-Wild Side zoo. In the afternoon they were headed for Lake Coeur d'Alene for a day in the sun.

As she often did, Gretchen decided to run before the kids were up.

Her route took her down Thirty-third and over to High Drive.

"I first saw him on Thirty-third," she said.

"He was walking and wearing sweat clothes and sun glasses."

On this cool, sunny morning Gretchen didn't think it strange.

She felt safe. Houses look out across most of High Drive. Other joggers regularly passed her as she plodded along.

But the South Hill rapist knew his evil business.

He waited and watched until the other joggers were out of sight and Gretchen cut through an undeveloped acre of the South Hill rim.

The hillside dropped off so steeply drivers passing by wouldn't have been able to see.

He pounced with premeditated accuracy.

"I think he had the spot picked out," Gretchen said. "It just happened to be in the most deadly spot on the South Hill. One second I was jogging, the next second we were over the edge."

Choking Gretchen around the neck, the rapist tumbled down the steep embankment.

"I've got a knife," he said. "If you so much as look at me once, I'm going to kill you."

Over the edge, out of sight, Gretchen dug her heels into the dirt to stop sliding.

The rapist told her to take off her clothes.

And he kept warning her not to look at him.

"He had two voices," she said.

"He was rough and mean and vicious when he ordered me not to look at him. But he had a modulated, sort of loving voice when he called me beautiful."

With her hand flattened across her eyes, Gretchen kept her cool.

She tried to talk to her attacker.

"I told him I had been gone a long time and my husband would come looking for me," she said. "I told him I had an

18-year-old son who was out looking for me. Those were lies. My husband had gone to work and my son is 14. But I thought I could get out of it."

The talk infuriated her attacker.

He blamed her for being unable to get on with his business.

He asked her, "Do you know what it feels like to have a knife in your chest?"

Gretchen quit talking and tried to remember details.

He was about 5-10 and in his 20s.

She noted he used no swear words and spoke with perfect grammar.

His jogging shoes were dirty, more like everyday shoes, not running wear.

And his hands were feminine and unkempt.

His sordid sexual desires fit a pattern of other South Hill rapes.

But she did not look at his face.

"He was so violent and horrible," she said.

"If someone like this guy had whopped you and threw you over a cliff and threatened to stab you if you looked, what would you have done?" she asked.

"I decided I wanted to live."

After half an hour, he ordered her to get up and walk away.

Nude, with weeds sticking in her hair, she stumbled down the hillside. When she finally looked back, he was gone.

At police headquarters, Gretchen's story reminded detective McGougan once again of the difficulty police face in breaking the South Hill rape cases.

The cops don't know who they are looking for.

"She has a better memory than most," he said. "But they are all the same.

"We feel very insecure about crime witness identification. If she had skin of the person under her fingernails, it would be something.

"But all of our witnesses have been in a position where they can't see the attacker either because of darkness or a mask or out of fear."

As a result, the police files contain half a dozen descriptions of attackers.

In each case, some details match, others do not.

"We're trying to paint a picture," the detective said. "But we could be looking for one man or ten."

Police do believe at least two men have taken up a similar mode of operation on the South Hill.

A special detective squad has been reorganized.

The detectives spent much of last week pouring over the files again, looking for a pattern, a clue.

Lieutenant McGougan wasn't optimistic.

"He's got everything in his favor on the South Hill," McGougan said.

There are older homes, many converted to apartments.

"They are filled with young women working downtown, walking at all hours, and a lot of them are jogging."

And there is 50 years of brush accumulated.

So women, beware. Change your jogging patterns, carry Mace, run with a friend.

The South Hill rapist – or, probably, the South Hill rapists – have grabbed the upper hand.

And, women, take heed.

One of the rapists came close to erring when he threw Gretchen over the hillside.

Because she, maybe unlike others of you, was loquacious, cool-headed, more willing to seek a pound of flesh.

"If I could identify him, I would do whatever I could," she said. "I'm furious."

Women on the South Hill, be furious together.

Look for clues, find the courage to open your eyes, press charges if you can.

Otherwise, creeps will prevail.

Rape joke not all that funny

If Detective Captain Richard Olberding ever looks for a new job, it probably shouldn't be as a comedian.

His gags just aren't getting the laughs.

Especially among women.

Captain Olberding is in charge of the Spokane Police Department's South Hill rape investigation.

For two years now, an unknown rapist has been jumping out of bushes and attacking mostly young, dark-haired women in Spokane.

And inside the houses and apartments along the wooded streets of the South Hill, fear flows like the spring runoff. Women are armed to the earrings with Mace.

Almost no one is laughing.

Information about the South Hill rapist is worth the price of gold to the women who live in his stalking ground.

And that is why Flo Jonic, a reporter for KXLY-TV, went to Spokane Police a few weeks ago. She wanted to know if the police had any leads, had organized a special task force or could offer any words of advice to women who live in terror of the rapist.

One morning about 9:30 a.m., Jonic met Olberding in the hallway of the Police Department.

Flo Jonic stopped him and asked for an interview.

The captain said he was busy.

And he made it no secret he thought reporters who always pressed for more details about the rape investigation are making it harder for him to catch the rapist. But Jonic kept at it. She said women needed to know where things stood. She said women needed advice on what they could do to keep from being raped.

Captain Olberding said he had to go to a meeting.

And on his way he asked Flo Jonic a question. "Flo," he said, "don't you know how to keep from being raped?"

Flo said no, she did not.

155

The captain replied, "You just lie back and enjoy it."

Then the spokesman for the city's rape investigation squad chuckled off.

Miss Jonic, who lives on the South Hill, didn't crack a smile.

"I was pretty amazed," she said. "And I was indignant."

That night she planned to air the captain's remarks. Technical problems ruined her tape. Then some of the male employees at KXLY-TV told her to forget the comment.

They said it was a joke, a man's off-the-cuff expression that didn't mean a thing.

So Flo sat on it.

But Jonic, who will leave Spokane this weekend for a new job at a TV station in Portland, kept mentioning the line to women friends and they were horrified.

Her friends said the "lie back and enjoy it" comment was symbolic of the Police Department's attitude toward rape.

So Monday morning, during the local news break on *Good Morning, America*, Flo Jonic decided to deliver a parting shot.

Reading a wire service story put together by another reporter about the South Hill rapes, she came to a section that outlined some of the difficulties reporters have had getting information about the rape investigation.

She came to the paragraphs discussing Olberding. He was paraphrased as saying the media have written too much about the cases.

"I felt the police were working against the press and the public," Jonic remembered.

"I thought they had a cavalier attitude about the crimes. I thought they had resisted the media at every step.

"So I ad libbed it.

"I put in the line about him saying that women should 'lay back and enjoy it' when they are being raped."

Well, the effect was as if someone yelled fire in a crowded movie theater.

Phone lines started lighting up at KXLY.

Soon the mayor had to comment, then the police chief, and then the letters started rolling into the newspapers.

"Olberding is an insult to the male race," one of them began.

"I wonder if he would 'lay back and enjoy it' if someone stuck a hot poker up his —."

Others in the media have chosen up sides.

A radio station editorialized that Jonic was unprofessional. Others have editorialized the captain had it coming.

Maybe Flo Jonic overstepped some mythical journalistic rule by pulling an old quote out of the closet.

But, then again, maybe she has a point.

"There is some responsibility in the media to tell people not only the workings of a police force, but the attitudes," Flo Jonic said. "And that is the crux of this story."

She said women must depend on a mostly male police force. And women have to believe the men in charge of rape investigations are serious and sensitive.

Flo Jonic doesn't think the man in charge of the South Hill investigation is either sensitive or serious.

The man in charge isn't talking.

"It's better not to say anything," Captain Olberding said Wednesday.

"I made a joke I heard 20 years ago," he said. "I think nothing should be said about it."

I think the captain needs to say something more if he wants to save the reputation of his rape investigation unit.

He needs to restore confidence in his credentials as a cop.

Of course, it's hard to talk with a foot lodged in the mouth.

But he ought to try.

Fred Coe's one man media blitz

Fred Coe sat in the front pew of a nearly empty courtroom.

Relaxed, smiling, the events of the morning had yet to dent his confident demeanor.

Moments before, a 16-year-old girl had taken the witness stand across the hall.

Crying softly, she told a hushed courtroom, "He put his hand in my mouth. He had gloves on, dark, leather gloves. I could make no sound. I wasn't able to scream. He told me he would stick a knife in me and kill me if I wasn't quiet . . ."

The teenager's description of her assault fit a pattern of rapes on Spokane's South Hill in the last three years.

When the prosecutor asked her if the man who attacked her was in the courtroom, she replied, "Yes, sir."

She pointed at Fred Coe. He stood. The eyes of the jury focused on him.

Afterward, the handsome, articulate son of a newspaper editor admitted it was an agonizing moment.

"It came as something of a shock," he said on the second day of his trial on six counts of rape.

"It's no fun to stand there and have a woman you have never seen and (who) has never seen you get up and say you attacked her."

The defendant in the South Hill rapist trial has emerged as an unusual and fascinating man.

Charged with the most spectacular series of crimes in Spokane in years, Fred Coe doesn't hide his face with his hands when the TV cameras are turned his way.

He smiles and nods. He strides confidently to and from the courtroom.

Several weeks ago he made contact with the *Seattle Times* and gave a long interview to a reporter.

Since the opening day of his trial, Coe has appeared on KXLY-TV in Spokane in segments of a taped interview.

On the nightly news he discusses what he considers to be the railroad on which he has been forced to take a seat.

Fred Coe maintains the women who are accusing him have been carefully coached by the prosecutor.

He says they are being forced to tell the grotesque details of their rapes simply so the prosecutor can win a conviction of an innocent man.

"As someone who is into women's causes, it's hideous," Coe said on the morning of the second day of his trial.

"I feel sorry for (those women). They are being used and abused a second time around.

"The police and the prosecution are not interested in women's causes. They are interested in getting a conviction."

Fred Coe's one-man public relations campaign in the middle of his trial has puzzled some people.

The judge in his case, who tried hard to keep the media from interfering with Coe's right to a fair trial, admits he was surprised the defendant has talked so freely about his trial.

"But my only concern was that he get a fair trial," Judge George Shields shrugged one morning in his chambers.

"I guess now that the jury is sequestered it doesn't matter what the defendant says."

Some attorneys are simply amazed at Coe's tactics.

"I think it does him more harm than good," said David Henault, a prominent Spokane defense lawyer.

"It makes people wonder how the case is going in court.

"The first thing I say to my clients is don't talk. I like to have control of my client. I tell them I'll do the talking."

Coe's appearances on TV and interviews in the newspapers have occurred without the support of his own attorneys, too.

"It's against my advice," admitted Roger Gigler, chief of Coe's defense team. "It's against my advice, not because of the press necessarily, but because it gives the prosecution a hand.

"If he says something to the TV or the newspapers and (it appears) contradictory to what he says in the stand, then it all could come out in the trial."

Prosecutor Donald Brockett smiled when asked what he thought of Coe's public interviews.

"We're watching them very closely," the prosecutor said.

Yet Fred Coe will not be dissuaded.

"Having spent 11 years in the media, I know what is appropriate to say and what isn't," he said during a recess on the third day of his trial.

"My attorney is running my trial, he's not running my life."

To Coe, enough cannot be said about his innocence.

He appears compelled to tell anyone, anywhere, anytime that he isn't the South Hill rapist.

He believes 300,000 people in Eastern Washington thought he was guilty before he had even gone to trial. That seems unfair to him and some of his family.

The bigger story, in their minds, is how Fred Coe came to trial in the first place.

"The frightening thing is that you may think your past is as clear as a bell, but in the courtroom it will be presented in such a way as to look bad," he said one morning as his sister met with him in the empty courtroom.

On television and in each of his interviews, Coe says the police threw him in a rigged lineup.

"I was up there shaking like a leaf. My voice was three octaves too high," he said.

He has suggested the prosecutor leaked all kinds of damaging information to the press about the six women identifying him, thereby souring the media on his defense.

Believing he was set up and confronted by a hostile media, Fred Coe decided to become his own best friend.

One reason probably is that since shortly after his arrest, Coe's sister began sending him clippings from a rape case in Seattle where the wrong man was arrested, tried and convicted.

Earlier this year, Steve Gary Titus was charged with the rape of a 17-year-old Seattle woman.

The woman picked Titus out of a photo lineup just as some of Coe's accusers have done.

The Seattle woman identified Titus in court just as Coe's accusers have.

But a reporter in Seattle kept on the Titus case. He was bothered that the victim's identification was weak and that some evidence had been overlooked.

The Titus case and the role the media played in it have become extremely important issues to Fred Coe.

"It could be you they were after," he laughed.

"You have the bushy mustache and the longer hair," he told me. "It could happen to you. You could be amazed at the smear Peck campaign."

"We should never forget the Titus case," the man accused of being the South Hill rapist said as he walked back across the hall and into the torrid courtroom.

Fred Coe's trial and its aftermath

Fred Coe has left an indelible mark on his hometown.

Everyone in Spokane knows his handsome features now: the prominent jaw line, the soothing, articulate voice.

After studying the man convicted as the South Hill rapist, there remains an impression that, deep down, Fred Coe considers his notoriety almost worth it.

Not that Coe admits he is guilty.

"The South Hill rapist is still out there," he said near the end of the trial.

Until the moment he was led to jail, Coe maintained the case against him was a setup, a railroad job. The coincidence that the string of two dozen South Hill rapes ended with his arrest suggested nothing.

"My own theory is that what finally ended the South Hill rapes is that all the women were armed," Coe said.

"Picture yourself as a rapist for a moment. Suddenly there are all these women who are carrying guns and maces. My theory is the rapist got scared."

Fred Coe has always had theories.

By age 15, friends recall Coe considered himself cannier than the average kid.

"It was amazing the things he thought he could get away with," one classmate remembered of the kid called Coco who became Spokane's most celebrated criminal defendant in years.

"As a teenager, he would argue with everybody. In junior high algebra class, he would come up with completely different answers from those his teacher had. Then he would argue forever about how his logic and theories were better."

If someone had called Fred Coe's bluff a long time ago, he might not have ended up in court.

But no one could do that.

Fred Coe was the son of a well-loved man in Spokane, a powerful man, the editor of the afternoon newspaper.

Classmates said teachers didn't want to risk alienating the family by making him toe the line.

So Fred Coe was never convinced he was anything but right.

"He would always pummel you with words and facts," one classmate remembered. "He had the feeling he could convince you of anything."

It was the same in court, 20 years later.

Coe's ears never burned red when he was being accused of rape.

When six women pointed to him as the one who jumped from the darkness, stuffed two fingers in their mouths and told them to talk about their families as he violated them, he coolly took the other side of the debate.

For a while, the jury was with him.

"On first impression, I perceived Mr. Coe as a very well-educated, super-fantastic . . . guy," jury foreman David Barkman remembered from the opening day of the trial.

"As far as I was concerned, the gentleman was innocent. I couldn't believe a fellow who looked like he did, talked like he did and came from the background he had, could be guilty."

From the beginning, Fred Coe was convinced he could win the hearts of the jury.

Soon after his arrest, when some family members suggested a high-powered defense attorney, Fred Coe said no.

He belittled the expertise of the prosecutor. He said he could win on his own. He often ignored the advice of his attorneys.

"My attorney is running my trial; he's not running my life," Coe added during his trial.

In court Coe was the showpiece of his own defense.

He spoke of his "11 years of media experience" and his work with "three of the top real estate men" in Spokane.

He surmised his arrest was part of a desperate plan by police to arrest him as a means of getting back at his father's newspaper, which had been partially responsible for the retirement of a well-liked detective, Jerry McGougan.

For all the salesmanship, Fred Coe probably convicted himself.

"I was left with an impression after he spoke, that he was trying to tell us he was lily white," foreman Barkman recalled. "But nobody is lily white. My own mother isn't."

What happened in court was not much different from what has happened to Fred Coe all his life.

Fred Coe has the looks, the mind and the family to be the All-American middle-class hero.

He auditioned for the part year after year. But he never landed the leading role.

Instead, he left Washington State University after two years. He left Gonzaga University after a semester. He had little success as a radio disc jockey and failed in his first marriage.

The day before his arrest, his last employer signed him off the company payroll "because he never worked."

His latest girlfriend contemplated turning him in as a suspect in the South Hill rapes.

That is not to say Coe wasn't good enough to protect that shadow of a doubt.

Flashing his orthodontically perfect teeth at the bright lights of the media, he succeeded in making the rape convictions hang like an ill-fitting shirt on a man who should have had it all.

By convincing his family to cling to him through it all, to the point of selling the family Cadillac to post bail, Fred Coe has held onto the possibility he is innocent.

Yet a family could not be asked to see what others have come to perceive.

It is the image of a man who long ago slipped into a strange, unknown place where he concentrated with a brilliant intensity on deceit.

Finally, it was that perception that caught up with Fred Coe.

His attorneys couldn't produce a single friend or confidant who would say he was, indeed, the All-American good guy.

No one but his family could say that Coe's only oddity was that, at age 34, he still ate all his breakfasts and dinners with his mother.

When the midnight verdict came in, Fred Coe stood all alone, still convinced he was smarter than the rest.

An old friend told a fitting last story about Fred Coe.

"I can remember in high school, doing history reports," he said. "I was working in study hall for hours, doing research.

"The last couple of days Fred came in, whipped out the *Encyclopedia Britannica* and started writing stuff down word for word.

"I remember him telling me I wasn't going to get anywhere in life.

"He said, 'You aren't going to be a success because you didn't know how to play the game.'"

Sadly, Fred Coe hasn't learned the game either.

Ruth Coe talks about her son

"They have taken a fine, clean, upstanding young man and ruined him," Ruth Coe said.

Wearing high heels and flesh-colored fingernail polish, she spoke in the hallway outside the courtroom where her son, Fred Coe, was being convicted of multiple rapes.

It was a sunny morning in July. The mother of the man implicated in dozens of sexual assaults on Spokane's South Hill had decided the world should know her feelings.

For nearly an hour, Ruth Coe talked about herself. She flayed her town, the police, the press.

After she had grown calm again, she asked that her angry words be held until some "appropriate time."

She and Gordon might be leaving the city after the trial, and perhaps then her story could be told.

But today, Ruth Coe sits in jail, charged with trying to arrange the murders of the judge and the prosecuting attorney who put her son behind bars.

For her sake, to help others understand her state of mind, today seems the appropriate time to recall the words and feelings

165

she nurtured toward the police, the legal system and the city where she has always lived.

From the public record, it will be remembered Ruth Coe was her son's only line of defense.

And on that early morning in July, she began by passionately explaining again how her son had many girlfriends, was well-adjusted and had, in fact, played sleuth with her – trying to catch the actual South Hill rapist.

But she understood that, in the courtroom, almost no one believed her.

She knew the gallery, from the first, assumed the convicted rapist's mother was knowingly lying for her son. Mothers do that. Mothers have to.

The woman who valiantly tried to put on her happy face every day allowed that she was stung by the judgment of her peers.

"I'm not an overbearing mother," she said. "(Fred) and I have a very normal relationship.

"And my son has never put me in a position where I had to lie for him," she stormed in an intimate and until now unpublished interview.

"Do you think (mothers) think (their sons) are Mr. Perfect?" she asked. "They don't. A mother looks at a son with a very realistic eye."

Mrs. Coe recounted how the night her son was arrested she questioned him closely about the charges. "It was the first question we asked," she said.

Ruth Coe said her son had always told her the truth. It was that simple. When Fred swore he was innocent, she believed him.

From that point, she admitted she became his most tenacious defender. "From the time I would get up in the morning until I went to bed at night, his defense (was) my life," she said.

That is because Ruth Coe considers herself a good mother. From her son's earliest school years, she attended parent-teacher meetings. A good mother does that.

Later, when her son went off to college and didn't like fraternity life, a good mother would have taken a son back home and helped him get on with life. She did as much.

At his trial, she felt Fred needed her, because he was innocent and because it hurt him to see the Coe family drawn and quartered by a vindictive police, a sensationalist press, a judgmental public.

The seeds that led to her arrest were sown early in the trial of her son.

Mrs. Coe said in July she worried that police were personally out to get her family and ruin her husband's career.

She believed some police officers had a "vendetta" against her husband because he was, at the time, managing editor of the *Spokane Daily Chronicle*.

"I think police are capable of the (most) vicious acts in the world," she stormed. "That's the real story here."

And on that same sunny morning, she singled out Spokane County Prosecutor Don Brockett for particular scorn.

"We live in Brockettsville," she said. "It's sinful for one man to have so much power."

The night her son was brought in on the first rape charge, Ruth Coe remembered prosecutor Brockett "looked like a storm trooper."

"He acted viciously," she said of her confrontation with the prosecutor at the Spokane Public Safety Building. "It was like dropping into Nazi Germany."

Still, Ruth Coe said she once believed the judicial system would exonerate her son.

But as weeks passed, and Judge George Shields repeatedly refused defense requests to admit certain evidence, she became convinced the system was stacked against her son.

"From hindsight, in retrospect, I would never try to play fair again," she said. "Because the law doesn't play fair."

"I'm telling you, from what I know now, I (should have) told my son to run. I (should) have got in my car and driven him over the border."

Instead, Ruth Coe, who insisted she was never a socialite, said she counted on the good sense of the city of Spokane to give her son a chance.

"Because Gordon (her husband) had such a beautiful career," she said.

"He has been loved and respected and he returned that affection.

"Now, that has been ruined. I see that as one of the saddest tragedies I have ever read."

By the time of her son's trial, Ruth Coe's affection for Spokane had clearly waned. "The love I have for Spokane will never be the same," she said.

"For a long time I didn't understand how people in this world could not go out and lend a helping hand.

"Now I do. (My family) offered a helping hand and has been slapped in the face. But tell them they are not going to run me out of this town."

Indeed, the public didn't run Ruth Coe out. The public simply dismissed her as a mother who lied for her son.

Only Ruth Coe didn't believe she had lied. And she couldn't forget what had happened.

Now, it would seem she has raged for months against the forces which sentenced her son to life plus 75 years in prison.

Other mothers surely will not condone what the police say Ruth Coe has done.

Yet, if a poll were taken, would not other women with sons and husbands privately confess an understanding of how a mother could entertain murderous thoughts about the men she felt destroyed her family?

Perhaps if some mothers had been able to talk with Ruth Coe, quietly remind her that fantasies of revenge should not be spoken in public, she would not be in jail today.

But there Ruth Coe sits, a sad and tragic figure who believes to this hour her son is innocent.

Coe press conference in Walla Walla

WALLA WALLA – When he opened his mouth to speak, I felt sorry.

For him. For us. For the sad state of our criminal justice system.

Three years in a maximum security cell at the Washington State Penitentiary haven't changed Kevin Coe.

If anything, the years alone with his typewriter, his telephone, his weights and his fantastic thoughts have given Spokane's most articulate criminal time to polish and perfect his yarns about a conspiratorial prosecutor and vicious police department.

On his most perfect day, the day the Washington Supreme Court patched together some technicalities and reversed his four first-degree rape convictions, Kevin Coe was ready.

Barely 15 minutes into his prison press conference, the man so soundly convicted and now so tenuously vindicated as the "South Hill rapist" hit stride.

"My case is one of those things that happens once in the history of this planet," he said, interrupting his attorney.

"This decision is a great victory for truth and justice, a triumph for civil liberties," Kevin Coe said, framing his sad and sordid affairs in the context of a cosmic event.

He had blown his hair dry.

He was wearing newly washed jeans and a black T-shirt, pressed and tucked in.

He looked, as always, handsome, self-assured.

By the end, his performance rated a 10. He was smoother than before. More in control. More relaxed.

And when he takes the stand a second time in his second trial, Kevin Coe will come off as the most poised witness in his own defense.

And for that I felt sorry.

If prison had made him less self-assured, less cocky, less gloating, then a larger seed of doubt might have crept into my mind about his guilt or innocence.

But to me, on the day the high court made him news again, Kevin Coe seemed to be the same cunning man who single-handedly had convinced his hometown of his guilt.

Judgment on his guilt or innocence, of course, must be withheld.

The Washington Supreme Court has seen to that.

The highest rulers from Olympia set aside questions of guilt or innocence, ignored public demands for justice, for the glory of making law.

But after reading and rereading the court's arguments and postulations, I am disappointed in the glory of the law.

Though hairs were split and legalistic definitions were honed, one sterling truth remains unbowed, unaddressed by the high court.

Since March 1981 when Coe was arrested, the rapes on Spokane's South Hill have stopped.

"There have been absolutely none," said Detective Roy Allen, who personally tracked Coe in the final days before his arrest and knows the South Hill rape files better than anyone else.

"There have been no more hand-down-the-mouth rapes, no more grabs in the night or early morning, nothing.

"Not one rape since then even slightly resembles any of the ones we had up there for years and years."

Allen says police records suggest at least 40 women were thrown to the ground, bloodied, threatened and raped by an oven-mitted attacker who spoke clear, perfect English.

For those 40 women, I feel particularly sorry.

They didn't need the fear to well up in them again.

They didn't need to begin fidgeting through their purses for the Mace again.

One vision must guide the South Hill rape victims – and all Spokanites – as they prepare to shudder through a rerun of our most sordid scandal.

This time, we must demand that our prosecutors and judges do it right.

If Kevin Coe is innocent, if, as he claims, "any levelheaded person will see" his innocence, we must tell our legal representatives to let the exculpatory rivers flood the courtroom and wash away the stinking mountains of doubt.

If Kevin Coe is guilty, then no effort can be spared to find every man, woman or child who can add ammunition to the case against him.

This sad chapter in our city's history should have been resolved in one cathartic spasm. That it was not will make us cry in pain.

The old wounds will reopen.

The paranoia, the hurt, the psychic damage will crush in again.

No matter what the ultimate verdict, a second trial of Kevin Coe will burn up dollars, dreams and civic energy like a blazing gasoline inferno.

For that, Spokane, I am deeply sorry for us all.

Second Coe trial and verdict

The most chilling yet tragic part is that Kevin Coe has never blinked.

Two juries have nailed him. More than 40 sexual assaults have been tied by computer and police analysis to his name.

Yet, as Coe was led from the courtroom after being found guilty a second time on multiple rape charges last week, I'd bet his mind was free.

What an injustice, I expect he thought, that such a successful, handsome, articulate real-estate salesman has been so mistreated.

Those of us who toil under burdens of guilt and regret, who suffer when we push at the boundaries of public acceptance, have unending difficulty comprehending the obliviousness of Kevin Coe.

We know – the world knows – that he raped, mutilated and terrorized women in his hometown for years. Yet, he denies all.

He denies and evades even though his history of sexual deviance dates back to the 1960s.

As a teenager, he was picked up as a Peeping Tom.

A high school teacher remembers how Coe got his kicks by taking unsuspecting girlfriends downtown and trying to force them to make love beneath the street lights where bums could watch.

Handsome, articulate, well-connected as the son of a newspaper editor, Kevin Coe should have had it all. Yet, he failed miserably and in the most sinister ways.

It's still hard for his past friends to figure out why.

"I know that a lot of people are saying he was weird and they knew it all along," D. Jay Williams, Coe's closest friend from childhood, said.

"That's too easy. He didn't wear around a sign saying he was a psychopath. He was bright, fun to be around. There was really no evidence that he had anything but a loving, close family relationship."

Love. That wasn't the problem.

Kevin Coe's parents loved him. To this day, his parents defend him and proclaim his innocence.

But Coe's life offers the sternest possible example that love does not cure all, conquer all.

Indeed, the bond between Coe and his parents suggests that heartstrings may draw so tight and become so twisted that they strangle rather than free the soul.

"Even before all this happened, it seemed to me that Fred's relationship with his mother and his family was a time bomb," Coe's former brother-in-law remembered.

"Fred (who changed his name to Kevin in 1982) had these illusions of grandeur, and his parents never said anything. When he failed, they would take him back. Ruth would coddle him; Gordon would slip him money. And that was the way it always had been."

Don't all good mothers and fathers love and protect their children?

Of course.

But psychiatrists who have counseled and observed Coe sketch a picture of a family where the degree of rationalization and denial was dangerously overdone.

"A family needs to have control. And a family must draw the parameters," explained on Spokane psychiatrist who had counseled Coe. "Kevin's family didn't do that. All along, the Coes' bag has been to deny any wrongdoing."

For that, Kevin Coe's parents must be viewed as tragic figures.

They believed too deeply in their son.

They believed, but Kevin deceived.

The deception began immediately after his arrest.

From the first day, Kevin Coe masterfully spun improbable tales to his parents.

Yet, rather than calling his number, they spent long hours embellishing his fantasies.

Friends and in-laws were called to the Coe home and asked to distort the truth. They could not. All they could do was watch and listen in disbelief as the family:

- Constructed the tale of Kevin and his mother following buses and looking for clues to the "real identity" of the South Hill rapist.

- Manufactured the times when Kevin ate his breakfasts and dinners at home and, therefore, couldn't have been pillaging the South Hill.

- Pieced together a phony story that the parents and Kevin were together previewing real estate the day Kevin was trapped with his dildo in a parkway near Washington Water Power Company headquarters in 1981.

At his trials, Ruth and Gordon Coe testified to all of that. Again and again, they went further for their son than most parents would ever deem necessary.

Psychiatrists suggest the Coe family's inability to set boundaries for Kevin and its constant rationalizations and denials of his problems may be related to the flawed attraction between Kevin and his mother.

"Kevin and his mother had a sort of seductive, adoring relationship," one doctor said. "And it was a dynamite situation."

Ruth Coe had difficulty with all the women in her son's life. Friends and in-laws recall that when Kevin attempted to pay attention to another woman, his mother often would shout life-threatening comments to the woman, would lock Kevin out of the house or would lock herself in her room and scream that he wasn't her son.

There is no way to know all that drove Kevin Coe to become the South Hill rapist.

Maybe this weird and tortured man simply was predisposed to crime.

Maybe his strange diets or daily use of beauty soaps did him in.

To me, it seems that his lifetime of horribly mixed signals from his family surely fueled an unimaginable personal anger.

174

Cut loose from many of the familial and social standards that hold most of society together, he lurked menacingly, with crystal convictions of his rightness, in the shadows.

The best that can be said about Frederick Harlan Coe is that his psychotic power put him in a class with Ted Bundy.

What a tragedy for a man, a family, a life.

Twelve Interesting People

Chapter Five

Dave Miller: 7-11 convenience clerk, murdered on the job

He died between the Bud and the barbecued potato chips.

The family buried him Friday and his epitaph should read: "Dave Miller, felled in a murder of convenience."

Untoward death takes untold forms. Yet Dave Miller's murder cleaves together the worst images of senseless loss of life.

The weirdo who put two bullets in Miller's brain at a Seven-Eleven all-night store ended up with $50 for his effort.

Investigators estimate the robbery-homicide took only 60 seconds, in-and-out, bang-bang, no clues or suspects in sight. The $50 murderer may never be found.

On top of all this, Dave Miller shouldn't even have been working the night he died.

His regular shift ended at midnight, but last week he agreed to work the graveyard hours for his best friend who landed a temporary job out-of-state.

"We could take it if it had been an accident, or a wreck or an illness," Dave's grandmother said before his funeral, "but this, this is hard to take."

In a way society double-crossed Dave Miller.

On one hand, no one wanted his job. Clerks at all-night groceries last only a few months on average. This is grunt work of the worst kind.

Yet someone must do the work for the convenience of the rest of us who wouldn't be caught dead working at a Seven-Eleven.

For six solid years Dave Miller cleaned floors, made change for pinball machines, straightened out magazine racks and sold beer to late-night drunks.

He viewed the sale of slushy sugar drinks and cigarettes as honorable, decent work.

In the end he was gunned down by a killer who knew no decency.

More than that, Dave Miller found out the hard way how his business could turn people into sitting ducks for crime and yet pay them only $3 an hour to play the part.

Oh sure, the stores spell out the rules for clerks like Dave Miller. They explain that crime comes with the job, an average of maybe one robbery a month in a busy season.

Every clerk receives instructions on where to deposit money in a safe that they cannot open and how to recognize thieves.

New employees learn the rules of stick-ups before they learn how to run the cash register. Keep calm, cooperate, offer to get out of the way after the money changes hands.

Follow the rules and you won't get hurt.

People who know Dave Miller said he would have carried the entire store out to a robber's car if asked to do it. Dave knew the rules, and he believed in them.

He fell, double-crossed and dead.

Now the grieving has begun. The store has offered a $25,000 reward for information leading to the arrest of the killer.

But at the family farm outside Spokane, a grieving mother asked a question that even a $25,000 reward cannot answer.

Why, she wondered the day after her son's death, was her son sitting alone, unarmed in the middle of the night, guarding money in a brightly-lit store?

"We never used to have stores that stayed open all night," she said, "and we got along all right."

The dead clerk's mother has hit the most awkward element in the convenience murder of Dave Miller.

For whose convenience did he die?

What element of society, or business, or human nature required a 28-year-old man to wait for his executioner in an all-night store that sells 212 varieties of candy and gum?

The corporate answer sounded logical the day after Dave's murder.

"We're open at night simply to serve those people who are up between 2 a.m. and 5 a.m.," the public relations voice of Seven-Eleven said. "It's a firm corporate commitment."

A closed door means a lost sale, or so the theory goes.

In truth, the hours between 2 a.m. and 5 a.m. are barely profitable; a good night would be $150 in sales after midnight and before dawn. That barely pays salaries, utilities and operating expenses.

But dollars in the till aren't the only reason to stay open.

All-night clerks cost less than burglar alarms and plate glass windows.

Cashiers who don't ring up sales at night still may clean floors and restock coolers. (The job description for a graveyard clerk lists two full pages of janitorial duties at Seven-Eleven.)

So Dave Miller, on the night he died, functioned as a living, breathing burglar alarm and robot janitor. Just good business, that's all.

And he was something more. The night he died Dave Miller played pigeon for the carnivorous night people.

Every all-night clerk in a convenience store knows the night people, the whacked-out weirdos who seep from the woodwork after 2 a.m.

They appear after the bar crowd has gone home, after the swing shift rolls into bed, before the milk men and delivery boys rise for an early cup of coffee.

In the parlance of the convenience store, night people emerge in "dead time," the hours of 2 a.m. until 5 a.m.

Some of these walking dead shoot up and wander stoned into the fluorescent dream world of Big Gulp slushland.

Others drink away another day and come stumbling and stinking to the convenience store door at 3 a.m. for one last quart of Thunderbird.

And some night stalkers have lost touch with time, slipped over the edge and come giggling, and growling and painted green.

These were the people Dave Miller served in the last two hours of life. He warmed Butcher Boy burritos for them in a microwave oven.

Convenience store policy suggests night clerks greet every face that comes in, no matter how grotesque or lost.

Establishing eye contact, the theory goes, creates a human bond between customer and clerk and lets the casual robber know he has been seen.

Dave Miller probably tried that. He always played by the rules.

He may have looked his killer straight in the eye, and recognized him as one of the night people, and that explains why he is dead.

Or Dave Miller may not have seen his killer.

He talked to his grandmother early on the night he was shot and told her he planned to deliver a half-gallon of milk and a loaf of bread to her door when he left work at 4 a.m.

Police found his body near the refrigeration coolers with two bullets in the head. He didn't make it to the milk.

No one person may be blamed for his death – not the robber who killed for $50, not the store owner who wanted an extra dead time sale, not the rest of us who contract the munchies during the wee hours of the morning.

Yet all of us applied a little pressure to the trigger.

And as we mourn the death of Dave Miller, we realize this grief is not unique.

Murders of convenience are as American as a late night fruit pie.

Friends and family of Laura Daylie suffered through it last year.

Miss Daylie died in a similar robbery-homicide at a Seattle Seven-Eleven 13 months before.

As long as we are grieving, let us not forget to comfort Russ Whitaker who was blinded at 2:20 a.m. last July when an armed gunman robbed his convenience store in Payette, Idaho.

Today, no one wants more people to die for our convenience. Tonight, thousands of all-night groceries will glow like beacons in the night for those who forgot to buy a pack of cigarettes and can't wait until morning for a smoke.

When someone finds a reason for this thoughtless, compulsive urge to consume when it's convenient, send a note to Dave Miller's mother.

Tell her why good guys finish dead.

Robin Lee Graham: Youngest man to sail alone around the world

KALISPELL, Montana – He lives on a mountain, safe, dry, almost a mystic – the youngest man ever to sail alone around the world.

Many times, when the rigors of terrestrial life battered my sense of purpose, I have thought of him.

He captained the 24-foot *Dove*, then the smallest sailboat ever to complete a circumnavigation.

The winds of the Indian Ocean dismasted his sloop, washed him overboard, yet he managed to survive.

He speared fish for food, navigated with the accuracy of a marksman and met his bride, Patti, in the Fiji Islands.

National Geographic devoted four issues to his voyage. On the glossy pages he lived a life uncluttered by the mundane.

Almost 15 years to the day from when he sailed, we sat in the living room of his hand-hewn cabin and talked of what the good life should be.

"I don't talk about the trip much," said Robin Lee Graham.

"I don't talk about it because I remember a lot of hardship, a lot of loneliness."

The picture magazines didn't recount those episodes.

They portrayed him as a teen-age Columbus, bound for glory on a hammered-gold sea.

He was 16 when he left, July 27, 1965.

He sailed 30,600 miles – alone.

In 1970 he sailed back to Los Angeles Harbor a celebrity.

A ghostwriter helped write a book. Hollywood made a movie.

Home was the sailor, home from the sea and America was prepared to exalt him.

But America misunderstood Robin Lee Graham.

The youngest man ever to sail the world alone sought no bounty.

"That would have been a real bore, wouldn't it?" he said, sipping a cup of tea and setting it down on his handmade coffee table, "to always be Robin Lee Graham, teen-age sailor. You'd be sort of a storybook person."

Ten years ago, he seemed straight from the pages of Robert Louis Stevenson.

For 1,739 days he had taken sights with a sextant, set jibs on a stormy sea.

He sailed away from a domineering father and a school that couldn't hold him.

When he returned, he was their darling. Charter boats wanted him, the talk shows wanted him, Stanford University offered him a scholarship.

All mistook the magnificent loner. He had sailed for manhood, not for money.

"A lot of people depend on the crowd," Robin said, stroking his long beard in the elegant light of a Montana sunset. "I was just the opposite."

And he suffered the opposite of cruising blues.

The 40-foot seas he could face. The deck shoes and gin-and-tonics at Marina Del Rey he couldn't.

One weekend, he simply left.

Patti and he drove all night toward Montana, to shed the oilskins of a modern folk hero.

At first, it wasn't easy.

He was a high school dropout fresh from the tropics.

The first winter they lived in a tent and shot rabbits for food.

"I used to go into long periods of depression," Robin said.

"I knew I could care for my family on the sea, but I wasn't sure about earning a living here.

"I struggled a long time to learn to be a carpenter.

"Many people thought if only they had done what Robin and Patti had done, boy, would they be happy," he said, holding hands with the girl he met halfway around the world.

"We have done things many people only dream about. We've sailed around the world; we've seen a lot of places. But afterwards I felt, like that Peggy Lee song, you know, 'Is That All There Is'?

"I knew it wasn't."

He bought the second issue of the *Mother Earth News* and set sail again alone in a wilderness.

He built a house. Skidding the logs by himself, burning up the transmission in a battered old Jeep.

Progressing from wood butchery, to wood working, to cabinetry, he became known as one of the best carpenters in Kalispell.

Rivendell Builders, his cottage business is called. Rivendell is a village in the Tolkein world full of peace and security.

Robin Lee Graham all but forgot his trip.

In nine years no one in Montana has seen the 33,000 slides of his remarkable, historic trip.

He hasn't spoken to the Kalispell Kiwanis Club or given an interview.

When the movie *Dove* showed at the Liberty Theatre in downtown Kalispell, no one knew the hero lived eight miles west of the popcorn machine.

He has packed one of the most astounding adventures of our century away to experience – except for the storm.

The storm, he said, that changed his life.

"It was a catalyst," he began.

In the logbook of the *Dove* he noted the "weird black squall" October 11, 1967.

By nightfall the squall off the west coast of Africa had grown to a hurricane.

Robin had met his bride by then. He wanted to live. He was frightened to die.

"Seas are towering 40 to 50 feet," Robin spoke into his tape recorder that night.

"Everything loose was hurled about the cabin. The sea broke into a porthole and green water poured in."

The roar of mountainous waves rattled the *Dove* as she shuddered and moaned down the crest of the waves for hours.

The cockpit filled with water. The companionway doors cracked.

"I knew if the storm got any worse the boat would sink," Robin said quietly, looking down at Patti's hand.

"I cried out for help, and I received it," he said.

The towering waves abated. *Dove* sailed on. He felt God had saved him.

"The storm sped up my thinking of spirituality," he said. "Today, God and my family are my priorities."

And that is what happened to the boy sailor.

He is the same Robin Lee Graham who sailed alone around the world, still testing himself, alone.

He watches no TV. His 10-year-old daughter, Quimby, conceived at sea, does not attend public school.

"The things that I rebelled against were in public schools," he said, gazing out at the girl as she rode her horse around the pasture.

"If you don't fit the mold, if you are on the fringes of school, if you aren't average, you are left behind."

His new life was not unlike the sea in its solitude.

He has become the model of the backwoods survivalist.

Navigating life from a cabin built by hand, he sits out of sight of any highway, a Bible on the counter top, his sextant beneath the bed.

As I stood to leave, he answered my question about sailing being the cordial of contentment.

"Sailing isn't the key to life," he said. "The key is excellence.

"There are so many people who live at the level of mediocrity.

"I've found that if you don't work for excellence, it's hard to have a sense of fulfillment, a pride of self-worth."

At 31, the youngest man to sail alone around the world sees people reclining on their laurels, postponing a cabin in the woods, a trip across the sea.

All around him men are taking water aboard their dreams.

Robin Lee Graham hasn't foundered at all.

Gordon Vales: Brilliant artist trapped 20 years in mental institution

No crow's-feet crease the corners of his eyes.

In that sense Gordon Vales was fortunate to have grown up in a village for the retarded.

He had no worries.

He was fed, clothed, cared for in every way.

That he was an artistic genius who, if started on a different course, might now be renowned for his gifts rather than his limitations – well, that was the price of growing up in a society at first prejudiced against the retarded and then intent on shielding them from risk.

Gordon Vales has spent 44 years in mental institutions, foster homes and boarding houses.

"I look 24, don't you think?" he asked one summer night as sheet lightning backlit the downtown Spokane skyline.

He scanned the sky.

He didn't look at the construction paper in his hands, nor did he seem to notice the red-headed little boy who stood, awestruck, waiting for him to complete his work.

Soon, a clump of people had gathered in Spokane's Riverfront Park to watch the man who tears pictures.

Gordon Vales can tear perfect circles without looking.

He can tear detailed outlines of cowboys rearing on horses, Indians wearing headdresses.

One look at a human face, and he picks up a plain piece of cheap construction paper and creates a perfect silhouette image.

On one plane he is a genius.

On another plane Gordon is special. He speaks in the parlance of the retarded.

"Did Jesus like cowboy movies?" he suddenly asked.

He was institutionalized as an infant in 1935 or as a 5-year-old in 1940 – no one is quite sure.

He was kept in a room with retarded people at a time when care and custody overruled the chances for human growth, overprotected and underestimated for years.

He is a study in environmental retardation.

Yet he had a gift. He could tear pictures.

And after 44 years, Gordon Vales has finally decided to wager that his talent can overcome his limitations.

This summer he moved into an apartment, alone.

He is trying to live like the rest of us, on his own, earning a living.

"I am an artist," Gordon said the night he tore the picture of Jesus. "I want to live alone. I want to tear pictures."

The success of this 44-year-old retarded man's attempt to live a dignified life as an artist is tied, in some degree, to Spokane filmmaker Robin DuCrest.

This summer DuCrest received a $20,000 grant from the Washington Commission for the Humanities to shoot a 28-minute documentary entitled *The Silhouettes of Gordon Vales*.

With a bit of luck, the 16mm film will be telecast on the Public Broadcasting System, and maybe the major networks in the coming months.

The film already is scheduled to be shown in October at five different forums in Eastern Washington.

If the film succeeds, Gordon Vales one day may be exhibiting his silhouette art across the country, selling his remarkable hand-torn works to major galleries, earning enough money to care for himself without the support of the state.

As it is, *The Silhouettes of Gordon Vales* already serves as an instructive example of what happens when a society assumes people want to be protected at the expense of taking a chance to succeed on their own.

Gordon was hidden at Lakeland Village in Eastern Washington for more than 20 years – an institution shaped, as most are, by the most conventional and conservative elements in society.

He grew up before the major civil rights movement in the United States, before the de-institutionalizing drive in mental hospitals.

That he may yet find a place among the victorious, not the vanquished, is the result of individuals who saw beyond the institutional barriers.

One of these people was Rhoda Williams.

She was a farmer's wife from the little town of Edwall, Washington, who taught part-time at Lakeland Village.

She was one of the few who saw around the label of retardation Gordon Vales had carried for 20 years.

"I felt Gordon was there because of social problems," Mrs. Williams remembered of the first time she met Gordon.

"He was so curious. He was the only one who took an interest in the farm."

Although Gordon is black and Mrs. Williams lived in a conservative farming town, she offered to take Gordon out of Lakeland Village and into her home to help with housework.

"When we took him in, they said he would never work out," Mrs. Williams told me at the family farm a few miles southwest of Spokane.

"And when we took him in, they got a petition up in the church and asked us not to bring him out here. The children were afraid of him."

Yet Mrs. Williams gave Gordon Vales something no institution had given.

For seven years she provided him with a chance to overcome the fears and prejudices of a society.

He attended Sunday school and won the hearts of the farm kids by tearing silhouettes of them.

When the Edwall Lions Club asked him to tear silhouettes for their annual dinner, Gordon tore tiny pictures of Lions doing good works like mowing the lawn and helping people.

Now, Gordon wants to make it on his own.

Not all special people could have done as much as he. Not all have talents as recognizable as perfect silhouettes. Still, Gordon Vales serves as a profound metaphor for what can be done to retrieve this country from its institutional and individual malaise.

His life affirms that human development requires some room, entails some risk.

The same vision could be applied to everything from health care to the very organization and vision of government.

"Human dignity is one of the very heavy themes we pursue in this film," Robin DuCrest said late one night after showing a working print of *The Silhouettes of Gordon Vales*.

"It seems the direction the film is taking is to key on the notion that we need everyone in society, that we have to use all humans as resources," he said.

Gordon Vales wanted to risk something to become something.

That notion is one many in our safe, risk-free society have forsaken.

Ara H. Woodhurst: *Woody the bus driver retires after 37 years*

The other evening I noticed Woody was gone.

Woody drove the Cannon Hill bus at night.

If he had been the clock-watching, it's-just-a-job kind of public worker, I don't think his absence would have meant a thing.

But in the few months I had ridden with him, Woody demonstrated some unusual traits for a public servant.

He had mastered the uncommon knack of being pleasant no matter what the weather or world situation.

And he took a quiet pride in his work.

On the night run of the Cannon Hill bus, passengers rarely pulled the buzzer to get off.

Woody knew our stops and cheerily wished us well as we stepped off.

When a regular did not board, Woody took it upon himself to inquire if someone in the neighborhood was ill.

Very quickly, I felt a part of the family on Woody's bus, part of his vision of public service.

After 37 years at the wheel of a bus, Woody decided to settle into the easy chair at home and spectator's seat at the horse track.

Fearing his kind of public service may one day be gone, fascinated at how he managed to drive a bus 75,000 hours and not develop terminal grumpiness, I sought out Ara H. "Woody" Woodhurst in the first days of his retirement.

He worked mostly at night, looking into the galaxy of headlights on the major thoroughfares of the city, or creeping along black and empty residential streets. His flight plan rarely differed.

The last 17 years he drove south from Standard, across downtown and up the hill – the Cannon Hill route.

Before that, he spent eight years on the Minnehaha run.

Despite the routine, the sameness of it all, Woody never lost his love for the job.

"It never was boring," he said. "Because I love to drive. And I enjoy the public."

Recalling innumerable conversations with lifeless airline reservation clerks, insentient telephone operators and crabby gas station flunkies, I pondered the difference between Woody's attitude and that of others in the public realm.

Woody doesn't think we, the public, are a pain.

"I never had any trouble with people," he said. "It's rougher out there today. But I think you just gotta talk to people, that's all.

"The kids, especially. They are dying for attention. It's like they aren't getting attention at home."

Because of the nature of his job and because he cares about people, Woody became a 40-cent psychiatrist over the years.

He arranged numerous marriages and counseled dozens in divorce, all for the price of a fare.

192

"A lot of the passengers treat you like they would their bartenders," he said.

"People have a problem; they want to talk about it. Who is easier to talk to than the driver?

"I didn't give much advice. Lots of time I would know both partners involved.

"All you had to do was be a good listener."

Occasionally Wood was more than a good listener.

"One time a young Air Force guy was riding the bus," he said. "I stopped and this real attractive young woman got on.

"Well, I drove around the corner and I set this girl right down on the guy's lap. When he got off the bus, he gave me four-bits."

Woody's job, like all work, wasn't without its bad moments.

He carried compulsive talkers, manic-depressives, hoodlums and drunks.

He barely escaped a head-on collision and often slid off a slick road in the dead of winter.

"And one of the biggest troubles was finding a toilet," he said.

"There used to be so many service stations on Division and downtown. They aren't there anymore. If you had a touch of diarrhea, you really sweat."

Yet, after 975,000 miles of driving a bus, Woody Woodhurst still held to a simple philosophy of work.

"It was like any job, I suppose," he said. "If you were ornery, you got it back."

At the Spokane Transit System office, Woody's file offers a testimonial that orneriness rarely boarded the bus with him.

"He was rather the exception," transit Manager Bob Harder recalled.

"In our kind of business dealing with the public, you normally only hear the negative side.

"On this guy it wasn't unusual for people to write in and compliment his friendliness and his attitude."

On his last run, Woody's passengers brought him cookies, cards and best wishes.

Woody meant a great deal to his passengers.

They saw him for what he was – a servant of courtesy and good service in an era when the science of surliness abounds.

Walter Kinsey: A new groom at age 98

Their vision fading in dim December light, they married, indefatigable disciples of love at first sight.

"To me, Walter doesn't seem 98," said the bride hours before her wedding. "I don't think of him as old at all."

Flora read the gleam in Walter's eye as something more than sun reflecting on his bifocals.

He loved her. She loved him. So, they walked together down a chapel aisle.

It was a familiar holy place.

It was the very chapel where 78-year-old Flora Way and 98-year-old Walter Kinsey each sent their first spouses to the Great Beyond.

Chaplain Michael Wiser had spoken the last words over Flora's husband, Joe, and Walter's wife, Anne. So who but Chaplain Wiser could ask:

"Walter, will you take Flora to be your wedded wife, to live together after God's ordinance in the holy estate of matrimony?"

One month into his 99th year, Walt Kinsey said, "I will."

That he would astonished many residents at the Good Samaritan retirement home.

There, the average age is 84 and marriage rarer than mouths with the teeth God gave them.

Indeed, there has never been a resident marriage at Good Sam. "And a lot of people around here thought it was kind of silly to put on the dog like that," said one old codger in the lobby.

But it wasn't silliness. It was a pact born in the high spirit of Bertrand Russell who said, "of all forms of caution, caution in love is most fatal to true happiness."

Since 1882, Walt Kinsey has avoided the life of caution.

As a young man, he said goodbye to Ohio and traveled to a godforsaken, treeless desert in Central Washington. The year was 1910 and Walter was a homesteader.

Defying the custom of his day, he waited late to marry.

Not until age 44 did he meet the train of his mail-order bride from North Dakota. They wed on a rainy Christmas Eve in 1926 and stayed that way for 52 good years.

He wasn't rich, but resourceful.

The depression killed his job, but Walter escaped the hardship, packed up and moved to Kansas City to restart.

Once back on track, he moved west to Okanogan, Washington, bought stocks in the 1940s, took a job with the state auditor and dreamed of driving a Packard.

"He never mourned the past," his daughter Karen Barnes recalled. "It was the thing that kept him young."

He bought the Packard at age 68. He packed the Packard with wife and belongings and toured the United States.

"He stayed young in his thinking," his daughter said. "He had the ability and eagerness to experience whatever was new."

The experimenting continued through the years.

At about 80, Walter took up baking. He conquered zucchini bread and then learned to make jelly to spread on top of it.

Into his 90s he kept writing letters and walked a mile a day.

The problem was, he out-lived his first girl. The chaplain buried Anne Kinsey in 1978 and right away Walter felt lonely.

"I don't believe in sitting around and watching time go by," he said. One day he started looking for someone else.

Last summer, he found Flora.

Flora and Joe had been happily married.

But Joe had begun his decline even before he and Flora moved from Kennewick to Spokane three years ago.

He didn't recognize Flora anymore. He couldn't walk. After 59 years of marriage to his high school sweetheart from Des Moines, Iowa, Joe was in the final days of his life.

One hot, July night Walter Kinsey, silver-handled cane in palm, came striding around the grounds. A slow stride.

Flora Way was coming out of the nursing home, and they just bumped into each other.

He asked her to go for a walk. "The very first time we walked together we started holding hands," Walter said.

A few days later Joe died. After his funeral, Flora and Walter's walks became a daily regimen. The venerable love birds clung close together in the moonlight down by the cherry trees.

From time to time nurses dashed into the night and disturbed the doting doves, confusing them for wanderers who had strayed too far from a convalescent bed.

If Walter and Flora's senses were out of whack, it was due to the feelings budding inside their well-worn hearts.

Walter became one of the last of the red-hot courters.

He escorted his new lady to the institutional dining room. He picked her chokecherries and cooked them into jelly. He regaled her with stories of trips to Alaska.

One night, after they had dined out with Walter's ex-son-in-law, after they had laughed and hugged like 16-year-olds, they kissed outside room 512.

"No teenagers had a sweeter kiss than we did that night," Walter said.

The following day he brought her a rose.

And every week since, he has offered a new rose in celebration of that kiss.

At first Flora hesitated at the thought of marriage. Walter was 20 years her senior. And though he could cook and clean and listen, Walter couldn't dance.

Flora loved to dance. And at the Good Sam parties another suitor often twirled her 'round the floor.

There was competition for her affections – until Walter produced the ring.

Just before Flora left on a trip back to Des Moines, he slipped it on her finger.

"That was one for the book," he laughed later. "I knew if she tried it on she would say yes."

She did.

Out went the invitations, in came the granddaughters to be measured for velvet dresses.

Music and flowers, a full retinue of ushers and brides-maids, Flora held nothing back.

"Neither of us had that on our first wedding," she said. "My husband got one day off. And the same was true for Walter."

On Saturday, Chaplain Wiser called them together shortly after 3 p.m.

"I tried to counsel them," he shrugged. "But what could I say? Between them they have 111 years of marriage."

The chapel already was packed. Pew after pew filled with keenly interested matrons with newly permanented hair.

The men wore suits that hadn't been out of the closet for years.

Walter, in full tuxedo, got a bit nervous with the ring. And right in the middle of the service, he sneezed.

"I hadn't sneezed in weeks," he moaned afterward.

But altogether, it was smashing.

Flora wore red velvet and her sons Chuck and Joe, Jr. escorted her. Flora's great-granddaughter Melissa played flowergirl at age 3 1/2, dropping rose pedals as she went.

A few voices clucked and wheelchairs squeaked, but in the end, most everyone at the Good Sam Apartments and nursing home wished Flora and Walter well.

And if anyone had doubts about the marriage, Flora predicted it would last.

"This marriage business is give and take," she said. "And we don't have time to fight."

Now, they are off on a honeymoon at the regal Empress Hotel in Victoria. They will drink tea in the afternoon.

"We are trying to set an example for others who are sour and unhappy," Walter said before he left, reminding those who snipe at his desires that the ultimate tragedy of growing old is simply giving up.

Flora and Walter have not done that.

They live and love in the image of William Butler Yeats who said, "I pray that I may seem, though old, a foolish, passionate man."

Walter moved his double bed into Flora's apartment.

He confided to his daughter that Flora loved to cuddle.

As inspiration to those of you who have forgotten how, Walter and Flora Kinsey will cuddle until the end of time.

Jerome Johnson: Bum's funeral at Union Gospel Mission

The invisible people rose from gutters Monday.

The bums, hobos and tramps turned out to bury one of their own.

It was the first funeral in the 30-year history of the Union Gospel Mission.

As a rule, those who live on the skids don't attend the funerals of those who die there.

Usually, there are no funerals.

People who die with nothing but what they can carry in a paper sack don't have money for funerals.

The 10 to 20 people a month who end up dead in the gutters of this city are afforded a pine casket, a donated ambulance ride and a free plot at the cemetery.

That's all.

"But Mr. Johnson's son wanted the funeral here," mission director Harry Altmeyer explained Monday. "He said that all his daddy's friends were down here and that his daddy always said he wanted to be buried with his friends."

That's the way it happened.

Jerome Johnson's friends buried him the best they could.

In the alleys and under the freeway overpasses word spread that one of the street people had turned up face down in the garbage.

The hobos took up a collection.

It took them five days and a fair amount of panhandling to do it, but they raised $36.

The $36 bought the flowers for the casket.

And when the time came, they did what all of us do at funerals. They stopped what they were doing to pay their respect.

Monday, the invisible people pulled themselves up from the sidewalks and off the benches in Riverfront Park and filed into the chapel at the Union Gospel Mission.

Smelling of cheap liquor, they sent off a man from their midst.

Shortly after 11:30 a.m., Harry Altmeyer rose to thank 40 forgotten faces for coming to pay final respects.

"I consider it a privilege to have known Jerome Johnson," the mission director said.

As it turned out, many of the skid row family sitting in the folding metal chairs didn't know Jerome Johnson – not by name.

He was just someone who often showed up at one of the east-end taverns at 6 in the morning with the rest of them.

"He was a street person like me," Dennis Roberts said after the services.

"I saw him the day he died. We drank a few bottles of jug wine together. Then he just left, that's all."

When the pine casket opened and Jerome's cold, cold face appeared, some of the women gasped.

"Wake up, Jerome," sobbed Alberta Wakam as she filed past the casket.

Others just looked hard at the face.

Maybe they hoped to see some clue to their own fate.

Maybe they came to see if he looked any happier in the casket.

For 25 years Jerome Johnson, with his adopted son, Freeman Davis, had done what many of them had done.

He rode the boxcars into the broken glass and boarded up sections of Portland, Seattle and Spokane.

He was a Choctaw Indian from Oklahoma whose life calling was to abuse his liver.

When the abuse finally ended, the respectable types would say he died as far from honorably as a man can.

Garbage men found Jerome Johnson's body.

Jerome Johnson, 41, crawled into a Demster Dumpmaster to stay warm on the chilly night of March 10, 1981.

He never crawled out.

The coroner said he died of an epileptic seizure, his tongue jammed between his teeth, his body mixed in with the empty green bottles of Gibson's white port and decaying remnants of a few Big Macs.

A garbage truck picked him up in the trash container and unceremoniously transported him to the Indian Trail landfill along with the other throwaway stuff of this culture.

"He was like 100 other men who come in here," Union Gospel Mission director Altmeyer said.

"He didn't have no money; he had nothing except the clothes on his back.

"He had just got out of the hospital with pneumonia. And he had cirrhosis of the liver.

"Before he died, he talked with his son, Freeman. He said he didn't want to be buried in no suit. Just a shirt and a tie and a sweater."

He was loaded into the hearse in somebody's donated shirt, tie and sweater.

On the way to Fairmount Memorial Park there was no police escort. No long line of black limos.

By coincidence, only a garbage truck followed the hearse for most of the drive in the rain along Northwest Boulevard.

It was a sad, symbolic bit of irony that caravan of two.

Jerome Johnson was a throwaway.

And this culture has a tendency to assume men who haven't a nickel to their names and end up dying in a dump have no family, no friends, no honor left.

But that is wrong.

On Monday, Jerome Johnson got some respect.

Many eyes were red from another night out in the cold and one more glass of breakfast.

But just as many other eyes shone red with tears.

Gerry Lindgren: He's still running from Spokane

The shoes rest in the quiet of a trophy case in a hallway of John Rogers High School.

All leather, no padding, the old flats with the funny spikes always left blisters.

Yet to those who know their history, the red-and-white relics still send the heart thumping.

The Adidas under glass belonged to Gerry Lindgren.

Scripts like the Gerry Lindgren story don't come around very often.

He grew up in a poor and somewhat difficult environment with a father who drank too much.

It seemed a breath of good wind could have lifted his 112-pound frame into the air like a cinder.

Yet for an enchanting moment, the wisp of a boy defied the winds.

The 65 inches of Gerry Lindgren could assimilate oxygen into his lungs better than any runner in the world.

And something in his head allowed him to tolerate the pain of 150 miles a week of running, faster, harder, longer.

In 1964 the skinny little teenager from Spokane blew the socks off Billy Mills, Olympic champion at 10,000 meters, and Ron Clarke, world record holder in the six-mile run.

He set an untouchable national teenage record of 8 minutes 40 seconds for the two-mile run.

That is why someone saved his shoes.

Gerry Lindgren was a living teen-age legend.

And so it will be hard for some to understand how the boy who had it all has run in a direction so unexpected.

Sixteen months ago Gerry Lindgren, owner of the successful Stinky Foot shoe store in Tacoma, father of three children, Spokane's most famous distance runner, simply ran away from his family, friends and his past.

"I don't know where he is," his mother said from her North Spokane home a few nights ago. "I haven't heard from him since January 1980."

Gerry Lindgren's sad legacy probably must begin at John Rogers High School – and with Tracy Walters.

Tracy Walters coached the teen-age sensation. Tracy Walters was Gerry Lindgren's closest friend.

"I think people must think back to who Gerry was," Walters, now dean of students at Rogers, said a few days ago.

"He was the greatest distance runner of his time. And all he ever wanted to do was run."

The old coach said there was a difference between wanting to run and wanting to bask in the glory of winning.

"He didn't seem to get that big a rush from winning," Walters said. "In fact, I think it was more of a thrill for me to see the things he did than it was for Gerry.

"Off the track, all the people asking questions about him put him under pressure. And Gerry responded to that pressure with jokes and putting people on."

That was the mark of Gerry Lindgren.

Sometimes he would grant interviews with an English accent. Often he would show up at track meets with an artificial limp.

Once, when a *Sports Illustrated* reporter asked him why he was so good, Gerry blurted out that it was because he was "a left-footed runner."

On the track he was all business. Off the track he was all con.

It was a delicate balancing act. He won 11 NCAA running titles, held the world record in the three-mile run and lived with the reputation as a prankster and as someone who did not seriously consider who he was.

And after college at Washington State, the balance inside Gerry Lindgren began to quiver and shake.

The greatest legs in the world began to slow and break apart. Doctors told Gerry Lindgren to quit running.

Instead, it was symbolic of his love of running that Gerry sought someone who would tell him he could go on.

He found Glenn Turner, con man and supersalesman, who pushed a self-improvement scheme called "Dare to be Great."

It was Gerry Lindgren's philosophy.

So the famous runner hit the promotional tour, selling the theme that a man in the right frame of mind could do anything he wished, from owning a Cadillac to running at world-class pace again.

Later, "Dare to be Great" unfolded as one of the monumental swindles in America. It was a classic pyramid scheme designed most of all to make Glenn Turner a multimillionaire.

Gerry Lindgren was burned. But he didn't learn from his mistakes.

Well into his 20s, he still struggled with the transition from the boy who could run into a man who stayed in one place.

Holder of an education degree, a student of Russian, he refused to take a 9-to-5 job.

He told his wife, Betty, that he would only work a job where he could run twice a day.

Perhaps it was understandable.

Gerry Lindgren, as much as anyone, sparked the nation's imagination for distance running. By the mid-1970s, running had bloomed into a national passion. With everyone else running, maybe Gerry Lindgren had to.

He talked about a comeback, but made little progress as a runner and even less as a man.

While living in Oxnard, California, so he could train in a warm climate, Gerry became involved with a woman who claimed he fathered her child.

Gerry denied it.

Yet when it came time to appear in court in 1975 to argue against making child-support payments, Gerry simply disappeared.

For six months he hid in San Francisco without telling his family.

"So I finally thought I would put an ad in *Track and Field News* asking him to contact me because I knew he wouldn't give up running," his wife remembered. "The day I called to put in the ad, the magazine told me they knew where Gerry was and gave me his address."

Five months after being reunited with his wife and kids, Lindgren and his family returned to Spokane.

He talked about opening a store. He ran in the first Bloomsday.

Back home, he confronted the same old problem. People asked him a lot of questions about where he had been, what he was going to do and why he weighed 135 pounds and finished 39th.

He didn't come back home much after that.

Instead, he moved to Tacoma, worked in a few running stores and finally bought a place called the Stinky Foot.

Gerry wasn't much of a businessman, but the store went well enough. He was a legend and young runners flocked to see him.

He joked and clowned with his fans and sometimes stood on his head. It was as if he were 18 all over again.

Only by now he was 30. And by now Gerry's running had taken a decided turn for the worse.

"We would go running," a friend, Bob Skar of Redmond, Washington, remembered.

"He would run a race and maybe drop out. But then, when we came back, he told all the people he had won the race.

"He was never serious. He was always fooling around, making up some stories."

It was the flaw that had somehow become a fixture.

The protective cover – always joking and putting people on – had made him a kind of jester among his friends. Gerry Lindgren couldn't confide to anybody.

Indeed, not since Tracy Walters, his old high school coach, did the grown Gerry Lindgren seem to have talked seriously about himself.

In January 1980, authorities in Washington state discovered he was wanted in California for failure to pay child support.

The state ordered him to set a date in court.

A few days before he was to appear, Gerry told his wife he had to be out of town for a meeting. He left the house with less than $50 and one pair of running shoes.

That was the last time anyone heard from Gerry Lindgren.

Shortly before Christmas, the Stinky Foot went bankrupt. Betty and the kids moved in with her parents in Tacoma. "I tell the kids dad is on vacation," she said.

She sold the inventory to different running stores, including The Human Race in Spokane, run by Gerry's old roommate from Washington State, Rick Riley.

"Yeah, I have a theory why he left," Riley said one afternoon as he looked at the last Gerry Lindgren sweatshirt on his rack.

"He was the greatest collegiate runner of all time. He won three straight 5,000- and 10,000-meter championships in the NCAA.

"But I don't think he could cope with his own image.

"When at last he realized how good he once was and realized that he couldn't achieve that any more, he just ran.

"It became a whole lot easier for him to be someone else, have a new home, a new place, where he wasn't Gerry Lindgren anymore."

And there rests the tragedy, said Gerry's family and friends.

They said Gerry didn't have to hide. No matter what his problems and mistakes, they all said he could have come home to the place where he was still a hero.

And people would have understood. Teenage legends, like everyone else, grow old and make mistakes.

At Rogers High School Terry Walters walked past the trophy case where the red-and-white shoes lie, toes crossed.

"He had a gift," the coach said.

"He is a rather precious person, as a human being and an individual.

"And right now I'm afraid there is a lot of guilt out there with Gerry Lindgren, that he is feeling he let a lot of people down." The coach got out his pictures of Gerry setting the high school record in the two-mile, of Gerry beating the Russians, of Gerry running with Billy Miles.

"I want him to know that no matter what has happened to him, somebody loves him," Tracy Walters said. "Spokane loved him."

Jim Chase: Spokane's first black mayor

Jim Chase had just discovered a flat tire on his 1969 Chrysler Imperial.

At the last minute, he called to ask if we could change our luncheon date from downtown to somewhere closer to his home.

The Bend restaurant happens to be just up the hill from the 67-year-old candidate's house, and he could walk there for lunch.

I agreed to the change in plans. In retrospect, The Bend seemed appropriate.

It wasn't a high-falutin' place. It was a place where Jim Chase felt comfortable. As we walked in, the smiling waitress behind the buffet of deep-fried prawns instantly recognized him and wished him well.

The man considered by many to be the front-runner in the Spokane mayor's race was puffing a bit as we headed for a table in the corner. He had spent his morning loading wood.

He wore a tan, polyester sports coat and a yellow and black shirt, open at the collar. Almost immediately, he ordered the daily special.

"And give me a root beer," he told the waitress. "I feel real sporty."

Jim Chase has much to feel sporty about. He is riding a remarkable political wave, which has taken him from shining shoes in a barbershop to within one step of the leather mayor's chair in the second largest city in Washington.

207

The possibility, raised by his detractors, that he is not up to the job of governing a conservative, overwhelmingly white city desperately in need of leadership, doesn't appear to have occurred to Jim Chase.

Next Tuesday's election is something he can even joke about. "I'm planning on a landslide," he smiled. "And you know what a landslide is? Two votes more than my opponent."

He flashed the good-natured smile, took a bite of his tuna sandwich and picked up the story of how he came to be what he is.

Chase was born in 1914 in East Texas, the youngest of seven children in a family so poor that food was often in short supply. As a boy, he worked many hours in a bakery, for no wages, but all the cookies he could eat.

"As I tell it, I came from a rich family," he said. "Not in dollars and cents, but in that good old family spirit where we shared together, we respected our parents and they respected us."

Chase's formal schooling ended with some classes at an all-black high school in Ballinger, Texas. The school closed in the Depression. Jim Chase received no high school diploma.

"All my education came on my own. I was self-taught," he said.

As a young man, Chase bought his son the *World Book Encyclopedia*. He became so fascinated with the new books, he proceeded to read virtually the entire two dozen volumes himself.

"I liked it so well that when my kid was gone, I bought the new edition of the *World Book* and read it, too," he said.

Chase has compensated for his lack of formal education by developing a close network of friends who can teach him, and by being keenly observant of his surroundings.

Indeed, these two factors – friends and an awareness of his environment – have guided Chase most of his life.

In the dust bowl days of the Great Depression, Chase was working at a Civilian Conservation Corps in El Paso, Texas, when two friends suggested he come with them to Spokane.

These friends – Elmo Dalbert and Harry Blackwell – had written the Spokane Chamber of Commerce for literature about the city.

When the pamphlets arrived in Texas showing Spokane's mountains, trees and plains, it was Dalbert and Blackwell who convinced Chase to hop a freight train with them and come north.

Later, Blackwell convinced Chase, who had never so much as pounded out a fender, to put money into a body repair shop. Dalbert went to work in the business and was Chase's partner for nearly 40 years.

Chase and Dalbert sold their body shop several months ago for a tidy profit. But business acumen was not as easy to Chase as friendship.

His body shop was on the verge of closing many times in the early years. And an apartment complex he built in the 1970s eventually fell onto hard times due to low occupancy and was sold.

These difficulties were due, in part, to Chase being a black businessman in an overwhelmingly white town. Characteristically, he shies away from talk that color could be a factor in Tuesday's election.

"From a personal angle, I never knew much discrimination in Spokane," he said.

"Right now, I wouldn't be able to join the Spokane Country Club. But it's because I couldn't afford to pay the dues."

Chase believes surviving and prospering in a mostly white town represents an important qualification for his being mayor.

He believes he has shown a knack for finding allies and friends to help him overcome whatever barriers he might face in governing the city.

His ability to forge alliances with the white community began in the 1930s, he said, when he was befriended by Tony Grashio, head barber at the old Spokane Hotel.

"Tony Grashio helped me quite a bit," Chase recalled. "He told me about the customers, what they like and what they didn't like.

"Tony told me I was making more money shining shoes than a lot of my (professional) customers. He said, 'Jim, if you have a nice car, don't drive to work in it. Don't show off too much. If you show off, they will quit tipping you.'"

Chase said his father always attended a variety of functions and that prompted him to become active in public affairs, too. At first, his functions were exclusively part of the black community. His most notable effort was co-founding the Negro Active Club, which provided a framework for young black men and women to meet and socialize in Spokane.

By the late 1950s, Chase began to move into wider circles.

"I've worked in a lot of organizations," he said, noting his tenure as president of the Zoological Society, the NAACP and grand master of a Masonic lodge. "I have been second in command, I have been in command. I have always known my positions."

Chase also has served two terms on the Spokane City Council. He admits he has rarely introduced new ideas to city government. He considers that a plus.

"I came in with some of the old heads over there and I watched them," he said. "A lot of things I thought of, I didn't bring up without bouncing them off (other council members)."

As mayor, Chase says he wouldn't be a Lone Ranger or try to run everything. ("Being mayor) is too big a problem for one individual," he said. "The people have to do it."

One of the people who would closely advise Chase would be his wife, Eleanor, a third generation Spokanite whose grandfather was first pastor of the Calvary Baptist Church.

"I've got a lot from Eleanor; she has changed my opinion about a lot of things," the candidate said of his wife who is an accomplished singer, a veteran social worker in Spokane and a recently elected board member of Eastern Washington University.

If he loses, Chase says he won't be crushed. He knows he has traveled a great distance since his box car ride from Texas.

At the end of lunch, he ordered a piece of loganberry pie to go with his root beer and hinted for a ride home.

Chris Kopczynski: Spokane climber who topped Everest

The January issue of *Concrete Construction* magazine lay on his conference table. For a moment, it didn't fit.

Wasn't I in the office of the pope of the piton, king of the Khumbu glacier?

And only the night before, hadn't he stood before 2,500 goose-bumped admirers who gathered to venerate him for being only the ninth American to set a cramponed foot on the highest mountain on Earth?

Men such as this, even if their names do read like the left-overs from a can of alphabet soup, don't read *Concrete Construction*.

Those who, at 20,000 feet, can win arguments with Sherpas who have lost 10 toes to frostbite and want to quit hiking up Everest, have long ago set aside such things as making a living.

Or so I assumed.

Yet, there before one of oh-so-few who have gone sight-seeing at the top of the world lay the January issue of *Concrete Construction*.

211

And next to it sat Chris Kopczynski, mountain climber non-pareil, worrying out loud about the slump in the construction industry and the impact on his family business.

"I love construction," he was saying.

"It's the challenge of doing something, of creating something.

"And coming back here to take up construction, I really couldn't call that a letdown.

"It is just a totally different train of thought, that's all.

"Even when I was going up the mountain, my dad was sending me letters with bid results from jobs here in Spokane."

All of us savor an adventure story. A few nights ago, Chris Kopczynski told one that had nothing to do with *Concrete Construction.*

To a packed Spokane Opera House, he narrated the breathtaking pictures from his 1981 American Medical Research Expedition to Mount Everest.

He described the rumble of the Khumbu ice fall where 35 mountain climbers have died trying to scale Everest. He recalled the 100-mile-per-hour winds which prompted the Sherpa guides to erect prayer alters and cook rice offerings for Sagamatha, as Everest is known in the Buddhist faith.

As I listened to the tales, I imagined a man unbothered with Reaganomics, the cost of a cheeseburger or the public schools.

For that is one essential in any adventure story: to take us away from mundane and venal problems and into the misty landscape of super-human challenge.

Yet at the end of his hour and a half of slides and explanations, the ninth man to see the world from 29,028 feet abruptly came back to Earth.

And what he tried to say was, in many ways, more inspiration than even his snapshots from the most exclusive vista on the globe.

"I would like to take these last few minutes to share with you some of my own philosophies," he said as a slide of Everest at dawn flashed on the screen.

"People all over the world face challenges daily that, to others, seem unimportant or worthless.

"Getting out of bed in the morning is a challenge to some people.

"But each one has his own victory.

"Doing the best that you can do with what you have been given is what life has been to me. That philosophy has made me happy.

"And as long as man lives on this planet, there will always be Everests in his mind."

Then the applause rolled up around him. It thundered through the rafters like an avalanche.

Maybe we were all just softies for the old "do-your-best" theme.

But it seemed to me the man who had gone to Everest had managed, as few heroes are able, to relate something of his experience to the lives of those of us trying to live in swivel chairs or at kitchen sinks.

This centaur of the Himalayas seemed intent on making the point that from his perspective, there really isn't much difference between negotiating Everest and mastering the paperwork on your desk.

"To me, it's all relative," he said the morning after his momentous public showing of the Everest climb as he went back to drawing up bids for a new county shop building. "It gets down to a question of attitude.

"You don't have to do something special to be a success. But you have to have the right attitude."

It is an attitude, he said, of not concentrating on what you can't do, but on what you can.

"When my kids say can't, I just about kick 'em," he said. "I tell them, you change that word to something else."

Of course, there are other factors in Kopczynski's personal success besides elimination of one word from his vocabulary.

A good and supportive family helped him immeasurably. He recognized his talents and limitations. And luck was his ally.

Yet, after climbing the world's mightiest mountain, Chris Kopczynski came back home to emphasize one point above all.

"As for genius, I don't hardly believe in it," he said, looking down at the copy of *Concrete Construction*. "What it takes in this world is desire. That tends to override everything.

"Setting goals for yourself and striving to reach those goals – that is success."

It is a simple philosophy. Even corny.

But after 18 years of trying, it led one man to that special vantage on the border of Tibet and China five miles above sea level.

And in some fashion it is a philosophy that probably can serve a man just as well when he looks out the front door each morning.

Ellen Kremer: Single mom becomes #1 grad of Gonzaga Law School

When she gave up her other life for law school, some of Ellen Kremer's friends and family didn't understand.

Wasn't she a doctor's wife living in comfort?

Didn't she enjoy a satisfying life of volunteer work as a member of the Junior League?

If she wanted a career, why didn't she simply pick up on her mother's advice from years ago: earn a teaching degree and then find a job after the children are grown?

What was with this woman, anyway?

Why, at age 37, did she take off her wedding band and soon thereafter enroll in the Gonzaga University Law School just as her children were toiling with teenage-dom?

Why? Because Ellen Kremer woke up one morning and discovered that the neatly packaged plan of her life wasn't making her happy.

"I was economically very comfortable," she said. "I had social status. I was successful in my volunteer work. Maybe I would have continued if I had been happy in the marriage, but I wasn't. I was watching my children grow up in an environment that was not happy or helping. So I decided to make a change."

Ellen Kremer cut the cord linking her to security, social standing and success.

She plunged into the world of bitter divorce proceedings, single parenting and a statistical probability that her standard of living would fall like a hard biscuit.

Six years later, Ellen Kremer, 43, has emerged triumphant.

To the cheers of her classmates, children and friends, she graduated No. 1 in her class from the Gonzaga Law School's evening division a few days ago.

The same day, her daughter Lisa graduated from Washington State University as one of the 10 most outstanding women of the 1987 class.

Her son David has just been informed his name will be placed in the professional baseball draft.

And Matthew Kremer, the youngest in the family, will finish his sophomore year in high school with a 4.0 grade point average.

If the essence of Ellen Kremer could be bottled, a great many authors and hand-wringers who discuss the troubled condition of modern American women would be out of work.

A popular philosophy these days is that the superwoman of the 1980s is flawed and failed. The story goes that a woman who tries to juggle a career, parenting and a job ends up depressed, failed and strung-out.

But those who know Ellen Kremer know better.

"The thing that stands out for me when thinking about Ellen is her ability to organize and balance her life," says Jim Vache, dean of the Gonzaga Law School.

"It's hard to capture this, but she seems to accept the balancing as normal. She is able to combine what amounts to three jobs into one life activity."

Ellen Kremer's successes suggest that life consists of an ever-more-difficult juggling act and that the survivors must learn the routine.

Of course, not everyone can keep the pins up like Ellen Kremer does. Many women struggle with the same events and don't emerge from them as she has.

"I represented Ellen in her divorce action," recalled Eugene Annis, a Spokane attorney. "I was impressed with her ability to get through a difficult emotional time. She coped with the stress remarkably well.

"But many women become so devastated, they can't cope. They become so bitter that they expend all of their energies trying to make life miserable for an ex-husband or vilifying the legal procedures."

Ellen didn't succumb to those temptations. Rather, her classmates and professors say, she seemed to apply her life experiences to her new challenge: the study of law and the relationships between people and contracts and responsibilities.

Maybe Ellen Kremer's timing is the key. Her children are older, her maturity helped her and she entered the Gonzaga Law School at a time when the institution was ready to be flexible for a student who sometimes needed to miss classes for a high-school football game.

For these reasons and more, Ellen Kremer has become something of a pathfinder for other women.

"There is no question that being a single woman with children, who also is working on a career and holding down a job is not an easy road," she said.

"But it can be done. You can maintain yourself, your children. I even think my relationship with my children has grown stronger. As a family, we now have a lot more discussion about all major decisions.

"And I feel very uplifted," Ellen said of the years since her divorce, the years of law school, raising three teenagers and holding down a job.

"There were a few times when I felt overloaded, but more often I felt I was blessed because of my children, my job and my schooling.

"Women ask me, 'How do you do it?'

"I have this standard speech. I always say, 'If there is something you really, really want, you can get it.' The problem is, many women don't really know what they want.

"And once you are locked into something, it's very hard to make a major change."

Hard, yes. Impossible, no.

Ellen Kremer unlocked herself and changed her life. We can marvel at her example.

Chevy Pickup: Tells why her dad named her that and more

Earl Pickup died six weeks ago.

This will be the first holiday his only daughter, Chevy, will celebrate without him.

That's right.

Earl Pickup's daughter Carolyne introduces herself by her nickname, Chevy.

Her dad always got a laugh out of the handle hung on her years ago by a friend.

"I remember he always said it was better to introduce yourself when you have a last name like Pickup. That way people don't get an advantage over you. And he was right about that," she laughed a few days ago.

Warm recollections were part of what I had hoped Chevy Pickup would tell me about her father.

I called her because I wanted to talk to someone about coping with the loss of a loved one on Memorial Day.

Since the obituary in the paper carried the reference to Earl Pickup's daughter Chevy, I imagined this father-daughter story would be lighthearted and, perhaps, provide some uplift for those who remember their dead on Memorial Day.

But Chevy Pickup's story was much more than I anticipated.

It wasn't all laughs for Chevy Pickup and her father.

Their lives weren't a joke, or one big happy smile.

"How do I say this nicely?" she began. "My dad lost 40 years of his life to alcohol."

By day he sold tires and life insurance and medical policies. On weekends and most nights, he drank.

"All of my childhood he was an alcoholic," Chevy recalled. "As I was growing up, all we did was fight. When he was drinking, he told me, 'You are my worst enemy.' He needed a reason to drink and I was his reason."

In 1979 Chevy graduated from Spokane's Lewis and Clark High School. She began to take some classes at Spokane Falls Community College to become a counselor.

By the early 1980s, the classes had begun to unlock a riddle that she had not understood before. "I realized that my dad was an alcoholic and that as a result of that he would never deal with all the important things that we should deal with in life," she said.

"I realized that I wasn't dealing with them either."

For two years Chevy attended programs aimed at helping the adult children of alcoholics.

"I was a very afraid, very depressed person who didn't know what to do with her life. It was basically easier for me to wallow in my own self-pity that to find a direction and go with it," she said.

Over time, the counseling classes and her own personal journey led Chevy to a decision: she must confront her father.

One day she went home and said: "Dad, you are a drunk and you are killing yourself."

For months Chevy and her father met and argued.

He would yell and scream and cuss her out.

She would continue to hammer home what the drinking was doing to the family.

"One day I had on this beautiful sweater-coat," she recalled. "I was so mad at him that I took off that coat and ripped it apart right in front of him."

That act of separation, combined with the months of confrontation, led to a turning point.

At age 63, Earl Pickup stopped drinking.

"And he began to do this wonderful thing," Chevy remembered. "Suddenly, he started to re-create himself."

As he sobered up with the help of a 12-step program, the angry, depressed man began to change.

He began reading books again, including Shakespeare.

He traveled to Europe.

Most important of all, he reached out to his daughter.

"That meant that I couldn't use him as my excuse for being a screwed-up human being," Chevy said. "During that period when he was changing, I was changing, too. In time we became friends."

They argued less and less, and the father began to listen and to hope.

"We would just talk," she said. "We would have these philosophical conversations, and he would listen and act like he actually was interested in my side of an issue."

When Earl developed a bad case of pneumonia six months ago, he told his daughter that he was a much happier man than he had ever been.

He said he now had done what he really wanted in his life and only wished someone had told him sooner what he needed to hear about his drinking.

The last time she saw him, Chevy leaned over and spoke into his ear: "I will always love you."

His ashes sit in her house.

"I have someone now to think about on Memorial Day," she said.

The memory brings peace to Chevy Pickup's heart.

Alex Khan: Afgan refugee excited about first presidential vote

Two days from now the greatest country in the world will elect Bill Clinton or Bob Dole as President. Alex Khan thinks this is a big deal, even if many Americans don't.

"I'm excited. I can hardly wait to vote," said the 32-year-old finance officer at Foothills Lincoln Mercury Mazda.

The 1996 election will be Alex Khan's first opportunity to vote for President of the United States. "I became an American citizen on January 10," he said.

"I never thought I would be emotional by what some people might think were little things. But when the judge asked me to take the oath for becoming an American citizen, I got all teary-eyed. In other parts of the world I think everyone has a dream, in some ways, of coming to America, and here I am."

A strange part of America for Alex Khan is the incessant gloom and negativity that surrounds politics.

"It's the one thing that bothers me here," said the young man who remembers when the military overthrew and executed the president of Pakistan.

Khan grew up on the border between Pakistan and Afghanistan. Politics there were not just dirty; they were murderous, scandalous and rigged.

"I was very young when Watergate occurred in this country," Khan recalled of the time in 1974 when he and his father were listening to short-wave radio and trying to get news of events around the world.

"I remember we were all amazed that in America, a president was forced to resign because he did something unethical. To us this was a tremendous sign that the American system truly worked. Where I grew up, everybody looked up to America as the champion of democracy."

So it has been a bit of a shock for Khan to see all the negative advertising, hear all the bashing of the presidential candidates, and endure the proclamations of people that they are fed up and aren't going to vote.

The gift of democracy, of being able to choose a political course peacefully, is one that Khan values because of what he has seen and experienced elsewhere.

As a child, he lived in Pakistan when president Zulfikar Ali Bhutto was overthrown, then executed by the military.

At 20 Khan took up arms against the Russian Army in Afghanistan. For nearly four years he fought in the guerrilla war against Russian troops occupying his family's homeland.

Though he hears the protestations about the media being biased, he remembers huddling with family and friends every night at 9 p.m. hoping to pick up a thread of news from the British Broadcasting Corporation or the Voice of America.

"There is so much that is taken for granted in this country about politics," he said. "Even now, we are sitting here talking about where the money comes from in American politics. We talk about it, read about it, debate whether it is right or wrong.

Hey, in other countries the president's plane would be blown up rather than let people talk about this stuff."

Alex Khan arrived at Eastern Washington University in 1988 without a job, with little money and with only one friend in the area.

"I was frightened," he remembered. "All I know about this country came from the TV show *Miami Vice*. You step out your door, and you're dead."

His mother told him before he left to be sure he was home by 7 p.m. with the door locked. "I couldn't tell her my first job as a security guard didn't start until 11 p.m.," he recalled with a laugh.

He made $3.80 an hour working nights guarding the campus. He had never made that much money in his life back in Pakistan.

"Then I started meeting people here who genuinely care, people who are willing to help you," he said.

"My image of America changed."

He went to school.

He got a job selling cars. He moved up to being a finance officer.

Less than a decade later, Alex Khan's life in America is good and getting better. "Every single year my living standards have gone up, up, up," he said.

"In America, if you have a desire to work, the United States gives you a chance."

People around his work often ask Alex Khan why he is so happy.

"I'm in a country where I can make good money," he replies when people ask. "I have a nice house. I have a job that lets me care for my family. My wife is expecting a baby.

"And in this country we make our political choices and the system doesn't get off track. I'm having a hard time waiting for Election Day."

Newspaper Issues

Chapter Six

The power of words

Faggot. Spic. Baby-killer. Right-winger. Wimp. Nazi. Commie. Robber-baron. Slav. Serb. Jew.

Just words.

Spit out and powered with degrading adjectives, they pack the wallop of a mortar shell.

Every day on every continent of our world, words incite violence, anger and hatred.

Yet there are other words with other powers.

Peace. Hope. Respect. Forgiveness. Tolerance. Liberty. Truth.

Strung together with grace and supported by objective explanation, these words can inspire and uplift, destroy barriers and build bridges.

The Fourth of July, perhaps, is the best time to consider the power of words.

On this day in 1776 the Continental Congress adopted the words of Thomas Jefferson, who largely wrote the Declaration of Independence. Those words defined the character of this nation: "We hold these truths to be self-evident, that all men are created equal, that they are endowed by their Creator with certain unalienable rights, that among these are life, liberty and the pursuit of happiness."

This nation fought a war to protect the ideas expressed by these words. The revolutionary founders of our land pledged their lives to the cause of not allowing government, the courts or the King of England to bar Jefferson's words from being spoken or supported.

Two centuries later, our nation is expending a great deal of time and energy fiddling around with mechanisms to extinguish and contain words some people find offensive.

We don't like the lyrics to songs, so we go to the legislature and ask for laws to invoke limitations and bans.

Only last week, the U.S. Supreme Court was asked to rule on a Minnesota law that wanted to punish racist groups for words and actions that conveyed messages of hate.

But the court checked the Constitution and the history books. Then the justices ruled 9-0 against a Minnesota law that attempted to outlaw hateful words.

"The First Amendment does not permit (this nation) to impose special prohibitions on those speakers who express views on disfavored subjects," wrote Justice Antonin Scalia.

How much easier it would be to defend Thomas Jefferson's words than the words of a racist hate group.

How much more uplifting to promote the national anthem than the rhetoric of rap artist Sister Souljah who suggests, "If black people kill black people every day, why not have a week and kill white people?"

But the tonic to hateful speech isn't to be found in legislatures and courts.

The antidote can be extracted from the same substance as the venom: words.

To his credit, Bill Clinton took just that course when he challenged Sister Souljah. "Her comments were filled with a kind of hatred that you do not honor today and tonight," he told an audience of Jesse Jackson's Rainbow Coalition. "If you took the words 'black' and 'white' and reversed them, you might think that David Duke is giving that speech."

Sadly, the fact that Clinton tried to use uplifting words to neutralize destructive ones was viewed as politically naive and stupid.

This nation's greatest leaders always have understood and used the power of words. In a recent essay on Abraham Lincoln, author Garry Wills suggests that the 272 words of the Gettysburg Address re-cast American history at a critical moment.

In a few, short phrases, Lincoln re-framed the very intent of the U.S. Constitution, the Declaration of Independence and the Civil War, Wills suggests. That speech, Wills argues, defined America as a nation where the struggle for equality was the most important commitment of the people.

Those words changed a nation.

Words ill-spoken can also change a nation. Their power may be so pervasive that well-meaning citizens will try to use courts and legislatures to limit their destructive power.

Instead of laws limiting speech, this nation needs orators, spokesmen and eloquent voices that can use words to their highest purpose.

The potential for such leaders can be seen every day in the rising support for Ross Perot. He is no Jefferson or Lincoln, but his use of symbols, myths and personal reminiscences has tapped into the tremendous hunger for words that break through the safe, unintelligible and uninspiring bureaucratic babble.

At the same time, we must be careful about what we hear. We have grown somewhat hard of hearing in this age when sound bites and visual imagery try to substitute for words.

Difficult ideas need not just good timing, but precise, clear, illuminating expression.

As Mark Twain said, the difference between the right word and the nearly right one is the difference between lightning and a lightning bug.

What we need are lightning words to jolt us into action, not lightning bugs buzzing around and trying to illuminate.

Pizza offered to citizens who will gather to discuss future

The train has left the station toward a new destination for the Inland Northwest.

The price of an average house in Spokane just topped $100,000.

Coeur d'Alene lakefront homes are more than double that.

More than 400 new school children will enter Spokane city schools this fall.

Lake City High, Coeur d'Alene's second high school, will open in September, 1994.

Spokane International Airport traffic is up 32 percent in the first six months of 1993.

And just try to find a vacant boat slip on one of North Idaho's big lakes. You can't.

Change is in the air, on the water and tying up traffic in neighborhoods from Airway Heights to Dalton Gardens.

The region has embarked on the most significant decade of growth and change in 100 years. But is anyone driving this train?

On one hand, the region has plenty of engineers-in-training:

• Spokane County freeholders are busily at work on a new structure for Spokane's regional government;

• Proponents of a new city in the Spokane Valley again are pressing their case for a vote this fall;

• Kootenai County is wrestling with a new land-use plan;

• The State of Washington has told Spokane to implement the Growth Management Act;

• And dozens of developers, builders and entrepreneurs along Interstate 90 are busily crafting their own plans.

But a very real question remains over whether these varied, disparate and disconnected groups abide by any road map – any guiding principles – as they make decisions affecting the future of the region.

So, *The Spokesman-Review* has begun work on what we are calling the "Values for a Growth Decade" project.

The mission is simple: help Spokane and North Idaho build a consensus on some guiding principles for the 21st century.

The newspaper isn't trying to steer the region in a particular direction. Rather, the paper desires to help lay the tracks on which the region can travel wherever it wants to go.

We're not pushing an agenda for anybody. We're pushing the idea that people can, if given a chance, agree on the ground rules.

The lack of any guiding principles has been painfully evident in recent months during exchanges that dominate meetings in city hall and the uneasy conversations in dozens of neighborhoods about a perceived change in the region's quality of life.

It seems clear people in Spokane and Kootenai counties don't want to simply be buffeted by the winds of change. They would rather sail through them with a clear destination in mind.

That's what the "Values for a Growth Decade" project will try to help the region do: set a course, decide what matters most, and then urge decision makers to adjust their plans according to these new bearings.

And as the country song says, "There ain't no future in the past."

That's a twangy way to suggest that the planners and dreamers who pulled together Expo '74 and the Coeur d'Alene Resort aren't necessarily the ones to set the guiding principles for the future.

For things have changed. The future belongs to neighborhood activists, newcomers, young people and those who live here even if they don't have fat bank accounts.

In order for new guiding principles to be established, though, people have to let their ideas be known. That's step number one of the "Values for a Growth Decade" project.

Basically, *The Spokesman-Review* is extending an invitation to you to get involved in agreeing on some guiding principles for the 1990s.

And we'll even buy you pizza if you will participate.

Today's "IN Life" section of *The Spokesman-Review* outlines a fun, easy and unfiltered way for you and your friends in Spokane or Kootenai counties to have a say in what you hope this region will become.

If you will invite a few friends and neighbors over to talk about what you like and don't like about the region and what you wish would happen in your town in the next decade, we'll buy you a pizza.

Write up a one-page summary of your ideas and send it to us. We're calling this work the *Pizza Papers*.

The *Pizza Papers* will be shared with regional political and business leaders in the "Values for a Growth Decade" project.

But there is more.

In September *The Spokesman-Review* and a number of key sponsors in the region will bring in noted urban expert Neal Peirce.

Over ten days, Peirce will interview dozens of residents in the region about their views of our problems and promise.

As he has done for Seattle, Dallas, St. Paul and Phoenix, Peirce will then draft a comprehensive report on the region. He will assess the region's politics, social challenges and opportunities and compare our situation with that of other cities around the country.

In November *The Spokesman-Review* will publish the Peirce report, along with the best of the *Pizza Papers*.

All of those interviewed by Peirce, and all who participate in the *Pizza Papers*, will be invited to community forums in North Idaho and Spokane County to discuss how to devise some guiding principles to help direct the changes headed our way.

The "Values for a Growth Decade" project will, with your help, become a way for citizens rich and poor, young and old, just arrived or always been here, to help build a new community vision.

That's what this region needs right now.

If we pull it off, the politicians and other decision makers will have a clear sense of what matters most to us. With your help, our children and grandchildren will thank us for giving them the best in the 21st century.

Music director of Spokane Symphony diagnosed with AIDS

Weeks before he died, *The Spokesman-Review* learned Bruce Ferden was suffering from complications related to AIDS.

What to do?

The former music director of the Spokane Symphony would be the most prominent person known by many Inland Northwest residents to suffer from AIDS.

Was his illness a story? Certainly Ferden's familiar grin and six years of performances conducting the symphony made him a public figure.

In the last few months Ferden's decline had led to cancellations of a number of public performances.

On this basis, most newspapers would claim a right to publish the information.

But the terminally ill conductor also had made it clear he did not want the details of his condition to be highly publicized.

An important debate began at the newspaper. It wasn't whether the paper had the legal right to print news about Ferden. That right was well-established. The issue was whether publishing sensitive information about Ferden was the right thing to do.

After a number of meetings and conversations, the decision was made to honor Ferden's wishes until his death.

A brief note appeared a few days ago about his illness, but no direct mention of AIDS was made until he had died. Then the cause of death was published.

Was this the right call? Should the newspaper have paid more homage to a dying man's wishes than to a public's right to know?

There's nowhere to look up the answer.

Instead, newsrooms from Maine to California engage in such discussions every week. Issues of privacy, relevance and appropriateness (aka political correctness) have overtaken the more traditional discussions of how to get news in the paper.

This shift is frustrating to some reporters and editors. The news business is different from the nice business.

How does a newspaper put a happy face on David Koresh?

Maybe mama suggested saying something nice or nothing at all, but it just doesn't work in a world with wars in Bosnia and Somalia.

A newspaper does publish comics, football scores and "Hints from Heloise." But the foundation of a free press rests not on entertainment, but on hard facts and public discussion of society's shortcomings.

Yet, it is out there where the news gets rugged that the public appears to have become discomforted.

The media unquestionably are being bashed for doing things they thought people wanted and understood.

An example: Spokane Mayor Sheri Barnard recently finished last in the city's primary election.

The morning after the vote, the headline read, "Barnard finishes dead last." Beneath the headline appeared a picture showing the mayor responding to the news.

Right away, the letters began to arrive. "I did not vote for her, but I found the headline extremely insensitive," wrote Virginia Williams. "And that unflattering photo below the headline was just too much. It saddens me that the once proud newspaper stoops to such low, hurtful reporting and photography."

All we said was that the mayor was last and all we showed was a picture of how it felt. To us, these seemed proper, traditional roles for a newspaper.

But maybe those roles are beginning to change.

The public seems fatigued by the world's troubles. And there surely is a feeling throughout society of the need to provide solutions, not just underscore problems.

All around this country, editors are receiving letters from people like Virginia Williams. As a result, many newspapers have begun to review again their internal codes of ethics – if they have them.

The Spokesman-Review has a detailed code of ethics developed a few years ago.

In coming weeks our reporters and editors will be asked to review it and consider whether our current standards for reporting and editing are meeting the expectations of our readers and community.

Once we have reviewed our ethical code, we're going to print it. We'll even send it to you if you like.

We know the bottom line in this business is credibility.

Credibility rests, first and foremost, on good reporting and accuracy.

It depends, as well, on community-based judgments about what constitutes news of value to readers and what is simply gossip or irrelevant.

Finally, to stand the test of public scrutiny, the third leg of credibility must be solidly set on policies that define ethical standards for our craft.

We know this. Every day *The Spokesman-Review* works to find this balance.

Never stop helping us stay focused on this task.

Mark Fuhrman rips the buttons off an S-R photographer

Los Angeles Police Detective Mark Fuhrman ripped the buttons off a newspaper photographer's shirt a few days ago.

I understand the instinct.

Every day I work around photographers.

They can be annoying, temperamental and demanding human beings.

The same goes for editorial cartoonists, sports writers and editors.

Some days I just want to grab their collars and yank.

Maybe that's why journalists are fond of T-shirts – no buttons.

My urge to rip off buttons doesn't end at the office.

At home I often encounter some good targets for a button-trimming: my kids.

When they are sassing me, bad-mouthing their mother or have left their ice skates where my stubbed toe now resides, I think of buttons flying like small insects through the air.

Hasn't everybody wanted to pop the buttons off somebody's shirt at one time or another? That's why some readers have called and asked why the paper even mentioned the fact that detective Fuhrman popped a few buttons off a photographer's shirt.

Life has its frustrations, stresses and strains, so shouldn't Mark Fuhrman get a break? Doesn't he have some privacy? If his name had been Mark Smith or Mark Jones, popping somebody's buttons in Spokane wouldn't make news.

But this is Mark Fuhrman, lead detective in the investigation of the murders of Nicole Simpson and Ronald Goldman.

Because of that, he has lost a significant part of his privacy for the moment.

He's getting his 15 minutes of fame. He may not want it; he may resent it. But he's getting it.

That's why the photographer and the reporter met Fuhrman at the airport. He's a guy in the news who shows up here on a house-hunting trip for his retirement years.

People are interested in this stuff. The plan initially was to give Fuhrman similar coverage as was given Patty Duke when she moved to Coeur d'Alene or General Norman Schwarzkopf when he came to town to join the Washington Water Power Company board.

Unlike Patty Duke or the general, however, Fuhrman made some news on his own.

By ripping the buttons off a photographer's shirt, he thrust himself back into the limelight of the O. J. Simpson trial.

Simpson's attorneys have darkly suggested the button-popping incident shows a character flaw in Fuhrman that bears on his conduct in the investigation of Nicole Simpson's murder.

They are implying that Fuhrman's choice of relocation to mostly-white Idaho has some racial undercurrent.

Nothing Fuhrman said at the airport suggested these things.

Paul Quinnett, an anger-management counselor in Spokane, warns it would be a mistake to jump to a conclusion about Fuhrman's character on the basis of the popped buttons incident. "I don't think any single incident allows us to draw a conclusion on whether an individual has trouble managing anger," Quinnett said.

So don't rush to judgment about Mark Fuhrman. We aren't.

Don't rush to judgment about that lousy, blood-sucking press, either.

Fuhrman is a national figure in the middle of a once-in-a-century case where the defense has raised the suggestion that Fuhrman could be a rogue cop.

That's the reality.

When Fuhrman lost it at the airport with a 28-year-old photographer, he threw himself into the feeding frenzy of the national press.

I bet detective Fuhrman has kept his cool on the streets of Los Angeles in some very tough situations. If he had done the same in Spokane, there would be no uproar.

True, what happened in Spokane may have more to do with the fact that people in tough jobs often put on a kind of armor for their work, then take off that armor in their private time.

As Spokane County Sheriff John Goldman explained, "In law enforcement, you kind of psyche yourself up for the job. Once you step out of the job, you assume a different, more relaxed role."

Maybe Fuhrman thought he was on relaxed, private time in Spokane on a house-hunting trip.

He wasn't. He can't be. Until the Simpson trial is over, the detective will be on the job 24 hours a day.

As Goldman also notes, law enforcement officers receive intense training on how deal with difficult people who spit on them, curse at them or threaten them. "And we are trained not to react," the sheriff said.

The photographer didn't spit or curse or threaten. He just took a picture.

Fuhrman reacted. That made news.

One day soon Mark Fuhrman and his family hope to get away from it all by moving to Sandpoint.

The folks who met them a few days ago speak highly of the Fuhrmans.

They likely will be fine neighbors.

Once resettled, Mark Fuhrman will regain his privacy.

He will be comforted as he gazes out across Lake Pend Oreille.

A peaceful time will come.

It cannot be here just yet.

Is news dead? Is news a dinosaur?

Put another way, will the Darwinian forces of a fed-up public, 50 channels of all movies and a new generation dazzled by their own home pages simply squeeze out that species known as news?

The disappearance of the news as we know it may seem implausible, or not much of a loss.

It is both. And, by some measures, news already belongs on the endangered species list.

On a recent business trip to Denver I channel-surfed cable TV. Content broke down this way: mostly movie channels, 12; mostly talk, music or advice, 10; mostly half-hour TV shows, 10; sports, 5; religion, 3; news and how to have buns of steel, 2 each.

The news is still there. It just occupies the Galapagos Islands while the dominant media are evolving away from news as quickly as Ted Turner can colorize movies or another teenage couple can be found to talk about their love lives (coming soon on line).

Even the news channels are becoming something quite different from reporting on events, issues and ideas that inform real people.

On TV, celebrity news has never been bigger. Spectacular famines, fires and disasters around the world make good video. On radio, the fabulous sports babes, health advisers and entertaining political commentators reign. News has been reduced to five minutes at the top of the hour or a celebrity profile at 5 and 11.

Another challenge to news these days is the home computer and its networking capabilities. This emerging medium clearly is attracting the big bucks and the big marketing.

Jumbo players in media, from Bill Gates at Microsoft to cable guy John Malone at TCI, are spending billions to install infrastructure that links every home and business with a telephone/TV/computer line.

One box will give consumers access to computers and computer-based information around the world. You can call or e-mail or search documents, chat about your sex life, make plane reservations, and, oh yeah, get the news.

Again, the news most often appears pasted on the end of a long list of available options.

The news is more than e-mail or a home page. The news isn't just access to every college library in America.

News and information, while related, aren't twins. News and interaction with others bear some resemblance to each other, but aren't interchangeable.

Telling people what you think about the world is a long way from news. The news attempts to objectively, truthfully, fairly and accurately report what is happening in the world. The news isn't just your opinions, your feelings or your thoughts.

Today, no one can predict with certainty how the computer-networked future will work.

There seems little doubt, however, that a medium of networked computers is not well suited to the concept of news.

For 200 years news has been defined and practiced as an organized effort to record events and ideas, test them against what is known or suspected, then synthesize the information and present it in a coherent way to a geographically defined audience.

At its most basic, news is making sense of what happened next door to the people who live there.

Of course, there is more to it. There is the making sense of what happens around the world and how it relates to what happens next door.

But the making sense of it all, the truth-testing, the telling in a coherent and speedy way are elements of news gathering that have served citizens very well.

Yet these elements aren't easy to replicate on line.

Paradoxically, because so much about everything can be found on networked computers, the news becomes more difficult to access.

Everyone on line can try to be a source of news, be a reporter, an editor or a commentator. This further blurs the line between reliable, accurate news, gossip and hearsay.

Not everyone will be a reliable reporter or good editor on line. Lies, half-truths and propaganda could easily be mistaken for the news. This will further confuse people about the nature of news and could lead to a news-illiterate generation that has no concept of the difference between news, opinion and somebody's wishful or fuzzy thinking.

An open, democratic society needs news. Despite the wonders of cyberspace and the warmth of old movies, we all live in real places occupied by real people.

This guarantees that we will have conflict, debate and disagreement. This is news. The news needs to be sorted out and told to all so citizens can make good decisions.

Telling about a community of people, examining the facts, reporting in clear, concise ways to all who live in a place is the news.

The news doesn't come bundled in your software.

The news isn't a movie rerun.

The news is fuel for good citizenship. It must be kept alive, not relegated to a place next to the dinosaurs.

City responds to call for help from Romania

Charity ranks high among human virtues.

Recent events in Spokane suggest charity is neither threatened nor endangered.

In early 1996, *The Spokesman-Review* published the story of Anni Ryan Meyer and her heroic effort to aid children living horrible lives in Romania.

She and a team of 12 volunteers from the Inland Northwest traveled 4,000 miles to a series of broken-down orphanages around the Romanian capital of Bucharest in Eastern Europe.

They found hundreds of children trapped in vermin-infested, unheated dormitories with no glass in the windows, no hot water in the pipes and little food on the table.

The children had no shoes.

They had not bathed in weeks.

Lice and chronic diarrhea made working in the orphanages a challenge to the senses.

But work they did. Meyer and her band repaired 22 toilets, 27 sinks, 17 showers and put glass in hundreds of windows.

They came home and told their story. Since then, the outpouring of charity has astounded Anni and her husband.

"We have about six tons of material already boxed up and ready to be shipped to Romania – everything from medical supplies to clothing and linens, to toys," said David Meyer. "To date, we have in excess of $50,000 donated to these orphans."

People were touched. They wanted to help. They did.

But the milk of human kindness isn't all the needy of this world require. A plane would help. And an honest bureaucrat at the border.

The last thing Anni Meyer or any of the hundreds of charitable donors would want is to lose track of 180 boxes of donated materials and $50,000 in cash as they wend across a big nation, a big ocean and through a corrupt customs system in Romania.

So, at the moment, much of donated material sits safely in the Meyers' garage.

"Anni has been in contact with many political delegations," her husband said. "We have had contacts with the State Department and private airlines. We don't want people to be frustrated or discouraged. Anni said she will make sure it all gets there."

She will, no doubt.

Yet her uncommon effort points out the limits of what one person, or one team of volunteers, can do.

Anni Ryan Meyer needs help to save the 100,000 orphans in Romania alone. Those needy children, along with the hungry and deprived children who live in every corner of the world, including the corner just around from your house and mine, depend on a network of impassioned, charitable people supported by public and private organizations, bureaucracies and resources.

This need for infrastructure has all but been lost in our recently politicized, often mean-spirited discussions about foreign aid, welfare and the size of government.

Right now, Anni Ryan Meyer could use the hand of a big government, and the belly of a big government plane.

Maybe she will get it.

Vice-president Al Gore is visiting Spokane Monday.

Representative George Nethercutt is up for re-election.

The old-fashioned politics of looking good at election time could kick in.

Anni Ryan Meyer accomplished a great deal. Her team, working through the Spokane Chapter of Northwest Medical Teams, offers a strong example of what private, charitable efforts can do.

Her success was based on establishing a genuine bond with those she decided to help.

Her bond to Sabina, a 5-year-old Romanian girl, was so strong that Ryan Meyer wanted to move mountains for her.

Ryan Meyer gave the girl the little red shoes she had purchased for her own daughter back in Spokane. The story and picture of Ryan Meyer with Sabina was a big part of what compelled hundreds of people to donate to her cause.

Yet how many people of means honestly ever make such a bond?

Instead, we send a coat. We write a check. That is wonderful, charitable. It is not enough.

The problems of the truly needy are that their homes are in disrepair, their health is bad, and they often have few of the basic reading, writing, personal hygiene or life skills needed to care for themselves.

Needy people need expertise, skills and lots of time and money from successful, busy people.

And if you can't go to Romania, you could at least go next door.

Spokane's third legislative district, the one that includes the heart of downtown and most of the affluent South Hill, has the highest percent of people relying on public assistance of any legislative district in the state of Washington.

Go there.

Bond with someone.

Give of your talents.

Anni Ryan Meyer's example can be tried at home.

M. L. King's lessons need to be taught today, says Flip Schulke

At Spokane's African American Forum luncheon a few days ago, Rob Fukai asked a question about the Martin Luther King holiday that probably is on many minds.

"What does Martin Luther King mean to me?" he wondered.

Fukai, vice president of external affairs for Washington Water Power, is a Japanese-American who grew up in Spokane and really didn't know much about King.

Not until Fukai went away to college did he learn about King's work for civil rights.

Only after King was assassinated in the spring of 1968, did then-college student Fukai begin to read about King. Only then did Fukai think back on growing up in Spokane in the 1950s and begin to understand the broad impact King's civil rights movement had across the country. For it wasn't just African-American families in the South that suffered indignities and injustices in the 1950s and 1960s.

In 1952 when he was only 3 years old, Fukai recalled the day neighbors visited his parents and asked them to move away because Japanese weren't welcome in that part of Spokane.

His parents moved.

He remembered the day in 1960 when he was thirsty after playing backyard football with friends.

"I went into a little cafe on Third Avenue in Spokane and couldn't buy a Coke," Fukai recounted.

The sign on the wall said, "No Japs Allowed."

He was 11 years old and didn't know what to do. He left.

That was the way much of America treated people of color and people of different ethnic heritages. Those ways were what Martin Luther King, Jr. resisted.

About 200 people heard Fukai deliver his moving, personal account of how King's life's work related to his childhood in Spokane.

Unfortunately, any meaning or historic significance of the King holiday will be lost on many other people in the region this year. After all, skiing will be good on Monday. And a few after-Christmas sales are still in full swing.

If there is any discussion at all about the King holiday, it likely will simmer around the old debate over whether King's birthday should have been a national holiday in the first place or include some grousing that the holiday comes too soon after Christmas.

This lack of awareness for why banks are closed and offices dark on the Monday nearest January 15, which was King's actual birthday, seems most unfortunate in our part of the world.

The blatant signs of racism and discrimination from Rob Fukai's childhood have disappeared, but the Inland Northwest very recently has suffered through acts of violence, intolerance and injustice that have shaken our faith.

Hate crimes and anonymous hate-related literature still pop up on college campuses and in street graffiti with sickening frequency.

In the last year bombs from anti-government, white separatist terrorists have twice ripped through U.S. Bank, destroyed a Planned Parenthood Clinic in the Spokane Valley and shattered the windows of *The Spokesman-Review's* Spokane Valley office.

Our region has been horribly stereotyped as a place where ethnic minorities are not welcome. If there was ever a place and a time where King's core message would have meaning, it would seem to be today across the Inland Northwest.

For King opposed violence as a vehicle for social change. Though he was attacked, bombed and eventually assassinated, he steadfastly maintained that violence had no place in a democracy. King opposed hate. He based his non-violence on Christian teachings and spoke often of a time when people with different views and backgrounds could find a common ground.

King didn't counsel special rights, special treatment or special accommodations. An excellent student, he did so well in school that he skipped both ninth grade and 12th grade and went on to earn his doctorate in theology.

His crusade for giving blacks the right to vote, to be educated and be allowed access to the everyday commerce of America didn't assume that the oppressed wouldn't have to work or achieve.

This history isn't getting through very well. Just ask a school kid.

The things that Fukai talked about from his childhood in Spokane aren't part of the local history lessons. Many people who heard him speak had no idea what Spokane had been like.

These are some of the reasons *The Spokesman-Review* has sponsored several living history slide presentations by photo-journalist Flip Schulke.

Schulke photographed King for national magazines and eventually became King's most trusted photographer.

Schulke took pictures of America in the 1950s and 1960s when blacks couldn't vote, couldn't ride a bus, couldn't send their children to some schools.

He has documented a part of history and the deeds of a man who changed history. This history, this story, this part of America needs to be told and remembered.

Fukai helped Spokane remember the significance of Dr. Martin Luther King, Jr.

Our hope is that Flip Schulke can do the same.

Pointed cartoon showing Idaho kids in Klan hats had a point

Jaime Johnson, 16, attends Post Falls High School and has a black father.

She also has met with Milt Priggee, editorial cartoonist for *The Spokesman-Review*.

She seemed to be an ideal person to speak about the way young people in Idaho struggle with the label of residing in a bigoted state.

Jaime's outstanding connections and leadership skills at Post Falls High made her a good barometer for reactions to a Priggee cartoon that poked a pen at this image of Idaho as a home for bigots.

The cartoon showed the start of Junior Bloomsday. A kid in the front row is asking, "Did you see the kids from Idaho . . . ?" In the back of the race, some pointy Ku Klux Klan hats are visible.

"My classmates were bothered by the cartoon," Jaime said. "I know that they don't all think of themselves as racist."

And, of course, they aren't all racists. Not by a long shot. Idaho's young people reflect a wide range of attitudes about diversity, tolerance and the races.

Jaime says her personal experiences as a person of color at Post Falls High have been mostly good.

"Overall, my experience in high school has been great," she said.

Then she paused.

"But there are a few people that don't exactly have the same thoughts as the Aryan Nations, but who use the word 'nigger' and feel it is OK."

For a girl who is on the prom committee, who runs school fund drives, who considers most people her friends, the shock of this occasional hallway chatter still sets her back.

"Being a person of color, when I'm around people and they happen to say something like that, I look at them hard and say, 'I can't believe you said that.'"

And that's the tough part for many people in Idaho. It's hard to believe this state has developed such a bad reputation.

About 350 people from business, education and government showed up at a leadership forum to show their concern.

Speaker after speaker that night said Idaho's reputation as a haven for hate groups has now become a factor in business recruitment, a factor in the tourism industry, a point of discussion in federal and state government agencies.

And come to think of it, that reputation is why Priggee sharpened up his pen.

Of course, Priggee's cartoon was a gross exaggeration. That's the way of cartoonists. Take a little kernel from the news and stretch it, exaggerate it, push it to one side in the hope of making a point.

Cartoonists express outrageous opinions with a pen, opinions that are their own, like talk radio hosts or political columnists.

Milt Priggee doesn't speak for *The Spokesman-Review*.

In fact, the voice of this paper's editorial board consistently has praised Idaho's efforts to combat hateful words and despicable acts. The editorials have supported efforts of Governor Phil Batt to draft the toughest anti-harassment laws of any state. The voice of the paper has lauded the efforts of the Kootenai County Task Force on Human Relations and its work to counter hate messages that can be heard any day on the Idaho Aryan Hotline in Coeur d'Alene.

And in its news coverage, *The Spokesman-Review* has done more than any paper in the country to shine a light on the hate crimes perpetrated by white supremacists and their supporters in the region.

And we're going to do more to help this region confront and overcome its image as a hate-filled, intolerant place.

This year one of the paper's most important civic outreach efforts has been to help organize the Inland Northwest's first-ever Community Congress on Race Relations.

More than 20,000 groups and individuals have been sent letters asking them to come to the Spokane Convention Center to discuss ways this region can make a commitment to improve race relations.

After the leadership gathering in Coeur d'Alene, *The Spokesman-Review* contacted Doug Cresswell, the incoming chairman of the Kootenai County Task Force on Human Relations and volunteered to help the task force develop plans for changing the image of North Idaho.

And don't forget Jaime's reminder.

"I think Milt's cartoon kind of puts into a reality what a lot of people think about Idaho," she said. "The reality is that these Aryan Nations kind of people are right here, right next door."

For what it's worth, Priggee will go to North Idaho high schools and meet his critics face-to-face. His boss already has contacted the schools.

The more important discussions, however, won't involve a newspaper cartoonist and whether he should be strung up by the thumbs.

The important conversations must be among people across the Inland Northwest, who need to be talking right now about what it will take to confront the realities and then change the image of this misunderstood region.

Personal Views on Life, Family and Home

Chapter Seven

American Flyer boys outdo Lionel crowd

Strip away college degrees and inheritances, and the prominent differences between American men hinge on whether they grew up American Flyer or Lionel.

From 1906, when Lionel first produced its standard gauge electric toy train, until 1966, when the last, genuine American Flyer train was sold, the two titans of the tinplate lines warred for the loyalties of boyhood.

An American Flyer engineer since age 5, I feel qualified to briefly summarize the dissimilarities between men raised Flyer and those raised Lionel.

To begin with, the Lionel boys are bullies and brats.

They have outnumbered us Flyers for 60 years and all that time have delighted in reminding us how Lionel catalogs had more locomotives and a wider selection of boxcars.

No doubt these former Lionel boys drive only four-door sedans and eat corn flakes for breakfast – no flair at 5, no flair at 50.

Also, the Lionel boys undoubtedly have grown into gray, unimaginative types who go to Las Vegas and play on the nickel slot machines.

Their miserable caution goes back to the days when Lionel fathers told their Lionel sons not to run their expensive Lionel trains at full speeds around curves.

You see, Lionel trains always cost more than American Flyers and a lifetime of caution arrived in every peacock blue Lionel box, along with the 12 sections of tracks.

Finally, Lionel kids have a tendency to be I-told-you-sos.

American Flyer types have a penchant for speed and derring-do. Once our track went down, the dial of our transformers went to 120 miles-per-hour and we let 'em run.

Granted, this love of the crackling rails increased the American Flyer down time some Christmases.

Elmer's glue worked only so fast at repairing the die-cast mold of those Flyer locomotives that jumped the track on a curve and plunged off the ping pong table onto the hard, family room floor.

But we American Flyers learned from these experiences, something the Lionel I-told-you-sos could never fathom.

As a result of our upbringing, we Flyers understand the virtues – and dangers – of recklessness. When the big crash comes, count on the Flyers to pick up the pieces.

But enough of this historic nit-picking.

On one point, all boy trainmen will agree: Lionels and American Flyers served admirably as the preeminent toys for boys of any age.

Evidence of memorable toy train loyalties pop up every year.

Only a few days ago, for example, the Spokane American Flyers Club had a Christmas party. And these trainmen weren't kids.

"You're really not old enough to have a train until you are 30 or 40," Flyer aficionado John Kelley said before his party. Kelley's basement contains maybe the best American Flyer layout in Spokane, at least of post-war trains. Kelley is near retirement age.

About a dozen other old friends of Flyer ate cookies and talked trains in Kelley's knotty pine basement room, and they all said the same.

Trains were the toys they remembered most vividly from childhood.

And something else came through about toy trains.

"I bought my kid an American Flyer train when he was two years old," Ernie Horr, publisher of Spokane's little

American Flyer 'S' gauge newsletter, said at the party. "I thought he was old enough to enjoy it."

The truth was, Ernie was old enough to enjoy it.

That was the enduring attraction of trains. They were fun for dad.

They clanged and chugged and whistled and offered the right combination of mechanics and entertainment.

More than that, dad looked good when he put up the train.

Only he could haul the boxes out each Christmas and string the track together.

The trestles had to be fixed to each section; the cow-on-the-track and barrel loading accessories had to be wired; and lastly, the cars had to be unwrapped from the newspapers and placed in a certain order on the rails. That was all dad's work.

Trains carried on a tradition year to year. Father and son could talk over new accessories and then dad could make sure Christmas day was an instant success when the new electric switches arrived.

Yet, the people at the American Flyer Christmas party reflect the deep trouble in trainland.

Only one train buff under 20 was there to watch the old American Flyers.

In the toy stores, it's computerized Space Wars and talking chess boards that fill the shelves.

Business Week magazine, quoting a computer whiz in California, predicts the talking, bleeping computerized gizmos will become "the railroad trains of the '80s."

And where are the trains?

American Flyer is long gone. The last sets disappeared 10 years ago with the bankruptcy of A. C. Gilbert.

Collectors get up to $3,000 for the surviving trains.

Lionel bought the old American Flyer molds, but then General Mills, the cereal people, bought Lionel. Now Lionel is cheap and poorly marketed.

Now dad has to be into computers.

Maybe it's up-to-date, but it won't be as fun. And dad will feel dumb trying to learn computertalk – particularly Lionel men. They were never good at putting together stations on Christmas Eve.

Bah, humbug. Save the rec room for trains.

Fishing with dad following his open heart surgery

VANCOUVER, Washington – It was 5:30 a.m. and the guy in the next bed had been snoring for hours.

If it had been anyone but my father, I would have asked the desk clerk for my $22 back.

Not that we were registered at the Park Hilton.

Our roadside room was the kind where you should drink three beers in a hurry and pray for sleep. Otherwise, the diesels rolling down the highway a few centimeters from your bed might bounce you off the lumpy mattress.

And honestly, my father calling the geese in his sleep was, all things considered, one of the happiest sounds I can remember.

Exactly a year ago from that morning in the motel, I watched him being wheeled away to have his chest sawed open.

Thirty years in the newspaper business clogged three of his arteries and blocked 90 percent of the blood supply to the left side of his heart.

Surgeons last February had warned that the muscle in his chest might be damaged and the surgery was a life-giving necessity.

The day he left for the hospital, my father walked slowly from tree to tree at the place where I grew up, hugging each big cottonwood as he passed.

He and I planted those trees 24 years ago and the family half-believed he wouldn't be seeing his trees, or any of us, again.

A few mornings ago I knew better. There he lay, breathing with the regularity of a quartz watch at 5:30 a.m.

On the anniversary of his surgery, we ripped up our respective schedules, jumped a couple of airplanes and met at the banks of the Lewis River for two days of steelhead fishing.

It was odd, in a way. Sharing a flea-bitten room outside Vancouver, Washington, was decidedly outside each of our life patterns.

That's not to suggest we hadn't fished before. We had, a few times, on family vacations.

And we had *talked* about fishing for the big one for 20 years.

It's just that so often the trips had been postponed for things my father has taken most seriously: his job, his civic projects, breadwinning for his family.

Since he passed his serious-mindedness on to his son, recently it was I who seemed to set back the adventures to work on some column or other.

Who of us doesn't do that?

Life can be so time-consuming. First we have growing up to do. Then comes going to school and finding a spouse, making one's fortune.

And then one morning you discover your father has gone out to hug his trees and leave for the hospital not knowing if he will come back.

Then the numbers on the priority list inevitably start jumping around like Mexican beans.

Only then did I really begin to realize that the names in life stay the same, but the faces change.

Sons grow up, grow beards, move away. Fathers grow richer, more Republican, and one day call about the pains in their chests.

So you might say I considered myself fortunate at being kept awake at 5:30 a.m. by someone snoring in a shabby motel.

By some accident, by some twist of a surgeon's knife and turn of luck, my father and I understood that Christmas waders don't ever make it out of the box unless someone takes them out, puts them on and kisses off routines and patterns of the past.

Besides, the snoring ended at 6 a.m.

At that unsightly hour, we struggled into our soggy felt-lined boots and headed for Joyce's 24-hour cafe for a bowl of cereal and juice.

We made excuses to our guide about the fog being so thick we couldn't make it exactly at 5:30.

And then we were off down the river, squeezing live shrimp on our hooks, laughing about how anybody could think sitting in a boat in the drizzle at $100 a day could be fun.

For excitement, we swapped lies with other fishermen. For education, we worked on the fouled-up wads of fish line on our reels.

We spent too much money. We left on a moment's notice and didn't quite have our work done.

A person could ask what good it was.

As I sit here in my damp wool socks, rushing to get this down on paper, I can answer that one.

I can say that we were a father and a son who got lucky. The river still had a fish in it for us, and time hadn't quite slipped around the bend.

College roommate returns to rural roots

KAHLOTUS, Washington – The radio reception gave out just after the turnoff to Washtucna.

For 20 miles more, only the yellow line of a no-name highway bisected the faintly green winter wheat fields.

Finally, two pheasants and 90 minutes southwest of Spokane, the blue spruce trees of the Rice Ranch poked over the horizon.

The planning for my visit to the 6,000-acre wheat factory in Franklin County began 15 years ago.

I was a rural kid from Wyoming then, on my way to college in California.

My first friend was a precocious city boy from Seattle.

The son of a doctor, a high school quarterback for the Mercer Island Islanders, his name was John Rice, and the only thing he knew about the country came from summers spent at Rice Ranch.

John and I hit it off as few people ever do.

In the next four years, we broke away to adulthood together. We bought the motorcycles our parents didn't want us to ride; we went to the concerts they didn't think were music.

Many nights, we just stayed up late, talking about our families, our lives and, inevitably, Rice Ranch.

Though he never had lived there, Rice Ranch clearly was the place where John's rootstock had sunk deepest. The ranch is the place where his family reunions have been celebrated, where family deaths have been solemnized.

After college, my friend went to New York to pursue the dreams of an actor, masher and gadabout.

Yet every so often, the phone would ring late at night. John would be calling, and Rice Ranch once again would become the yeast of conversation starter.

One day, we vowed, we would get together at the bend in the Lind-Kahlotus Road.

One day in late October, we did.

John was standing in the driveway beneath the blue spruce trees when I pulled up.

I hadn't seen him in a year, maybe more. Polishing a newspaper career, investing in house payments, providing for the new baby don't leave much time for old friends.

John wasn't the best for staying in touch, either. His life has been charted by the wind, propelled by free spirit.

He's known a legion of attractive women, but hasn't found the perfect one.

He's waited a hundred tables, traveled cross country half a dozen times and won occasional rave reviews for his acting.

Yet at 33, he still hasn't cracked the nut that would allow him more than a six-pack of beer and a share of the rent.

But we hadn't come to Rice Ranch to share *curricula vitae*.

We were there as old friends, making good on a promise.

At the heart of Rice Ranch for the last 68 years has been John's grandmother, Emma.

Emma Rice came from the mold God used to turn out grandmas.

She arrived in the Washington wheat country in 1915, joining her uncle on his 160-acre homestead.

She and the country were equally young and exciting then. The farm boys came a-courting, the dances at the Sandhills Grange lasted late into the night and Emma always kept her dresses in a hotel room in Kahlotus so they wouldn't get dusty out on the farm.

At 86 Emma still had the good sense and good planning to have dinner ready the night I arrived – pickled beets, pork chops and homemade pies in plenitude.

It was the least she could do, she said. It was the way her generation always had made other generations feel at home.

After dinner, John and I walked off the last piece of pie and ice cream.

We began talking of the differences in generations and how time has a way of slipping away, of changing people, testing friendships and bending every stalk of wheat in between.

"This is the scene I remember most from childhood – every curve, every dip in the land," John said out in the stubble at sunset.

"There was a time when I thought this was so ugly, so barren. I couldn't wait to leave this place.

"But no more. Now, it's beautiful. You don't know how much it means to me."

For a moment, John wished times were earlier.

If only we had been there before harvest, to see the glory of the grain, the beauty would be more evident.

Then, he wished that time were slower. If we hadn't let the sun go down, we could have viewed the old barns in the light.

Finally, John wished that times simply were different. If his father hadn't moved away, if he hadn't seen the city lights, he might have taken another path that would have led him back to the land.

He began telling the stories of the family.

He talked about the meteorite hitting his grandfather's field and being carted away to Washington State University.

Down in the basement of the farmhouse, we searched the root cellar and found his grandfather's sweat-stained farm hats, still hanging untouched 10 years after his death.

John told me some very private things about his family.

It was a special, intimate moment for him, for us. For an instant, we again touched the magic of a true and lasting friendship.

Back upstairs, Emma told us of the contentment she had nurtured from spending 68 years on the ranch.

"You know, I really never thought about leaving this place," she said as her black poodle, Cinderella, jumped into her lap.

"I've never been hungry here. We always had our beef, our eggs, our chickens – even when we didn't have money. And we've had the land. I would never sell the land, no matter what."

On the way back home, I realized that Emma's life itself was what drew me – and, more importantly, my friend John – to Rice Ranch.

Emma's life was fundamentally different from ours.

At age 20, Emma had set her course, made her commitments.

Most conflicts between selfishness and responsibility, any delusions about when adolescence ended and "real life" began had been disposed of early in Emma's years.

She was to be a farm wife, living on the land, and she would dedicate her soul and energy to it.

The ranch, above all, was an example of the value of commitment and what it means to be a human being.

A few weeks have passed now, and John hasn't written.

I'm not sure where he is.

Our friendship once again has begun to show the strains of separation, of casual affiliation.

But before we left the wide, quiet spaces, he grabbed my arm and said, "Let's get together at the ranch again."

And to that, two old friends from the 1960s made a commitment.

Dad, *daughter survive head-on crash*

On a shining, sunny morning in May, my daughter and I came within an angel's breath of death.

The driver of the other car thought we could have been killed. Paramedics said circumstances suggested we should have been.

May 19, 1986, began as most days do for my family. Up at about 7 a.m., I shook off the sandman with a quick jog around the neighborhood. Then came breakfast, a shower and a word of encouragement to my 4-year-old that she not wear her tutu to preschool.

For the first time in weeks, Sarah and I left the house early. By 9:20, we were in the car.

At 9:25, less than a mile from home, somebody ran a stop sign. In the three-quarters of a second between the time I saw the car and the moment of impact, I swerved.

Good news. The twist of the wheel carried me away from the car careening through the stop sign.

Onlookers recounted the bad news. They said I swerved directly into the path of an oncoming van. We hit with a velocity of 50 miles-per-hour, head-on.

My head splattered against the windshield, splintering the glass into a spider-web nightmare. My legs jammed against the dashboard, fracturing my right hip in a star burst of broken bone.

In the back seat my daughter's head slammed forward. A sharpened edge gashed her forehead and cut through her eyebrow to the bone; blood gushed from her eye. Her tiny pelvis was fractured as the seat belt fought desperately to keep her body stationary and whole.

Neighbors rushed to the street. Someone had the good sense to call 911.

I lay unconscious on the front seat. Sarah screamed in terror in the back.

Until two Mondays ago, I subscribed to a kind of mid-30s macho view of life. Days weren't long enough to accomplish all that needed to be done. But no matter. Time could be stretched, extended. When job, family, friends or Bloomsday demanded extra attention, my answer was simply to get up earlier, work harder, push out the boundaries of living.

Death? No time to think of it. These were wine-and-roses days to revel in the energy that accompanies good fortune and health.

But today, my 14th in a hospital bed, I think less of pushing out the parameters of time. I lie, instead, listening to the sparrows and the wind in the trees. I revel only in salty-eyed knowledge that my girl and my broken body likely will heal.

CHRIS PECK

Over the years, I have not entertained many thoughts about the powers of a supreme being. But at this moment, while nursing a patchwork of bruises that could serve as a template for every protrusion inside a Volkswagen Rabbit, I wonder: "Why? What good fortune allowed me to live? How is it that my lovely daughter was spared when so many children in similar accidents are not?"

At Northwestern University, Dr. Thad Aycock's specialty is reconstructing automobile accidents. He can look at shattered glass, bent metal, scorched rubber, and determine how an accident happened and how people were injured.

But he couldn't tell me why I had survived.

"In any accident, there are so many variables that it is impossible to say why some people live and some do not," he said. "The speed at the moment of impact, the make of the cars involved, the direction of thrust after the crash – all of these things are factors."

Aycock says I probably was saved because my relatively new car was designed to absorb most of the impact of the crash while it collapsed like an accordion. And he speculated that I have a hard head.

He guesses the women in the other vehicle lived because they were wearing their seat belts.

And if we had died, well, Aycock wouldn't have blamed the automobiles. "Basically, we have the technology to design safe cars," he said. "Our problem is designing a foolproof driver."

Late at night, when I feel like 40 miles of rough road and the image of my child's torn face fills my memory, it is easy to fan the spark of animosity I feel toward the man who blew through the stop sign. Still, for all I know, his lapse may have been the only mistake he has ever made as a driver.

And have we not all committed the error of inattention behind the wheel? Maybe the kids are fussing or the dog is acting up or a pretty girl is walking on the sidewalk, and we have looked away. That's what gets us.

262

"I would guess that 90 percent of the accidents we see are the result of inattention on the part of a driver," Maynard Gillespie, a traffic analyst for the Spokane Police Department, said.

"Everyone is guilt of inattention at one time or another. Sometimes, an accident results."

We worry a great deal in this country about nuclear war, AIDS and living downwind from Hanford. Most of the time, we don't even think about getting into our cars.

Last year in the city of Spokane alone, 2,529 men, women and children were injured in car accidents. Seven people a day, every day of the year.

Good people, caring people, like Della Wright, who was driving the van I tried to flatten.

"I was driving to Ogden Hall (a shelter for battered women and unwed mothers) to wallpaper a room that our church sponsors there," Mrs. Wright said of the circumstances that had put her van on Boone Avenue that morning. "Our ladies' group had set money aside to help make Ogden Hall a little more cheerful.

"All of a sudden, I saw the car coming through the stop sign. I was concentrating on trying to get the van stopped when we hit."

Mrs. Wright suffered leg, chest and head injuries. Her passenger twisted her sciatic nerve, damaged her lower back and spent six days in the hospital.

Mrs. Wright says she thinks the accident may have been God's way of telling her she was trying to do too much.

"And I've become kind of a fanatic about wearing seat belts," she said.

I'm not sure what God was telling me. Except that I was lucky. That fate's hand may touch you at the most innocuous neighborhood intersection.

Life is precious. I am reminded each time I roll over in pain that it is never too soon to stop and kiss your daughter on the cheek.

Hospital nurses make it possible to recover

Allow me to sing praise to nurses.

Nurses who work nights, holidays and weekends. Nurses who manage to stay chipper even when the bedpan chirps.

Let me sound the hurrahs for all those nurses who, despite the high tech and high cost of medicine, hold fast to their mission of service to patients.

Just these kinds of nurses worked the fifth floor of Sacred Heart Medical Center during my recent recuperation.

Some, like Mary Messer, turned me when I couldn't roll over; others, like Debbie Williams, cheered me from the depths of the blues. And late at night, when I couldn't bear the solitude of my own heartbeat, the likes of Leon Keller or Earleen Uber came hustling after the buzz of a call button.

Since 1854 when Florence Nightingale organized 34 women to care for English casualties of the Crimean War, nursing has stood as the grandmother of what we now call "the service economy."

By the year 2000, labor analysts project, nine of 10 jobs in this country will be clustered under this heading. By century's end, almost everyone will be gone from the steel mills, automobile assembly lines and aluminum works.

Jobs in the service-driven economy will be based not on hard goods, but on soft people and their assorted problems and dreams.

In time, then, most of us will be introduced to the people-based perils and rewards that nurses have confronted for more than a century.

To look at nursing today is to view the challenges associated with service-based employment.

In many respects, service-sector jobs have been oversold. These jobs aren't easy, aren't necessarily rewarding and may carry a high degree of stress. Women familiar with nursing as a profession know the downside all too well.

And while new jobs in the service economy have grown, interest in nursing appears to be on the decline.

Look at applications to nursing schools: Nationally, the numbers are down 30 percent; in Spokane, applications for admission to the Intercollegiate Center for Nursing Education have declined, too. As recently as 1983, about 175 high-school graduates applied for fall admission to the nursing school. Last fall, however, only 120 applicants filled out the forms.

"We attribute a lot of this decline to the fact that other professions appear to be open to women and appear more attractive," said Pauline Bruno, associate dean of undergraduate studies for the center.

Rolling over IRAs for a bank apparently sounds more exciting to many bright young women today than the idea of turning patients.

"It is one end result of the women's liberation movement," said Jean Stevens, assistant director of nursing at Sacred Heart. "Women have grown more attracted to professions like banking, finance and law.

"And, of course, the hours for nurses never improve; and there is a fair amount of stress in the lifestyle."

The stress on nurses has risen on the same curve as technology and costs in medicine, according to nursing administrators.

"Today, nurses are dealing with patients who are much more acutely ill or injured than in the past," said Alice Hansberry, head nurse on Sacred Heart's 5-South wing.

Medical technology has advanced so fast that many patients who would have died 10 years ago are being kept alive now, but are seriously ill.

A spin-off of the new technology has been an inexorable rise in the cost of hospitalization.

Such luxuries as checking in patients for observation or rest or to obtain nursing care have disappeared. No one can afford such care now.

Patients who can leave the hospital do; patients who stay have little choice.

I learned this lesson firsthand. After my automobile accident, I couldn't walk or roll over. As a result, I was wheeled into a room with a man who suffered from diabetes and heart problems. The day I checked in, he answered the phone for me. The next day, he died in his bed as I watched in helpless horror.

For nurses, there clearly was no letup in the intensity of the work. So, perhaps, it is small wonder that nursing no longer attracts the numbers it once did.

The hours are long, the stress may be high – and there is always the question of money. After what often is four years of college course work in biology, chemistry and anatomy, a staff registered nurse at Sacred Heart can look forward to starting out at about $11 an hour. Add 81 cents if you work from 11 p.m. to 7 a.m. *[Ed. note: This column was written in 1986]*

From this perspective, banking, law or some brand of social-work consulting may look better.

But after having been in the company of nurses, I have to wonder if the work of data processors, bank vice presidents or divorce attorneys can possibly carry the same sense of purpose felt by the best nurses.

The services of nursing simply cannot be questioned. They are essential, vital and, at times lifesaving.

The person filling out your house-insurance form cannot say that. In fact, many of the service-sector jobs anticipated in the next 15 years strike me as non-essential and, perhaps, damaging to our society.

The raw commodity of the service economy is human need. The more screwed up our society can be made to seem, the more need we will have for consultants, experts and advisers.

To grow, the service-based economy requires our society to mine itself for more human deficiencies, more unmet needs. Thus, we have counselors for raising our pets, and we have more fast-food outlets offering square, round and double-thick hamburgers.

I fear that such an effort to find more and more needs will provide more jobs for more people to do less and less meaningful work.

And that is where nursing has an edge.

What nurses do matters. Their work isn't artificial. Nurses assist human beings in times of genuine crisis and pain.

Their success can be measured every day as they struggle one-on-one to help individuals deal with profound changes in their lives.

The core function of nursing matters more than finding somebody a high-yield mutual fund. The need for nurses is real; the service they render, priceless.

Just ask anyone who has been in a hospital.

Toy guns still toys and OK for boys

For my son the Christmas season has turned into a holiday of guns.

He has discovered candy canes make fine pistols.

Ski poles serve him well as rifles.

When we talk to Santa about his shopping list, my 3-year-old doesn't hesitate. "Guns," he says to anybody in a beard and red suit who inquires what he wants for Christmas.

For a father this raises troubling questions. Are guns compatible with peace on Earth, good will toward men?

A few days ago some members of Spokane's Peace and Justice Action League offered their statement about guns at Christmas. Standing in front of a big toy sore, these concerned parents passed out leaflets urging Santa's helpers to forgo war toys this year.

"I think it is very important that we attempt to teach our children to play more creatively," explained Nancy Nelson, mother of a 9-year-old boy who has never found a toy gun under the tree.

The Nelson family has concluded that war toys occupy a spot on the continuum that cascades from squirt gun to .22 to M-1 tank. "Playing with guns as a child made it a lot easier, simpler for me to find myself carrying a rifle in a combat situation," explained Rusty Nelson, father of the 9-year-old boy. "Everything just seemed to be a natural flow. You move up the scale: your cap pistol turns into a BB gun; your BB gun turns into your first .22 rifle. The mindset is all there."

It's Construx and kaleidoscopes for the Nelson kids this year.

But I'm not convinced.

As a kid, I took guns to Sunday school. In the summer no game could top a romp outside between the cowboys and outlaws who were my friends.

Thirty years later I haven't joined the National Rifle Association and don't own a Saturday Night Special.

So, for Santa's convenience I've come up with 10 reasons why I think it's acceptable to bring my boy a toy gun for Christmas:

1. He wants one. Popularity matters on Christmas morning. This day needs some magic and fulfillment. Nothing is sadder than a boy who rips open his special packages only to find a button-down shirt and a fruit cake.

2. It beats watching TV. Guns aren't the problem with childhood play these days, television is. Freewheeling, imaginative play has been supplanted by sedate video games and Saturday-morning cartoons. At least with a toy gun, a kid is likely to get up and run around.

3. Play time isn't political. For a 3-year-old, play means freedom from imposed rules. Fantasy is the key, not political correctness. If being a cowboy or policeman is part of the fantasy, it's normal.

4. Kids need to rid themselves of aggression. Peace is better and non-violent decision-making should win out by the time he turns 18. But when your big sister eats the last M&M and then shuts you out of her room, a boy feels the need to get the wiggles out by shooting a pop gun at the gremlins.

5. Other kids play the game. Don't make your child a social outcast. Imagine him standing up among his buddies and saying, "Sorry, guns kill people and I don't condone this childish activity."

6. Playing with guns can be morally instructive. Every kid remembers pointing a toy gun at his mom who then said, "Don't point guns at people you don't want to kill." Elementary peacemaking begins.

7. Guns are part of learning about good guys, bad guys. Kids divide up their world into a place of us versus them. These simple divisions aren't a sign of a budding Hitler, but appear to be the first, tentative steps toward trying to figure out right and wrong, good and evil. Besides, kids take turns being bad guys and good guys. Don't we all?

8. Kids who play with toy guns rarely turn into killers. To assume a connection supposes too much. Playing with blocks doesn't suggest a career in architecture.

9. Parents shouldn't be anxious. A worst option for mom and dad is to suggest to a kid that his playing with guns makes him a bad example of humanity. Growing up is hard enough

without carrying around a suitcase of guilt handed down from your parents.

   10. Men inevitably learn about guns. Hiding away toy guns won't change a world that is overstuffed with weapons much worse. Rather than shield your child, try to direct him. Just as sex education should begin at home, so should discussions about violence and war.

Before the gun nuts send me a box of ammo for the holidays, I think it important to note that when my son grows up I hope he doesn't fight a war.

On Christmas Eve I pray for his embrace of Christian ethics.

My dream for him would be that our planet one day will be free of strife and aggression.

And because of the words and example I expect to give him as he grows, I fully anticipate his adult energy will be directed to the side of secure, peaceful coexistence and non-violent conflict resolution.

But this Christmas, he's a little boy.

His ripe imagination predates Rambo by a thousand years. A boy experiments with moral identities. Such acting out probably allows him to progress toward his adult self.

If Santa brings him a bit of plastic for playing bang-bang, I don't think my son's life will be the worse for it.

Working in basement with son, Cody

My son, Cody, pounds nails like a journeyman.

He and I have been practicing in the basement the past few nights.

Nail-pounding with a 4-year-old has given me a Fulghumesque view of the world.

Working in basement with son, Cody

Robert Fulghum is the Seattle minister-turned-philosopher who wrote the book, *All I Really Need to Know I Learned in Kindergarten.*

Close, Bob. But it starts earlier – at age 4 in the basement.

Or maybe the learning comes later, like at 39 when you are a dad and see again what it is like to be very, very young.

Fulghum made a million on his book and homey advice. All I'm hoping for is to end up with a spare bedroom for my mother-in-law.

But even if the walls aren't square and the dry wall is dented, I have learned much down there. So has my son. We have hit on some eternal truths that don't bend no matter how hard, or how badly, we hit at them.

To begin with, we've learned that boys are different from girls.

We're talking a whole different wiring. Different blue-prints. Wholly different materials from top to bottom.

That's not sexism – it's plain fact.

Girls don't go down to basements to pound nails.

They go down to look, yes.

They go down to play "Star Wars" in the storage closet; they even go down to climb around the stud walls and shinny up the posts.

But then they go back upstairs.

Boys hang around at dinner time waiting to get going. And they are there until the very end of the work night, long past bedtime.

My boy first lines up the hacksaw, screwdriver, wrecking bar, level, drill, chisel, claw hammer and pliers on a work bench. Then he picks out a handful of nails without complaining about the pokes in his palm and proceeds to pound.

This is fun. This is life's work. This beats Barbies and stuffed animals all to heck.

"Glasses on!" one of us calls when the Skil saw whirs and the sawdust flies.

271

CHRIS PECK

That's the next thing about working with a 4-year-old. A kid would just as soon learn the right way to do things. You tell a 4-year-old kid to put on the goggles and he does it. Kids assume, for a while, that you know what you are talking about.

But don't let them down.

I didn't put the goggles on.

In a hurry and being a big macho dad, I just cut into a 6-by-6 beam with the whirling saw and promptly inherited two eyes full of dust and wood chips.

Staggering upstairs, I rinsed my eyes and then struggled through a restless night. The next day the doctor assured me I would have to wear an eye patch for only 24 hours.

"Why didn't you wear your glasses, Dad?" Cody asked when I came home with the patch.

Why? Because when you grow up, you sometimes forget the basics. You speak them but you don't practice them.

Don't drink and drive, you tell your kids. Then you proceed to get smashed on New Year's Eve and swerve the car home.

Put things back where they belong, you say. Then you spend half the night searching the shop for the tape measure.

Wear your safety goggles, you say, squeezing the trigger on the saw. Then you end up wearing an eye patch until the antiseptic wash flushes the dust from your sockets.

Kids see that. They want to be just like you. So is it any wonder that people sometimes turn out less than perfect?

The other night Cody pounded his thumb. His flesh turned the color of grapes.

We talked about what had happened.

The hammer was too big for him. Pounding nails takes practice. And you have to pay attention to what you are doing.

Kissing it makes it better, we decided.

Each night, we listen to the news on the radio. There are many sad stories out there.

The news often tells of ruined lives, of people who end up cheating and stealing rather than working and earning.

Wasted lives that have sunk into the endless maze of drugs or alcohol rather than the comfort of love and friendship.

Short-circuited lives that come up short after somebody has dropped out of school, married too early or beaten up his own children.

Many people don't figure out the basics of the basement.

At 4 years old or at 40, and probably at 80, the basics remain the same.

Find someone you love and work next to him or her.

Take pleasure in what you do and try to do it well.

Sweep up. Plan ahead. Take a break when you are tired.

Be good to yourself.

And wear your goggles.

Best friend's third wedding

In Coeur d'Alene a few nights ago, the best man at my wedding was married.

This was his third time down the aisle.

Third weddings draw smaller crowds.

More kids attend.

The men have less hair; the women, more wrinkles at the eyes.

Everyone is relaxed. They know the script. They have lived it.

Raising a toast at dinner, I suggested the third time could be the charm. And why not?

The three-point shot counts most in basketball.

Three goals in a hockey game make you a star.

Then somebody shouted, "Yeah, but what about baseball and three strikes?"

Nervously, the mother-in-law laughed.

A friend's third wedding offers this reminder: never bet on how long love will last, when passion will flicker and die or when a new romance will sweep someone away again.

The odds aren't in your favor when guessing about affairs of the heart.

Third weddings suggest a stubborn optimism. Sure, people grow distant, separate and cry. But very soon, the human heart starts it all over again if possible.

Coco Chanel said there is nothing worse than the solitude of growing old without a shoulder to lean on. Marry, marry, she said, even if he's fat and boring.

Most of us follow that advice.

Eight marriages a day, on average, unfold in Spokane. And check the pictures of the newly united. Not everybody looks like Clark Gable or Marilyn Monroe.

It's not the marrying that's tough. It's the staying together. For every eight marriages, there are six divorces.

Why?

"I think the Lord intended us to go two-by-two," said family counselor Jannette Murray of the Life Directions Counseling Center in Spokane.

"But the fact is 95 percent of the population is dysfunctional to some degree in their human relationships."

The good news is that we all need somebody to love.

The bad news is we cannot master the art.

Murray says she believes the decisions we make about finding a mate spring from early experiences in life. We look around, observe our parents and build from there.

"Very often in patterns of marriage, work and friends, we attract someone who has many of the positive and many of the negative qualities of our own parents," Murray said. "We are kind of programmed that way.

"Then we adopt a role. We continue to attract people who allow us to play out our script. Unless we do some kind of reprogramming to change our patterns, most of us will go on our whole lives attracting the same kinds of people."

Maybe that's why my friend married a woman this time who shares many characteristics of the woman he married last time.

I have an optimist's view of my friend's new commitment. Everyone is more experienced this time around. The couple went into this with eyes open. They checked out the pluses and minuses of the relationship. I think it will work.

Counselor Murray also takes an optimistic view of love and relationships. "Really, you often have to go through some relationships to wake up to what is going on."

"Balance" is the word she uses to describe what keeps love and marriage alive.

"You can't give everything of yourself trying to make other people happy," she said of good relationships. "And, on the other hand, you can't look to someone else to fulfill every one of your own dreams.

"The key is finding a balance."

Often, there isn't much equality or balance or sense of sharing.

Look around your neighborhood, at your friends, your family. The inequities are out there like so many leaning towers of Pisa.

Over-nurturing women are trying to give everything of themselves to prove their worth. On the other end are suffocated men and children.

Distant husbands and lovers, addicted to their bottles, jobs or golf games, build walls to keep their feelings encased.

Co-dependent couples feed each other's habits, put up facades, make excuses, pour it all into civic duty, but don't tend the fire back home.

It might get kind of discouraging, except that we know that feeling loved and offering love, when it happens, make it worth it.

For Valentine's Day Jannette Murray's advice on love is rather simple: begin to speak truthfully to your partner and don't be so hard on yourself.

"You've got to get yourself into shape to save a relationship," she said. "If you aren't working on your own growth and sense of self-esteem, it won't happen.

"And the most important thing to do is open up the lines of communication. Whether things have been strained or not, whether you have a family that is or isn't warm or loving, go ahead and hug your dad or your mom or your husband. Say 'I love you.'"

My friend did just that. And I think this time it's going to stick.

Being a man in a suit isn't all that easy

The worst label to sew on a man these days is "just a suit."

The words often are spit out like a bad mouthful of bananas on a man's overstarched shirt.

I wear a suit most days of the week.

And I am paranoid every time I hear somebody talking about "a suit."

"Suits" just don't get it, the implication goes.

They are hollow, polyester shells with nothing inside but uptight, white, guy assumptions of who's in charge.

"Suits" get bricks from all quarters.

Women have had more than a full dose of their stiff-as-cardboard exteriors.

Co-workers grouse about privileged existences accorded the suits.

Upstairs, the CEOs grumble that their once loyal ranks of men-in-blue just aren't as loyal as they once were and that nobody in a suit, top-dogs included, gets much respect anymore.

But then, why should he? The case can be made rather convincingly that white guys in suits have a history of building a society that largely rewards the same.

And for that "the suits" are resented.

Yet on some levels men in suits already sense this.

In areas of culture and family life the suits are beginning to pick up the signals that maybe they should be tuned into a different frequency.

They worry that *Wayne's World* might not be a movie about an old cowboy named John. They at least wonder exactly who Wynnona is.

And, because men in suits have kids and wives and contacts with life outside the pin stripes, it has begun to dawn on many of them that they just may have lost touch with what really is happening and what really matters.

They feel the stares when the kids are busy watching two hours of music videos per day when they suggest somebody switch channels to public TV's *Nature* show.

They turn a little sheepish when a woman starts talking about Deborah Tannen and a "suit" makes a comment that suggests he thinks Tannen is a kind of yogurt.

Marching off behind ties with the knots a little too tight, most "suits" occasionally try to fill their minds with something other than tepid thoughts about mutual funds.

As they are buttoning themselves into a life of male competition, dragon slaying and toughing it out, they wistfully think of being sensitive, nice and in touch with their feelings.

A recent Roper survey of men's attitudes found that a full 71 percent of guys in suits really want to be more concerned about home, children and being sensitive.

Good intentions live in suits. But, of course, the people who criticize "suits" quickly point out the difference between the good intentions and real actions. And that's why "just another suit" has become so pejorative a term.

Not long ago I heard Tom Kochman, author of *Black & White: Styles in Conflict*, discuss why many white males are having a tough time getting much sympathy or understanding from almost anybody.

Kochman suggests the reason is that "suits" still put great value on good intentions, while a lot of other folks are looking for genuine change.

As a result, Kochman theorized, many men these days are stuck between wanting to change and not knowing how or why.

Men in suits want to be liked. They want to have their intentions respected. Yet they also want to defend much of what they have achieved and believe to be right about their management of the world.

Still, they also are often lonely, often dissatisfied with the materialistic, sterile aspects of their lives, and would like to change.

But where is the balance between the best and most alluring parts of modern man's life, and the shift to something that connects more with a world outside the suit?

These guys are trying to dance ballet in their wing tips.

They are experimenting with cooking up a new, sloppy spaghetti of life in clean white shirts.

They want to lambada in their ties, cuddle their children in a sports coat. They are drumming with their designer pens.

And even when they get close to really changing or really talking or really getting in touch, they will be apt to run and put on the suit.

Maybe it's a T-shirt and jeans, but "the suit" effect is one well-known to most men, a kind of armor where nothing gets to you.

Inside that gray flannel I think something is trying to burst out for a lot of these guys.

Maybe that's why they have taken to unbuttoning the tops of their shirts and wearing flowers on their ties.

How to keep the Christmas tree from falling over

I am looking at my new Christmas tree stand.

Emptying out the box, I count nine red and green pieces.

Only one piece is missing.

The piece that guarantees the stand will hold a tree upright.

True, this is a bargain stand purchased for $1.99 at The General Store in Spokane.

No matter.

That same crucial piece has been absent from stands I have purchased for $12.99, or more.

The Trilateral Commission secretly has been removing these critical pieces for years. It's their way of destabilizing American households from within.

And it's working.

Each year hundreds of holidays end in tears, ruin and divorce after parents come to blows over whether the tree is standing straight.

The walls of my garage are hung with sad reminders of my shattered American dream.

All of us have dreams. Mine is to enjoy one Christmas where friends and relatives can actually sit near the tree without fear of having to yell "Timber!"

I browse yard sales for Christmas tree stands.

In the heat of July I hoard them, believing I have stumbled upon the secret to conifer perpendicularity.

In the cold, dark days of December I learn their enduring, angular truth.

This is not a new vexation. As early as the 1600s, Germans were decorating Christmas trees in their homes.

Volumes of tragic, violent tales written by the Brothers Grimm suggest the seriousness of the childhood traumas suffered by young Germans back then as they struggled to cope with the tilting, listing and falling down of their sacred symbols.

Why haven't the engineers who sent men to the moon or made Barbie talk been able to devise a stand that holds a tree straight?

For the answer I sought out a Christmas tree stand expert, Bill Barany.

Since 1947, Bill has sold Christmas tree stands at The General Store.

He founded the store. His business has increased every year, as the public determinedly looks for the more perfect stands.

I found Bill hanging out near the Christmas tree stands a few days ago.

I sought his wisdom.

"I've had the same Christmas tree stand for 35 to 40 years," Bill said.

This weekend he will get it out once again. He expects no trouble.

I inquired how he was able to achieve this blissful state.

He began at the place where most of us remain: terrified that the tree won't stay erect.

"Sure, I remember the days when the kids knocked over the tree, the dog knocked over the tree, and the cat. Maybe even me," he said of the time long ago when he was plagued by unstable, off-center greenery.

"And what wife doesn't always have a suggestion on which way the tree needs to be tipped? They are all budding engineers," Bill went on.

"You see, there are basically two types of Christmas trees," he said. "Wild trees and cultured trees."

In my mind I saw a wild tree, bucking, twisting and wearing cowboy boots.

"Wild trees have narrow trunks," Bill said.

During the early part of this century most Christmas tree stands were built for wild trees, with narrow trunks, because that is what people went out and cut.

In time, we decided to stay home during holiday weekends and watch *It's a Wonderful Life* 43 times in a row.

That eliminated any time for stalking the wild fir. Now, we mostly run to the vacant lot and buy a cultured tree from a commercial grower.

"Cultured trees have wide trunks," Bill Barany explained, pointing to the fattened bare end of a domesticated Christmas tree outside The General Store. "And they are four times heavier than a wild tree."

But people still try to cram their cultured trees into the stands built for their wild cousins.

It doesn't work.

The stands wobble. The bows fade to one side.

Christmas ornaments crash and shatter.

Bill Barany won't buy a cultured tree.

"I hate them," he said. "They are so dense you can't hang anything in them."

This weekend Bill will travel to North Idaho, tromp through the powdered snow and cut his own wild tree to match his wild tree stand.

And is that his secret? No.

"I put a screw in the ceiling and tie a string from the top of the tree right into it," Bill admitted.

"I leave that screw up there all year. Who's going to see it? It's the best thing I know to keep the darn tree from falling over."

Beware the perils of home repair

The day began as a handyman's special.

Climbing the ladder to repair the rain gutter proved uneventful.

Nothing untoward happened with the garage trash.

But replacing the 10-cent washer in the shower?

That task will forever remind me of the limits of doing it yourself, the possibility of dying when you least expect it, and the value of living in the midst of the most expensive, but most accomplished health-care system in the world.

The plumber had looked at the dripping shower faucet a few months ago. "Needs a new seat," he said "But you can get by if you replace the washer every few weeks."

The sound of running water, so pleasant when out in a tent, had begun to keep us awake at night.

In the basement last Sunday I found a package labeled "bathroom repair kit."

A few trips up and down with wrenches, screwdrivers and washers resulted in an almost-fixed faucet.

The car already was packed for a last trip the lake. My wife had gone for groceries. I was at home with four kids under age 12.

I decided to take a shower.

Too soon, victory had been declared.

As I twisted the cold water off, the leak returned with a contemptuous drip-drip-drip.

The "get a bigger hammer" mind-set quickly kicked in.

With my right hand I pushed down hard on the handle. Bigger hammer. Brute strength. Man's will would prevail.

I don't remember the sound of the porcelain handle snapping off.

My mind focused only on the blood gushing and numbness in my fingers as the jagged edge ripped into the muscle, vessels and nerves of my palm.

Horror movie crews would have loved the scene. Blood from the severed artery spurted all over the shower curtain, the walls, the floor and the towels.

My feet were bloody. The carpet to the bedroom was marked by a bloody Hansel-and-Gretel trail of drips.

But I had to dress. A person simply cannot show up nude in the emergency room.

I was sick and lightheaded. My father always faints at the sight of blood. I felt I was my father's son.

I struggled into shorts and a T-shirt and called the Group Health urgent care center. "Can you be here in 15 minutes?" the voice in the care center asked.

If I were to make it to the hospital, someone would have to drive. But who? My 8-year-old son? The dog?

Later I would think of the difficulties faced by single parents or the elderly when they confronted a personal disaster or accident and had no one to help. I knew how scared and alone these people could feel.

In my truck I turned on the air conditioner to keep the sweat cool on my forehead.

I yelled in pain as I drove. Other drivers probably thought I was singing. This was dangerous, not just for me, but for them if I passed out.

At the care center they knew right away that this wasn't a Band-Aid-and-aspirin injury.

Their assessment was quick and sure. Call the surgeons, now.

The surgeons, like most of the rest of the Inland Northwest, had gone to the lake. Dr. Gerald Olmsted was relaxing at his Hayden Lake vacation home when the phone rang.

Patient with severed artery, numbness in fingers, bad flesh wound.

Dr. Olmsted said he would get cleaned up and drive to the emergency room.

My problems weren't the worst the staff in ER saw that afternoon. A transient had been stabbed. A pregnancy had developed complications.

The nurses told me to lie down and be patient.

A friend who is a doctor came in to see if he could help. He did.

My wife, after quickly cleaning up the blood in the carpet, managed to find a place for the kids, for the food in the cooler and for my truck.

She gently removed my wedding ring so it wouldn't be lost in surgery.

The thought of losing the use of a hand wasn't conducive to calm and patience.

I cried about it. How could I type? Play the piano? Hold my kids?

The doctor arrived from the lake and quickly tried to put my mind at ease. Nerves grow back one inch a month, he said.

283

The good news was I didn't need a blood transfusion and drugs would allow me to never remember the operation.

Five days later in his office, Dr. Olmsted took off the dressing and we looked at the pair of two-inch long incisions in my hand.

The 70 or so stitches had been used to sew up an artery, re-attach nerves to my thumb and index finger, stitch up the muscle and close my palm.

"It looks good," the doctor said.

I nearly threw up.

But I didn't. Nor did I bleed to death, ignominiously, in the shower.

I managed to type this into the computer with a bandaged, numbed right hand.

I've learned to tell the story with some humor.

Life has its abrupt and dangerous moments. What can we do but shrug and laugh and simply go on?

The worst part is the faucet still drips.

What love is, 18 years into a marriage

After a long day in real life I sat with my wife and ate a piece of Valentine's Day candy at midnight.

This sweet celebration at home marked 25 years of Valentine's Days spent together.

The quiet while kids were sleeping was the best gift we had.

In the living room, we took the opportunity to simply talk and reflect on the years and the tears and the triumphs.

After 25 years we're savvy to the hype and sugar high wrapped up in pop culture's cellophane packaging of love.

We've been there, done that: beautiful places, romantic dinners, and all the rest.

When time, money and a babysitter allow, we still get away.

But we know it's not room service or red wine that has held us together.

As any couple who has stuck with it will attest, only the heavy lifting of a relationship keeps it fit.

This isn't the message most people pick up about love and marriage.

From Boyz II Men to the various versions of *The Bridges of Madison County*, the boy-meets-girl story line generally begins with a passionate kiss and ends on a bended knee and a diamond.

Wonderful and essential as these moments are, they don't reflect reality or even the greatest rewards of a marriage.

That's why a bill being promoted by Washington state Senator Lorraine Wojahn this session appeals to me. In her bill Senator Wojahn attempts to write something of a reality check on marriage licenses.

"Marriage is not easy," Wojahn explained from her home in Tacoma a few days ago. "To succeed you have to work at it, and many people don't want to do that. They think if it doesn't work out they can just get out."

Senator Wojahn has asked the Legislature to pass a bill that would add these words to every marriage license issued in the state:

"The laws of the state of Washington affirm your right to enter into this marriage and at the same time to live within the marriage free from violence or abuse. Neither you nor your spouse is the property of the other.

"The laws against physical abuse, emotional or psychological abuse, sexual abuse and battery and assault, as well as other provisions of the criminal law of this state, are applicable to spouses or other family members."

Married herself for nearly 50 years before her husband died two years ago, Senator Wojahn acknowledges her bill is primarily designed to alert women to the dangers of domestic violence.

ChRIS PeCK

She hopes the sober wording on marriage licenses will cause prospective newlyweds to consider a full range of responsibilities and expectations.

"When you marry someone, it's serious business," she said. "When things get tough – and they will – you have to learn to listen to the other person, to see the other person's side."

Many people who get married forget these components.

They seem to approach their relationships much the way my seventh-grade daughter does: through what Paul McCartney called all the silly love songs.

Boyz II Men, Melissa Etheridge and Bon Jovi sing them these days. The themes remain as eternally shallow as a first heart throb.

One true love will make life wonderful and romantic forever.

A kiss and a full moon are all we need.

Right. But as Senator Wojahn noted, "shouting has its purpose, too."

Shouting, fighting, orneriness, vexation, frustration, giving in, not giving in, being told to sit down, pipe down, grow up, shut up, all these are part of a vital, enduring marriage.

For some, these struggles do lead to a loss of affection that propels people separate ways.

For others, the struggles build a foundation for an enduring and deepening partnership.

No question, some couples should be divorced and try again.

But in his best-selling book, *Care of the Soul*, Thomas Moore describes the difference between trying to fix, change or adjust life to perfection, versus remaining patiently in the present, close to life as it presents itself imperfectly day by day.

The first course, I'm convinced, can lead couples rather quickly to conclude they cannot stand their partners or their lives.

The second option leads, in time, to a soulfulness in a marriage, a Valentine's chocolate at midnight.

286

Deck project true indicator of summer

My most cherished bric-a-brac at the lake appears to be nothing more than a few weathered strips of moulding, shortened lengths of 2x4 and fragments of pine board.

These treasures lie, like untrained country kittens, beneath the almost-level deck my friend Ted Wert and I built 11 years ago on a cabin overlooking Lake Pend Oreille.

Over the years, the valuables have been collected from a variety of soon-to-be-finished projects: new patio doors, an enlarged window in the bedroom, the last of trying to hide the mistakes of an early addition.

At the end of these sweaty, not-quite-long-enough weekends, a few odds, ends and irregulars always remained scattered like puzzle pieces from these projects.

In town these leftovers would be trash.

At the cabin they must be viewed as opportunities for next year.

Now, next year is here.

Memorial Day weekend officially opens the season of good intentions at a cabin.

You could hear the gearing up of these good intentions from Harrison to Priest River.

Chainsaws whined, hammers banged, pick-up trucks laden with uncovered loads from last year's mess or carrying new materials for this year's project sped along the country roads, their happy captains of industry at the wheel.

This year, I simply went to the stash beneath the deck.

First came the work of plugging up the chewed-through hole where squirrels gained entry into what I'm sure they considered the Pend Oreille Hilton.

Through the winter, the squirrels managed to transport 50 pine cones from nature to the dresser drawers.

When my wife arrived at the cabin, the squirrels were none too happy to see her.

I thought for a moment the BB gun might be employed. Instead, loud shouting and the careful insertion of a cedar shingle across the opening of the rafters seems to have reclaimed the cabin for human habitation.

Next came a search for bon fire fodder and a suitable s'more stick.

The season's first campfire with s'mores could not be constructed until the fire pit had been cleaned and a combustible teepee constructed with more of the old shingles.

Once the fire raged, the s'more stick would provide the necessary safety gear to keep children from singeing off their eyebrows in pursuit of a crisper crust for a marshmallow.

But the most important, compelling and uplifting use of those remainders from projects past comes when they are used to sketch out projects yet to come.

This summer, the project talk runs to more deck.

Did you know decks are the hottest do-it-yourself project in America? And have you ever seen a cabin with too much deck? The first rule of building a deck remains constant: lay out the plan before you begin to build or buy.

Nothing assists in the planning of a deck at a cabin like a large supply of old boards, planks and mouldings.

Every design can be imagined as these pieces of past projects are pulled from the pile and placed along an imagined perimeter.

A level, a carpenter's string and batterboards might make this planning more exact.

But a project at a cabin on the first weekend of the season isn't about exactness or being plumb and square.

It is about possibilities.

This is not work you have to do, but long to do.

A project laid out with a few old boards relies on the mind and imagination, where friends are gathered at sunset, laughing and raising a toast to that new deck.

Over the weekend I laid out a dozen different designs.

At the end of the holiday I left my favorite outline lying there as a small memorial to big plans at the beginning of the summer.

Of course there is a boat to get in.

Bushes need trimming.

Fishing season is heating up.

My son wants to hike to the top of the ridge and my daughter wants to spend more time at Silverwood.

So, the odd boards lying there atop the pine needles may be the reminder of a new deck I see this season.

But summer is young and the possibilities boundless in those old boards.

Landscape isn't the same after mother's death

My mother's car rolled on a desolate stretch of Wyoming highway where the wind blows 50 and trucks drive 70.

The empty, rutted highway east of Rawlins is remarkable only because most drivers press hard on the accelerator, hoping to speed their way beyond the God-forsaken plains where my mother died. She never looked at it that way.

In a poem she wrote a few years ago, printed on the back of the funeral bulletin passed out at the Riverton Methodist Church last week, she said this of the place where she had lived:

> *I know you, Wyoming.*
> *I know your boundless, spreading plains,*
> *Your forsaken outposts with forgotten flames.*
> *I know your silvered Rocky peaks;*
> *I know your wind that ever speaks.*
> *Antelope running,*
> *Sunflowers sunning,*
> *Buttes and bluffs standing by,*

Larks thronging the splendid sky,
In boot and brim I ride the rim,
'Mid sage and painted flowers,
Grateful to the Giver,
For my Wyoming hours.

She admired poetry and read all the greats.

People didn't expect this from someone who lived 69 years within 50 miles of the place she was born, a place better known for deer and Yellowstone than Dickinson and Yeats.

Born in 1926, my mother grew up on cattle ranches without benefit of TV, movies or neighborhood amusements.

Looking out across the high plains stretching east from the Wind River mountains, she saw no lights and few signs of humanity.

This magnificent isolation became the subject of her stories and conversation with all her children.

On the morning of her funeral I arose from the bedroom where I slept 40 years ago and looked out the window at the plains and mountains she had imagined and described to me.

I recognized the place. Yet, it was altered.

The death of one's mother changes the landscape. What once seemed familiar suddenly seems changed.

The inevitability of biology makes good the chance that each of us in our adult lives will get a telephone call that begins, "I have some bad news."

A week after I received the phone call I am stunned by the intensity of this unavoidable, but somehow unanticipated event.

It is the mirror opposite of the birth of a child.

As a wedding inflates the future, this deflates it.

Memories that once seemed ordinary, now ache with meaning: this was my mother's bedroom; here are my mother's shoes; these were the spices my mother used to cook dinner.

I went into her closet and felt her sweaters.

I rifled her purse and took her library card for my wallet as a reminder of her love of books.

I dabbed my eyes with her handkerchief to remember her fragrance.

All last week the aunts, uncles and cousins kept saying something good could come of this.

And some has.

For three nights the families who live in New York, California and Wyoming laughed late into the night telling family stories.

New generations of children were introduced to family tales and listened in rapt amazement.

My daughter learned each of her uncles was a first-chair, all-state musician.

My son learned most men in his family had a decent jump shot when we all played a game of patio basketball.

Each of us who had let the years go by without enough correspondence or contact learned the value of staying close as a family.

Long-ago slights didn't matter anymore. The time had come to heal festering wounds.

This is an indulgence, writing about my mother. She wouldn't have liked it much. She would rather keep her private life out of the papers.

But mourning requires some outlet.

Some people will play music when their mother dies. Some will run or knit or drink.

I could write this.

It was a comfort. It was a bit of the old world that seemed familiar.

I wrote it in the small-town newspaper office where my father and brother come every day, where my mother picked up the mail, where I thought as a child all the world unfolded as it should.

The world changes.

The wind blows more bitterly cold in Wyoming than I remembered.

291

Finishing 50th in All-City race

Recently my son finished 50th at the Spokane All-City Cross Country Meet.

He was thrilled.

His mom and dad were thrilled.

We celebrated 50th place with hearty congratulations at the dinner table.

Still, no one is thinking college scholarship to the University of Oregon for distance running.

There can be no secret about the fact that 50th place is exactly 49 kids away from first.

My son's friend and classmate Garrett Mandeville finished in the mid-30s for their age group.

Matt Oye, a really fast kid from Garfield School, was second among the fifth-grade boys.

Katie Johnson, a sixth-grader from Hutton Elementary has won her all-city age group for six years in a row. She got her picture in the paper.

So, finishing 50th and being happy about it required some thought and explanation. Honestly, the life lessons related to finishing 50th can come none too soon.

Most of adulthood, it turns out, revolves around 50th place finishes.

The moments of going for the gold and actually grabbing the medal are few.

Thankfully, so are the boos and hisses of being a total failure.

More often, we all live in that gray zone where people say, "Good try." It's not easy to explain winning and losing in the same breath. Yet often, that's what we face in our lives.

To help understand what lessons can be learned from making all-city and finishing 50th, I went to an expert.

Kathy Blatt, elementary cross country coach and school librarian, has held the hands of hundreds who have tried yet not wholly succeeded to be the stars of running around the schoolyard.

"What I tell them is that they hung in there," Blatt explained. "They came to all the practices; they finished every race; and that's quite an accomplishment by itself."

A pearl of wisdom here, possibly a cultured pearl, but a pearl worthy of being strung for use later in life.

Simply showing up for life's daily run gives us the best chance of winning or doing well.

A whole lot of people never manage to show up.

They are too scared, too lazy, too hung up on the odds they will fail.

They freeze. They don't struggle to take a step. And this isn't just about kids running round the schools.

Blatt continued. "I also try not to stress the winning," she said. "Throughout life there are going to be a few times when you are number one and lots of times when you are not. So, we try to have some fun, try to get into good condition."

Another pearl suitable for later life. It isn't the winning, but the game, the practice, the striving to succeed that finally matters.

Following your passion is more important than getting a law degree, unless law is that passion. If the road to success is only a grind, an ulcer and a chore, the victory lap will be bitter and empty. "There really is nothing worse than a bad winner," Blatt observed.

Before the all-city qualifying runs, however, Blatt must tell her young and aspiring athletes that they do have to run fast.

The kids get three chances to finish in the top seven in competition with kids from half a dozen other schools.

Those that make it go on. Those that finish eighth or below do not.

At that point, if a kid's peer group says this is dumb, many kids drop out.

If parents say it's too cold, kids will bail.

But if kids say let's do it, and parents and teachers chime in, the race will be run.

Running a mile isn't really all that much fun as a kid.

Nor is taking the night shift or working weekends and holidays.

But most people who eventually make a success of themselves run the races time and again, even when the weather isn't perfect, the kids ahead of you are faster and a snack is waiting at home in front of the TV.

It's the same race that begins with doing your math homework in seventh grade and going to college thanks to a good score on the SATs.

My son finished 50th on the night the St. Louis Cardinals were blown out in the last game of the National League Championship Series.

He finished 50th on the night Bob Dole probably saw his presidential aspirations fade in the last presidential debate.

The point is that even at the highest level of achievement and success, there will be some wins and some losses.

But my kid was happy.

He felt he had taken a step.

He had his moment to compete with every fast kid in the city.

The night after the all-city run, his pride showed through in his homework and at the piano.

He zipped through a recitation of the 50 states.

He played 50 right notes on the piano.

All because he had a chance to compete, to strive to meet a personal goal, to take a turn at being part of something.

"Good try," I said, and I hoped he one day will truly understand what I meant.

Asking the President a question for my son

My question to Bill Clinton has entered our family history under the heading of a "dad moment. "

Positive dad moments, usually occurring when children are under age 13, are times when dad's presence seems larger than life.

Negative dad moments, ever-more frequent occurrences as children grow up, are the strung-together bits of evidence that a father also can be dumb, confused and imperfect.

Forgive me the recounting of a dad's moment with my son and the president. There is a message here for boys and men of all ages.

The dad moment began with a long flight to Washington, D.C., over spring break with my wife and 11-year-old son. On the last day of our trip, President Clinton addressed a convention of newspaper editors and I had tickets.

My son threw a fit over wearing a sport coat.

The plate of broccoli-stuffed pasta paraded before him didn't help his mood either.

Finally, the president arrived.

He hobbled along on crutches, thanks to the fall he had taken a few weeks before.

The air hung heavy with suspicions that Bill Clinton could be headed for an even bigger fall as a result of turning the Lincoln bedroom into a bed and breakfast for cheesy political fund-raising efforts.

The president rose at the head table and opened a black binder. He began to deliver a major policy statement on chemical weapons. Big. Important. Deadly dull.

My son drank two bottles of Pepsi and displayed a bad case of the wigglies.

The president closed his binder and announced he had time for a few questions. The room rustled with indecision.

Our table sat a few feet from a microphone.

I rose and approached the microphone.

"Mr. President," I began. "My son, Cody, age 11, is here with me today and his fifth-grade class will be voting in the presidential elections of 2004. What advice would you give Cody's class and the other young people of America about what they can do to prepare themselves to be productive citizens early in the next century?"

The president began to nod and smile and gather himself in that way that he does when his mind connects with wistful memories of the time he met JFK, a time before the brutal realities of politics and power had begun to corrupt his dreams.

He cared about chemical weapons, of course. But he felt rising in him a sermon, the voice of a preacher, the words of wisdom to the young.

He turned and looked at my son.

"First and foremost, be a good student," he began.

There was no hesitation. Not a single m-m-m or uh.

"Learn all you can. Learn the hard things as well as those that aren't hard for you. Stay out of trouble. Don't do something dumb like get involved with drugs or alcohol, or something that will wreck your life.

"Second, get to know people who are your age, but different from you. People of a different racial or ethnic group, people of different religions. You are going to live in the most multi-ethnic, multi-racial and multi-religious democracy in human history. How we handle that will determine whether the 21st century is also an American century.

"Third, learn as much as you can about the rest of the world because it will be a smaller world and you will need to know more about it.

"And the fourth thing I would say is to start to take the responsibilities of citizenship seriously. Find some way, even at age 11, to be of service in your community – whether it's helping some student in your school who is not learning as well as he or she should, or doing something on the weekends to help people who are unfortunate. I think we need to build an ethic of citizen service into our young people."

My son listened with every hair on his head.

He wasn't thinking about Whitewater just then or Webster Hubbell or the Lippo Group.

He was thinking about what the president of the United States had just said to him about what it meant to be a good citizen.

Back home, I got hate mail from someone who saw the president on CNN and wondered why I lofted such a softball when so many Clinton scandals need to be exposed.

The answer is simple. At 11, my son doesn't need a lesson in political scandals. He needs inspiration.

He needs guidance from people in authority about what it means to grow up and be a good citizen.

The president of the United States, an imperfect man, had risen briefly to an eloquent place where people desperately wish he could find his footing and remain and where my son imagined presidents always reside.

If Bill Clinton ends up disgraced, impeached or forgotten, well, that will afford another lesson for my son.

It will be the lesson of older men who know the wholeness of a person contains slivers of high character amid shovelsful of shameful banality, twinges of disappointment with a tincture of inspiration.

About the Author

Chris Peck's first journalism job was sweeping out the castoff linotype lead filings at the *Daily Riverton* (Wyoming) *Ranger*. That was in 1961. He was 11 and the co-owner's son.

Newspapering in his blood, he studied communication at Stanford, landed an editor's slot right after graduation at the *Wood River* (Idaho) *Journal*, and aimed at markets that were larger – but not big enough to displace him from the landscape of his beloved West. The progression was steady.

In 1977 he was named managing editor of the *Twin Falls* (Idaho) *Times-News*. Joining the Spokane *Spokesman-Review* as a news columnist in 1979, he was managing editor three years later, adding the same title at the *Spokane Chronicle* when the papers merged in 1983.

At the privately-held *The Spokesman-Review*, the largest newspaper between Minneapolis and Seattle, Peck directs a staff of 150 journalists and is a member of the company's four-person executive management team.

The Spokesman-Review won the General Excellence award as the best metro daily in the Inland Pacific Northwest for 10 years in a row.

A steelhead fisherman and a jogger, Peck is married to Kate Duignan, a self-employed fashion designer. They look after Sarah, 15, and Cody, 12, together.